D1498366

THE MORAL LIMITS OF MODERNITY

Also by Victor J. Seidler

A TRUER LIBERTY: Simone Weil and Marxism
RESPECT AND INJUSTICE: The Limits of Liberal Moral Theory
REDSICOVERING MASCULINITY: Reason, Language and Sexuality

The Moral Limits
of Modernity

Love, Inequality and Oppression

Victor J. Seidler

Senior Lecturer in Social Theory
Goldsmiths' College, University of London

St. Martin's Press
New York

© Victor J. Seidler 1991

All rights reserved. For information, write:
Scholarly and Reference Division,
St. Martin's Press, Inc., 175 Fifth Avenue,
New York, N.Y. 10010

First published in the United States of America in 1991

Printed in Hong Kong

ISBN 0–312–05596–X

Library of Congress Cataloging-in-Publication Data
Seidler, Victor J., 1945–
The moral limits of modernity : love, inequality, and oppression /
Victor J. Seidler.
p.   cm.
Includes bibliographical references (p.   ) and index.
ISBN 0–312–05596–X
1. Ethics. 2. Love. 3. Social justice. 4. Christian ethics—
Controversial literature. 5. Ethics, Modern. I. Title.
BJ1031.S42   1991
17—dc20   90–45271
                                                                CIP

In loving memory of
Paul Ickowitz
and Helen Placek Ickowitz

Contents

So show us how to spend our time
and acquire a heart of wisdom

Psalm 90:12

Preface

This study of *Love, Inequality and Oppression* is in many ways a challenge to prevailing forms of moral theory. A sense of the inadequacies of a rationalistic moral tradition to discern the moral realities that we face after Auschwitz and Hiroshima has slowly grown. In large part the intellectual culture that developed after the Second World War turned its face away from these events seeking to reconstruct itself as if these terrifying events had not taken place. Moral theory was to organise itself around Kant's question 'What ought I to do?' in the conviction that there is a right decision for individuals to follow, even if there was disagreement over whether Kant or utilitarianism provided the clearest path. It has taken over forty years in the wilderness to discern that our inherited Enlightenment frameworks might themselves be part of the problem. They tend to render invisible the sufferings that we face.

In *Kant, Respect and Injustice: The Limits of Liberal Moral Theory* I argued that a liberal moral culture talks easily about freedom, respect and individuality but that in reality it inherits from Kant a weak and attenuated conception of the person. It is only as rational selves that we can be acknowledged as moral agents. Our emotions, feelings and desires have no moral worth. They cannot be sources of knowledge nor can they have much to do with our dignity, integrity or self-respect. With Kant we inherit a secularised form of Protestantism with its disdain for human nature and emotional life.

But it can be difficult to uncover the Protestant sources of our Enlightenment tradition since this has been presented to us in secular and universal terms. It was part of the appeal of moral rationalism that it was apparently open to all, despite the religious, class or gender background. It has taken time to recognise that a secularised form of Protestantism has set the terms which have worked to marginalise the experience of, amongst others, women, Jews and blacks who have had to prove themselves as rational to enter the magic circle of humanity. I realised that it was important to acknowledge the continuing influence of Christian assumptions within a secularised moral and political tradition. As feminism had recognised the importance of women, acknowledging those difficulties of grasping women's consciousness and values within a man's world, so I gradually became aware of the importance of working through what it meant personally to grow up Jewish within a Christian world.

At the outset I was struck that there was no place for love within Kant's rationalism. His ambivalence has deep sources within a Christianity that had learnt to reject bodily emotions and to conceive of spirituality as a matter of overcoming an earthly body. So it was also for Kant that as we transcended selfish egoism in our growth into rational moral selves, we would leave behind the influence of our 'natural selves'. This echoes in another sphere the ways that Christianity was supposed to have superceded the revelations of Judaism.

As Christianity learnt to forsake its rootedness in Judaism to the extent of seeking to deny the Jewishness of Jesus, so a rationalistic moral tradition sought to sever its ground in our emotional and somatic experience. We were to learn to reject these parts of ourselves. To resist this trend was to subject oneself to the charge of being 'irrational'. The universality of reason became a force for centralising legitimate authority. The sovereignty of reason set the terms which would marginalise and invalidate differences.

Wittgenstein's later work provides the crucial challenge to a Cartesian rationalism. He rejects the idea of a single and unified conception of reason as an authority before which the different spheres of our lives have to prove themselves. He recognises the integrity of different 'language games'. We have to be wary of judging before we have really understood the nature of the activity that we are involved in. We have to discern the criteria that are appropriate. This does not mean relativism. It warns us against asserting a single standard of truth. There is a recognition of difference and plurality that set Wittgenstein in opposition to an Enlightenment tradition. It is part of the difficulty of constructing his work as a contribution to a 'philosophy of language' and it goes some way to explaining his sense of isolation and estrangement. With the developing discussions about the nature of modernity a more suitable context for interpretation could emerge.

In *Ethics and the Limits of Philosophy* Bernard Williams acknowledges that philosophy has traditionally shown a desire to reduce diversity. 'It has tended, first of all, to see all non-ethical considerations as reducible to egoism, the narrowest form of self-interest' (p. 15). He also recognises the strength of a pervasive desire to reduce all ethical considerations to one pattern, with other types being explained in terms of it. Interestingly he recognises that this reductivism is not merely a matter of intellectual error. The 'drive toward a rationalistic conception of rationality comes instead from features of the modern world, which impose on personal deliberation and on the idea of practical reason itself a model drawn from a particular understanding of public rationality. This understanding requires in principle every decision to be based on grounds that can be discursively explained' (p. 18). The assumption we make about rationality is that two considerations cannot be rationally weighed unless there is a common consideration in terms of which they can be compared. As Williams says, 'This assumption is at once very powerful and utterly baseless' (p. 17). Somehow the difficulties in finding a place for love within our moral theory are connected with the difficulties in illuminating inequalities. Since this is a difficulty shared in different ways both by liberal and Marxist moral and political theory it seems to reflect something significant about Enlightenment conceptions of modernity. We seem to inherit an inadequate moral psychology that is tied up with the notion of the rational self. This tends to present freedom as exclusively a matter of rational choice, equality as if it is a matter of access and justice as if it is exhausted by the notion of distributive justice. This makes it impossible meaningfully to connect issues of inequality with dignity, integrity and self-respect for we tend to construe these terms in rationalistic ways.

In some ways this weakness in our inherited traditions has been discerned by Iris Murdoch who opens her essay 'On "God" and "Good"' by saying that: 'A working philosophical psychology is needed which can at least attempt to connect modern psychological terminology with a terminology concerned with virtue. We need a moral philosophy which can speak significantly of Freud and Marx, and out of which aesthetic and political views can be generated. We need a moral philosophy in which the concept of love, so rarely mentioned now by philosophers, can once again be made central' (*The Sovereignty of Good*, p. 46). We shall have reason to recall these words again later.

I looked towards the writings of Kierkegaard and Simone Weil for voices within a Christian tradition that sought different ways of talking about love, inequality and oppression. In different ways they challenge the terms of an Enlightenment modernity and the rationalistic conception of the rational self. They both illuminate different aspects of our everyday moral experience, offering ways towards more substantial conceptions of the self. They provide images that illuminate the different ways that we can think and feel about inequality. They help to reflect the contradictions that we inherit with a liberal moral culture as we attempt to respect as equals those who are forced to survive in unequal conditions. Kierkegaard helps us appreciate that the attitude we have to ourselves reflects on the love we can have for others, so challenging the identification of morality with selflessness. Simone Weil helps us recognise that our material and spiritual needs have to be recognised in the everyday organisation of social life. She challenges an orthodox Marxism which would deny the autonomy and freedom of civil society, thinking that the realisation of individuals can somehow be identified with the interests of the state. It is crucial for her that individuals have to discern their own needs. Often this involves acknowledging the integrity of our emotions and feelings, rather than learning to discount them in the name of reason alone.

In exploring the complexities of a Christian inheritance I have sought to challenge the simple notion that it exclusively serves to block our grasp of underlying material inequalities. The orthodox Marxist notion of ideology, as Gramsci appreciated, offers too reductive an understanding of the workings of religion. Similarly the secularism of a liberal moral culture often suffers from a historical amnesia of the Christian sources that it carries in a tacit way. In coming to terms with the tensions and contradictions we are coming to terms with important aspects of experience. It is only through acknowledging their continuing hold that we can begin to free ourselves from certain aspects of traditions that can blind us to the realities of oppression and injustice.

But we can also grasp, as Weil understood, insights and values that we would want to cherish as we learn to understand our experience in different terms. In the concluding chapter I have sought to reassert some of the Jewish sources of Christianity, to argue that if pluralism is to be genuine it has to recognise the integrity of different traditions. Often it is from an experience of marginalisation that we can see the workings of the cultural relations of power. The universality of reason carried in a secular form the earlier universal claims of Christendom.

In these different visions of Kant, Kierkegaard and Simone Weil we meet different conceptions of the relationship between self and society. We also meet different levels of abstraction from prevailing relations of power and subordination. I have wanted to use these differences to argue against too sharp a contrast between a liberal individualism that conceives of the rational self as existing with given needs and wants prior to involvement in social relations and a communalism that would see our identities as constituted by larger social relations that leave us without a sense of what is important in our lives.

It is a strength of feminist work that it can help break the hold of this duality. It can speak a language of individuality while giving due recognition to shared conditions of oppression. Women have had to contest the prevailing definitions of their reality so that they could begin to affirm their own values even when they are only tentatively embodied in emerging personal and social relationships. Our moral and political theory is only beginning to come to terms with some of these feminist insights.

Both liberalism and Marxism have been shaped by a shared sense of progress as involving the domination of nature. If they have had different visions of inequality, they have both regarded oppression and injustice as a matter of the public sphere of politics. They are both threatened by Freud's sense of the suffering that is wrought by personal relationships. They have both been silent about the realms of intimacy, love and sexuality which they have sought to banish to the private sphere. Sustained by a Protestant ethic, we learn to deny our emotional needs to meet the ends that we have set for ourselves.

As we learn to be critical of ourselves so we are often critical of others. It becomes difficult to learn a self-acceptance that can recognise the dignity of our emotional lives. It also becomes difficult to recognise the value of human relationships as we learn to identify with individual achievement and success. We learn to distrust others as we become suspicious of our own motivations. As we begin to come to terms with this inheritance we recognise, as Weber did, the extent to which modernity has been created within a Protestant image.

As we learn to heal the fragmentation that an Enlightenment modernity has wrought between reason and nature we begin to remake a moral tradition out of fragments of the past. We learn of a conception of freedom that can acknowledge struggles against oppression and visions of individuality that can recognise the integrity of our emotional lives. These are connections that cannot simply be made intellectually for they call us to consider the quality of our everyday relationships. We begin to form a moral consciousness that can speak both of love and inequality.

By bringing Kierkegaard and Weil into critical relationship with a Kantian tradition that has been so formative in structuring liberal moral culture, we can learn to ask different questions. We learn to remake the connection between morality and politics in a way that makes central a concern for individual truth, dignity and integrity central. We become deadly suspicious of empty political rhetoric that fails to connect with the realities of people's everyday experience. As we learn to respect ourselves in new ways, so we can learn to respect others. If rationality no longer serves as a defining feature of our humanity because we have learnt to recognise the integrity of our emotional lives, so our relationship to the natural world – and to the planet more generally – is no longer a relationship of domination and control.

Many people have helped me on this path. In the early days of working with these ideas there were Peter Winch and Richard Wollheim, who encouraged me from their different perspectives. There were many conversations with Larry Blum, who shares an interest in many of these themes and whose friendship has sustained me through difficult times. At a later stage I have also received encouragement and support from

Isaiah Berlin, Carol Gilligan, David Hartman, David Heyd, Ted Honderich, Alan Montefiore, Iris Murdoch, Paul Morrison, David McLellan, Sheila Rowbotham, Michael Sandel, Charles Taylor and Michael Walzer.

Often it is difficult to trace the influences that shift the way we think and feel about issues. If philosophy as a love of wisdom has been thought about as a form of therapy by Wittgenstein, it can be equally true that an experience of therapy can transform the ways we think about philosophy. If therapy in part is also an exercise in learning how to love we can recognise connections that go back to Socrates, if not earlier. Therapy can help us face a truth that we would wish to avoid. Philosophy as a love of wisdom cannot dispense with a search for truth, even it is fashionable to think otherwise. In this way I would like to appreciate work that I have done over the years with David Boadella, Terry Cooper, Stanley Kellerman, Helen Davis, Anni and Bob Moore, Jenner Roth, and Myron Sharaf. I would also want to acknowledge 'the English group' in Denmark and the 'men for men' group in London. In their different ways they have given me the courage to follow my own path.

I would also like to thank Anna Ickowitz for her continuing love and support. It has not been easy with Simone Weil as another person in our lives. Our children Daniel and Lily have also had to bear all the pressures involved in bringing such a project to completion. I have appreciated their refusal to let me be distracted and their constant reminder of what matters in life. Janet Ransom has been constantly encouraging and insightful with the manuscript, and students doing the Sociology of Knowledge at Goldsmiths' College, University of London, have helped me sustain a sense of the importance of these questions, as together we struggled to bring more light to bear.

1 Introduction: Love, Inequality and Oppression

EQUALITY AND FREEDOM

In exploring the writings of Kant, Kierkegaard and Simone Weil on the relationship of love, inequality and oppression, I have investigated different and challenging Christian traditions of thought and feeling. I have set these against an implicit reference to tensions and contradictions within Kant's moral writings since they have a centrality to the ways we are brought up to think and feel about morality within a liberal moral culture.

The moral difficulties Kant acknowledges about relationships of inequality and dependency in the *Doctrine of Virtue* have become centrally challenging to liberal conceptions of respect and equality in a society in which class, gender and ethnic relations of power and subordination have become so crucial. As I argued in *Kant, Respect and Injustice: The Limits of Liberal Moral Theory*,[1] this shows up the difficulties of our inherited individualistic moral traditions to illuminate the realities of people's experience in the twentieth century. It becomes crucially important that Simone Weil faces some of these crucial issues in her writings.

I have drawn upon the influence of Christian writings on love and inequality not only to sharpen an awareness of a liberal inheritance but also to show the ways these traditions can make it difficult to appreciate the significance of the class, race and gender relations of power and subordination in people's everyday experience. This is one way of giving meaning to their ideological character.

At the same time I hope to show that those traditions of thought and feeling endure not only because they are in the interests of the ruling classes in society, but also because of how the poor and oppressed in society have used these traditions to validate elements of their experience. So, for instance, the notion of human dignity as an 'inner quality' can help people resist oppression and suffering, as it can also mystify people about the ways relationships of subordination and dependency can be continually working to undermine their trust and confidence in themselves. In a similar way Kierkegaard's idea that we can abstract ourselves from the structures of power and dependency we endure in our earthly lives, can strengthen

1

people's sense of self-respect, especially if we are also guaranteed equality in the eyes of God.

But again this can be at the cost of encouraging people to deny themselves fulfilment and realisation as individuals within their everyday social lives. As Nietzsche grasped, this can perpetuate its own tradition of self-denial as it minimises our expectations of what we can receive, deserve or are owed in our earthly lives. This is the more fundamental level at which Simone Weil's recognition of our earthly needs is a challenge to a Kantian tradition'.[2] This can help us focus upon the moral importance of the quality and meaningfulness of people's earthly lives.

Our sense of human equality has been deeply influenced by the Christian tradition. This has had a very deep historical influence upon the formation of our moral culture. Often we take its influence so much for granted in our thinking and feeling that it is difficult to become fully aware and conscious of its continuing influence, especially within a more secularised culture. This tradition is deeply contradictory in its influence upon our thinking and feeling about human equality.

Significantly the vision of human equality it created remained potentially subversive to the aristocratic conceptions of Greece which could so easily legitimate slavery. This was something Alexis de Tocqueville was aware of:

> All the great writers of antiquity belonged to the aristocracy of masters, or at least they saw that aristocracy established and uncontested before their eyes. Their mind, after it had expanded itself in several directions, was barred from further progress in this one, and the advent of Jesus Christ upon earth was required to teach that all members of the race are by nature equal and alike. (*Democracy in America*, vol. 2, p. 16)

Christianity created the possibility of a human community which embraced 'all members of the human race'. This was a revolutionary notion that potentially challenged the inequalities and distinctions of social life. It could give strength to movements which challenge the injustices of social life.

But the tradition has left a contradictory inheritance. Notions of Christian equality have implied contradictory ways of relating to the distinctions and differences of social life. Christianity has also been important in legitimating structures of social inequality. Through withdrawing people's interest and concern from the social world, people have been educated into implicitly accepting that what matters in their lives is the equality experienced before God. This is what comes to sustain and nourish us.

This is what gives us our sense of equality with others. This is what offers us salvation. This can help produce a profoundly ambiguous relationship to social life. In some periods it has meant accepting the social order as if it were a natural order ordained by God.[3] Human equality became an equality before God in which everyone is equally subject to God's authority. With the establishment of the medieval church, talk of human equality was made compatible with a society divided into different social orders. So Christianity could be used directly to legitimate a hierarchical social order. The relationship between the need for equality and the demands of hierarchy is central to our grasp of the continuing influence of Christianity in the ways we relate to the social world.

It has been difficult for Marxist theories of ideology, with the exception of the writings of Antonio Gramsci, to illuminate these contradictions.[4] This is partly because of the limits of its conception of human needs and its antagonism to religion and spirituality.[5] Gramsci's *Prison Notebooks* were centrally concerned with revitalising the moral vision of Marxism and it could be argued that an attention to spirituality is integral to a new or revitalised moral vision. It was a strength of Gramsci's Marxist theory that he could recognise that ideology is a lived reality and that religion is not merely epiphenomenal but has to be taken seriously in its own terms. He appreciated how the Catholic Christian tradition has been important in shaping Italian history and culture.

Similarly I would argue that Protestantism in Northern Europe and the United States has structured our sense of equality and therefore remains central to our moral and political understanding. This inheritance is a contradictory one, especially since its continuing influence is denied in a secular culture, and different elements of it can be carefully explored through the moral writings of Kant, Kierkegaard and Simone Weil. Each in their own way helps us explore how Christianity has shaped our sense of what is at issue in relationships of equality and subordination between people.

Central to the inheritance of Christianity is the conceptualisation of the individual that it leaves us with. A unifying concern is provided by the ways that Christianity has been limited in its capacity to see the individual as a *substantive* moral category. The different accounts and understandings that it offers of the relationship between the individual and the society are reflected in the different visions that it offers of the relationship between the 'inner' and the 'outer', the self and relationships, the soul and society. The three writers consequently have different senses of relationship and crucially different senses of the relationship of morality to politics.

With the development of Protestantism we discover a reassertion of the importance of an individual's relationship with God. This relationship is no longer to be mediated. This had a profound impact upon ideas of freedom and self-determination in the Enlightenment, especially in the writings of Kant. Kant's concern is with the interaction of essentially free autonomous individuals. This initiated a tradition in which relationships of authority and hierarchy have to find a different legitimation. Society has to foster individual freedom and self-determination. Institutions now have to be legitimated in terms of the interests, desires and needs of individuals. The authority of the state has to be grounded in a contract between the rulers and those they govern.

Different versions of a contract theory initially forged in the writings of Locke, Rousseau and Kant, still remain important in liberal conceptions of social justice and the legitimation of social inequality, though we often remain blind to the continuing impact of Christian conceptions within a supposedly secularised moral culture. Possibly the most impressive contemporary statement of this view, John Rawls' *A Theory of Justice*, rests heavily upon a theory of the social contract:[6]

> My aim is to present a conception of justice which generalizes and carries to a higher level of abstraction the familiar theory of social contract as found, say, in Locke, Rousseau and Kant. In order to do this we are not to think of the original contract as one to enter a particular society or to set up a particular form of government. Rather, the guiding idea is that the principles of justice for the basic structure of society are the object of the original agreement. They are the principles that free and rational persons concerned to further their own interests would accept in an initial position of equality as defining the fundamental terms of their association.   (*A Theory of Justice*, p. 11)

It has been the Protestant tradition that has made this conception of 'free and rational persons' intelligible to us. It is a setting we cannot afford to forget if we wish to grasp contradictions in our liberal inheritance.

Kant's ethical writings have been crucial in providing a secularised and systematic form of Christian ethics as the guiding moral theory of liberalism. It is presented as a rational and universal form of ethical theory that can be justified by reason alone. As rational agents a rational moral theory is available to us all so that we become blind to its Protestant assumptions. Within a liberal moral culture we grow up in its image, learning to see ourselves, whether Jew, Christian, Hindu or Moslem, through its eyes. It appropriates reason and rationality to itself, thereby unwittingly suppressing other traditions of thought and feeling that are cast as 'backward', 'traditional' or 'religious'. The break between religion and humanism is taken to be a defining feature of modernity. This is central to the project of the Enlightenment which was able to present a secularised form of Christianity as the universal voice of reason.[7]

As long as our moral theory remains within an Enlightenment tradition deeply influenced by Kant it remains fundamentally concerned with the decisions individuals make about how to live a moral life. This encourages us to give a particular meaning to our 'moral lives' as an autonomous and discrete realm of our experience. This makes us think that our moral decisions have to do, for instance, with those decisions that relate to an individual's relationship with the moral law. Morality becomes essentially an individual quest in which, for Kant, the individual has to prove his or her moral worth.

As I have shown in *Kant, Respect and Injustice*, this hides and mystifies the fundamentally moral character of the decision about am to live a moral life living in an unjust society. Kant was expressing a Protestant inheritance to conceive relationships as the outcome of individual decision and resolve, and so to abstract them from the character of the social relations of power and dominance within which they take place.

Within this framework we can no longer make sense of Plato's recognition that it was only in the context of a society that was organised in a just way that we *could* individually choose to have just relations with others. This is part of what is lost in Christian and liberal moral traditions of thought that assume it is simply a question of the moral qualities of an individual whether they choose to act morally. For Kant it was a question of an individual living up to the moral law, regardless of the social situation they find themselves in. As long as I am acting out of a sense of duty then the moral worth of my actions is guaranteed. As long as my life is full of moral actions then I am guaranteed the moral equivalent of salvation.

This tradition has enormous strengths in the support it can give to individuals to stand up for their beliefs and to resist relating simply to the consequences of their actions. At the same time this clarity is often given at the cost of simplifying the ways the prevailing inequalities of wealth and power shape the moral situations people are in. Kant came to the edge of considering these difficult issues in his consideration of the relations between rich and poor. It is important to highlight these difficult moments because they can throw into relief important contradictions within the moral consciousness of liberal society.[8]

Since for Kant respect is related to not interfering with others, setting out the implications of growing up to respect others, through distancing ourselves from others, can help us clarify a certain form of social relations we grow up to take very much for granted as part of a Protestant inheritance. But we also learn something about the formation of 'character' and 'personality' within a particular moral culture. So Kant's ethical writings can serve to reconcile us to a certain distance in our relations with others, and to thinking that the meaning of our lives is not going to come from our close relations with others, but rather from achieving the goals we have set for ourselves individually. We will often be left assuming that we should not really need the help and support of others, and that we will prove ourselves all the more if we are able to do things for ourselves.

We will also come to take for granted a rationalist conception of morality in which very little can be learned from our emotions and feelings. Rather at some level we will learn to subordinate our own wants and desires so that we are ready to do what is required of us. In its own way this will work to suppress our individuality, which we will too easily identify with achieving the goals we have set ourselves, rather than with the fulfilment and nourishment of our capacities, wants and needs.

Kant tends to assume that our characters simply express whatever individual qualities we have, so he never has to understand the ways these are influenced by the kind of social relations people grow up to take very much for granted. It is partly because for Kant it is possible to judge a person's 'character' by whether or not they act morally, that a person's moral life can be conceived more or less as a series of discrete moral actions. This has a deep influence upon the conception he develops of human relationships. Although in the *Doctrine of Virtue* he sometimes sketches a deeper recognition of the ways people need to reveal themselves to others, he is more concerned to recognise that others can take advantage of us.

He tends to assume that this is a necessary feature of social relations, rather than something which becomes particularly prevalent within a particular form of social relations, as, say, for instance, when we are brought up within competitive institutions to prove ourselves to gain our very sense of individual identity. This can easily make the fear we have of the use others will make of what we share with them 'rational'. It will also be reinforced if we are brought up to assume that needing to share ourselves with others is already a sign of weakness. Kant might have felt this himself in his earlier writings though he learnt to worry about this, possibly feeling the pull of different senses of Christian love:

> Man is a being meant for society (though he is also an unsociable one), and in cultivating social intercourse he feels strongly the need to reveal himself to others (even with no ulterior purpose). But on the other hand,

hemmed in and cautioned by fear of the misuse others may make of this disclosure of his thoughts, he finds himself constrained to *lock up* in himself a good part of his opinions (especially those about other people). (*The Doctrine of Virtue*, p. 471)

Kant does not think through the consequences of locking up in ourselves a good part of our opinions, especially when he also acknowledges that 'he feels strongly the need to reveal himself to others'. This is a contradiction within our experience that will inevitably have implications for the formation and development of our 'characters'.

It was particularly difficult for Kant even to begin to acknowledge this, since there is a deep tendency within his thought to regard the subordination of our needs and desires, our self-denial, to be near to the core of our moral experience. Acting morally can be very much a matter of learning to deny whatever thoughts and feelings we have personally, so that we can do what is required of us by the moral law. This is connected with the notion that we show our respect for others through keeping our distance from them.

This can make it easy for us to grow up within a moral tradition which systematically empties the moral significance of love and relationships with others as it denies the need which Kant partly recognises here, to be able to share ourselves with others. It only seems to be in Kant's later writings that he worries about the kind of limitations this puts on our relations with others, and sometimes about the ways this denies our need to reveal ourselves to others.

It is also because Kant tends to assume that we are equal before the moral law that he can think we are equal in what really matters in our lives. This makes it easier for him to discount the workings of the inequalities of wealth and power. I showed in *Kant, Respect and Injustice* how he is forced to rethink the assumption he makes about the autonomy of morals, about the equality he assumes within the moral realm for us to live moral lives, when he thinks about the relations between rich and poor. Since we often assume that structures of social inequality and class power belong solely to the empirical investigations of sociology, we are barely sensitive to the moral questions which they can raise.

This deep separation of morality and politics was unknown to the Greeks, but it has become almost definitional to the individualistic moral traditions we grow up to take very much for granted. It was also at the centre of Hegel's critique of Kant's moral writings. It is not simply that it is easier for those with wealth and power to live moral lives through doing good for others, it is also because the relations of class, sexual and racial power form and influence our personal and social relations with others. When Kant talks about the 'fear of the misuse others may make of this disclosure of his thoughts' he cannot assume that he is dealing with a relation between equals. This fear is deeply mediated through the social relations of power. It is harder to share myself with someone who has power over me, since it is easier for them to abuse this knowledge.

These issues are also keenly present in how we interpret the respect we owe to others. I explore different conceptualisations of respect, a formalised liberal sense of it, founded in Kant, as opposed to more substantive conceptions. If we can assume with Kant that we are equal as 'moral beings', then it is easier for us to think that it is simply a matter of individual choice whether we respect others in our relationships with them, since this will depend upon the attitude we individually choose to take up. It can be said that we are 'free' to take up whatever attitude we want towards others. Similarly it might be said that we are always 'free' to show respect for others by adopting 'the maxim of not abasing any other man to a mere means to my end (not demanding that the other degrade himself in order to slave for my end)' (*The Doctrine of Virtue*, p. 449).

But does this 'freedom' rely upon our being able to abstract from the social relations of power and inequality? This was the position which Kierkegaard took which helps explain how his insights into the transformation of moral relations were compatible with a radical denial of the significance of social relations. Is the attitude we want to take up towards others sometimes not *contradicted* by the nature of the relationship we are involved in? Is it simply enough for us individually to adopt a certain maxim in our relations with others? Does not the relationship itself sometimes have to be *transformed* since there might be no way within a certain kind of relationship for us *not* to use a person as a 'mere means to my end'? If this is not simply a question, as I have argued, of individual intentions, but relates to the very character of the relationship, *how* is this to be thought about? This is the issue I consider Simone Weil crucially helps illuminate, though somewhat paradoxically, within a Catholic tradition attuned to problems of hierarchy.

INEQUALITY AND INDIVIDUALISM

We can only become aware of some of the issues involved if we begin to bring out how the central tension within our liberal inheritance unwittingly draws upon Christian traditions to articulate both our sense of human equality and our sense of hierarchy and inequality. This is already ambiguously reflected in the ways we think about 'distance', both in terms of the respect that is due to people but also in the 'distance' that is experienced, say, between parents and children, teachers and pupils. We learn to respect our parents and teachers through learning to 'look up to them'. We acknowledge this respect by being careful to keep a certain distance from them. This can involve learning only to speak when we are spoken to, learning not to be too familiar or personal with someone we respect.

In this hierarchical notion of respect there is a sense of maintaining a certain 'social distance' between people. Often it is in these contexts that we think most easily about the nature of respect. Kant also talks about 'distance' when he talks about the respect we owe to others as equal human beings. In doing this, there is a danger of trading upon our understanding of what is going on in 'unequal relationships' between, say, parents and children, teachers and pupils. The character of the 'distance' within these relationships is different from the 'distance' we keep from others when we are careful not to infringe upon their rights. It is left unclear how much Kant wants to include a sense of deference within the sense of respect due to each person.

Sometimes it seems as if Kant is trading upon the hierarchical sense of respect, in clarifying the respect due to others as human beings. This is because, as I have already shown, he is often thinking about respect for the moral law. This could argue that we should give priority to this hierarchical sense of respect. But if we begin to think about these issues in the Protestant context of Kierkegaard it enriches our grasp and it also helps us understand the *abstract quality* of the respect that is given equally to others.

In Kant's individualism it does not involve a personal understanding of someone's needs and wants, emotions and feelings. Often it threatens to become an abstract acknowledgement of others, even though it seems to promise much more. In the very distance we have to maintain from others, it is easier for our acknowledgement of others to become *purely formal*. This relates to the notion of abstract rights which is so central to a liberal conception of an individual's relationship to social life.

It is this conception of an 'individual' which has a powerful influence upon liberal social thought. For Kant we are defined by our moral capacity but in a way that leaves us emotionally disempowered, depersonalised and hollow. This is what both Kierkegaard and Simone Weil, drawing on different resources within a Christian tradition, in their different ways can help to question as they can help foster a more substantial individualism.

This helps challenge a tradition which while talking about individual dignity and worth, can serve to *depersonalise* our conception of others who we implicitly see as clusters of abilities, qualities or capacities. If this reminds us we owe respect to people whatever their social background and position, it also makes us think that these are 'incidental' to our understanding and relationships with others.

Relatedly, for Kierkegaard, our differences that provide at some level for the substance of our individuality are not sources of morality. The absence of any sense of a structured level of societal power relationships in Kant and Kierkegaard seems to be what provides for these conceptualisations. Society seems to be a matter of individuals in contingent circumstances. In contrast, what is crucial for Weil is that she does attend to power: she acknowledges its reality and so develops a different understanding of the individual.

For Kierkegaard there is some sense of societal mediation of the quality of relationships, as I show for instance in terms of possessiveness, but this is seen as separate from political concerns. Both Kant and Kierkegaard collapse politics into difference; difference is the difference between individuals and structured relations of power shift to a space beyond moral concern. The issue then is *what is lost* in abstracting from the concrete form of relationships.

What is contingent for Kant and Kierkegaard is substantive for Weil, partly because she casts the relationship between the inner and the outer, individual and society, in different terms. Weil locates the sacred in the individual substantively, rather than abstracting it and thereby setting up a vision where we have to see difference as partiality and look through it to a spiritual realm which is radically separated from the social.

For Weil social structures not only mediate the quality of relations but actually operate at a level of identity so that whilst the sacred is still for her in some sense depersonalised, this is not in the sense that it is outside the concrete context of relationships. But this is to argue for a substantial individualism that is enriched, rather than compromised, in its connection with social relations of power and subordination.

Within the dominant tradition of liberal individualism which has grown in relation to a Protestant inheritance, our individuality is thought about very much in terms of 'the abstract and universal subject of the rights of man and the rights of the citizen' (*Anti-Semite and Jew*, p. 57).[9] Learning to think about ourselves in this way is taken as a sign of cultural maturity. In this way a person's Jewishness can only be a matter of individual beliefs he or she happens to hold. It can be no part of his or her individuality.

So in claiming our individuality we are called upon tacitly to renounce our Jewishness. It is this very universalism which is taken as a sign of moral maturity. This is embedded in the ways Kant conceives us to be individually subject to the moral law. This is partly why the 'defence of the Jew saves the latter as a man and annihilates him as a Jew' (p. 57). In learning to prove ourselves individually, we learn to distance ourselves from our cultural and historical heritage. Since this is no part of our individuality, it cannot be anything that we draw our strength and identity from. It is an individual's relationship with the moral law which, in Kant, works 'to persuade individuals that they exist in an isolated state'.

Kant's notion of respect as non-interference fundamentally assumes a Protestant idea that people need to be left alone to pursue their own ends. This is the way people will find happiness. This very much assumes that individuals enter social life with a set of pre-given wants, desires and ends. If utilitarianism talks more of satisfying our wants so that it does not need to separate human fulfilment into an independently defined moral realm, it shares with Kant a conception of the other person who is to be taken into account. This is something Charles Taylor learns from Hegel's critique of Kant's moral theory:

> Because he only has a formal notion of freedom, Kant cannot derive his notion of the polity from it. His political theory ends up borrowing from the utilitarians. Its input, we might say, is the utilitarian vision of a society of individuals each seeking happiness in his own way. The problem of politics is to find a way of limiting the negative freedom (*Willkur*) of each so that it can coexist with that of all others under a universal law . . . It takes its start from men as individuals seeking particular goals, and the demands of morality and rationality, i.e. universality, only enter as restrictions and limitations (*Beschrankungen*) imposed on these individuals from outside . . . (*Hegel*, pp. 371–2)

In *Kant, Respect and Injustice*, I questioned the broadly held assumption that the existence of a relationship of inequality does not present a moral issue or constitute a moral concern, but only presents a context in which moral issues arise. This questions the assumption that we are always free to relate to others with respect, since this is an attitude we can always choose to take up in our relationships with others. This is simply a question of fulfilling my individual duties within the social world. The social world becomes a *setting* in which I can make sure to obey the demands of the moral law. It is up to us individually to decide how we want to relate to others. It is simply a matter of whether I have the will and determination to do what I have set myself. Again it is a matter of proving my moral worth as an individual.

REASON AND MORALITY

Here, after treating themes of respect and love in Kant, I want to investigate two contrasting treatments of this situation which both draw heavily upon Christian traditions and which can help us think about this as a problematic inheritance sometimes sustaining and supporting, sometimes challenging and questioning, liberal moral and political theory. For Kierkegaard equality was something we could achieve through abstracting ourselves from the social and historical relationships we found ourselves in. The social world is seen here as an area of inequality and dependency. It is only if we are ready to abstract ourselves from this world that we can grant equal respect to others and relate to others as equals. The source of our moral duties comes from an independent realm.

Kant remains central to the formation of a liberal moral theory. He provides the basis for a secularised form of Protestantism the guiding presuppositions of which are taken for granted within the universality and rationalism of Kantian ethics. His moral theory underpins so much of what we take for granted in our relations with others as well as the fragmentation we inherit between reason and emotions and desires within ourselves.

The identification of reason with morality and a sense of ourselves as moral beings to the extent that we are rational beings has equally underpinned sexual and class relations of power in which it has been possible for men to appropriate reason to themselves as a defining feature of a dominant form of masculinity.[10] It is the split between reason and nature that is the source of the formalism that has remained an integral aspect of the rationalism we inherit within moral theory.

Identifying morality with reason establishes a framework in which morality can be separated from politics, for it means that individuals are free to respect others through being ready to *abstract* from the unequal social relations which form our relationships. Respect is an attitude of mind that we can freely adopt towards others so that the morality of relationships can be separated from issues of power and social inequality.

For Kant freedom is fundamentally an issue of reason. We are free to the extent that we refuse to be influenced by our natures but use our reason to rise above them. Both our desires and feelings, as well as the social relationships we live, are regarded by Kant as external, as parts of a nature that we have to learn to distance ourselves from. In contrast reason is taken to be an inner quality that is the source of our freedom and autonomy as individuals.

So it is that freedom is available to us if only we have the strength of will to resist the determinations of our desires or relationships, to act according to reason alone. This secularised a Protestant disdain for our natures, which are seen as leading us astray from the only true moral path. It is the source of a modernist vision for it dictates that there is a single path that as rational moral agents we are free to take. In this way civilization is appropriated by western culture, which assumes itself to be guided not by interests but by the impartial voice of reason alone.

The pervasive disdain for the body and for natural emotions and feelings is deeply embedded within Kant's formalistic writings for it separates reason as an independent and autonomous faculty which is defined *in opposition* to nature. Reason gives us access to a realm of moral law that is radically separated from everyday moral experience. It is this formulation of reason that sets people against themselves and which means that emotional life is threatening as a form of determination that takes us away from a path that we have set by reason alone. We learn that reason has the power to establish meaning and value in the goals and purposes that we set for ourselves individually. We learn to despise and put down our desires and inclinations as essentially selfish and egoistic.

Men in particular find themselves threatened by emotions since they challenge a vision of self-control which is formed through the identification of masculinity with reason. It also accounts for the ambivalence about love within western culture that can only be venerated within a Christian tradition that separates it from the body and sexuality. Kant is forced to conceive of love as a rational feeling so as to preserve it from the contamination of any contact with the body, emotions and desires.

This ambivalence about love is at the core of a Christian tradition that teaches the importance of 'love thy neighbour' while insisting upon a radical separation between bodily love and spiritual love. Love becomes disembodied within a tradition that finds it hard to revere and respect the teachings of the body. We have to deny our natures so that we can look in a different direction. Self-denial and a disdain for bodily experience are structured into our ethical theory.

There is little sense, as there is in some eastern traditions, of the transformation and transmutation of sexuality in its movement towards spirituality. Within the guiding dualism of the western tradition we test our love by separating it radically from the impulses of our natures. At best we are left with the classifications of different kinds of objects of love.[11]

Kant is thinking within a Cartesian tradition which gives a secular formulation to some of these guiding conceptions. For Descartes the body is part of the world of nature which is separated from reason and the mind which alone define our identities. The body is a machine that has to be used for it stands in an external relationship to our selves. The mind can no longer find a home in the world but has been estranged for as selves we have no place within the world. We can only find roots in our memories and so it is that within a modern philosophical tradition we learn to think of personal identity in terms of consciousness and mind.

Within an Enlightenment tradition we are rational selves who learn to guide our lives through reason alone. We exist as centres of consciousness within a natural world that has died around us. It is a profane world that is to be used at will to fulfil human needs.[12] As we learn to use our bodies to realise ends or goals we have set for ourselves so it is that we use the natural world around us.

As a profane world it is bereft of any meaning and value apart from the meanings and dignity that we can provide it with as human beings. We assume an instrumental attitude towards ourselves as well as to the natural world around us. It is part of the arrogance of a humanism that sees human reason as the only source of meaning and value within a disenchanted world, as Max Weber describes it.[13]

Descartes and Kant did not go unchallenged. There was the voice of Herder and a counter-Enlightenment that saw the fragmentation of Kant's vision as destroying the possibilities of a more expressive wholeness. For Herder we are not simply rational beings whose freedom lies in our realising ends and goals that have been set by reason alone.[14] This assumes the autonomy and integrity of a rational self that exists prior to relationships, traditions and community.

It is as if individuals enter social life already complete with pre-given purposes and goals. As rational selves we do not have to become ourselves, for we are already complete. This vision of the rational self and the idea of reason that defines it was challenged by Herder, as it was to be later by Wittgenstein, who sensed that the continuing dominance of a modernist Enlightenment tradition would make his writings inaccessible.[15]

For Herder it is only as we express ourselves through what we do that we can discover what it is that we need for ourselves. It is in the context of a particular history, community and tradition that we can want to explore our individualities. If we uproot ourselves from our language and tradition we do an injury to ourselves. Language is not universal but has to be grounded in history and culture. There are similar insights in Simone Weil's writings that allow us to explore some of these tensions within a Christian inheritance.

A modernist tradition is beginning to fragment and this helps to bring into focus some of the Protestant assumptions that have underpinned an Enlightenment identification of reason with science, of progress with the domination of nature. Gradually we are coming to appreciate the centrality of the moral issues about our relationship to the natural world. Love and morality do not simply concern a realm of personal relationships in which we are supposedly free to act towards others as equals.

As we have lost contact with a language of the soul in our relationship with ourselves, something that Keats in a romantic tradition wanted to nourish in his talk of soul-making, so we have lost contact with a sense of our bodies as alive and with nature as a source of meaning and value.[16] These are part of the same process since it is in the idea of self-control as the domination and silencing of our inclinations and desires that makes us less sensitive to the hurt and injury that we do to ourselves and so also to the hurt we do to others and the natural world around us. As we learn to be instrumental to ourselves so it is that we take for granted an instrumentality in our relations with others.

We no longer listen to ourselves and to others for we are falsely confident that it is only through reason that we can assign value. We test ourselves against others for our humanity is not to be revealed in a love and appreciation of nature but in the domination and control of nature that has to be transformed in our own image. In a disenchanted world, meaning and value are not waiting to be discovered in our experience of relationship with others and with nature. It is reason alone that provides a source of meaning and value.

Kant accepts this vision, thinking that reason will give us access to a realm of value that exists beyond the everyday empirical realm. This allowed him to be critical of existing institutions and relationships. Kant could also escape from Hume's conventionalism which said that morality was defined within the habits, culture and traditions of particular societies. But Kant's rationalism serves to isolate people from the natural and social worlds which are conceived as profane worlds of determination and unfreedom.

I show that individuals stand alone before the moral law and that Kant limits the dignity of our lives to the moral worth of our moral actions. Our feelings and desires can have no moral worth; nor can our love and concern for others. It is only our duty that can save us from our selfishness and egoism. We prove ourselves by rejecting our natures. This is a path of self-denial and self-rejection though its universal language often blinds us to this, for we often assume that it presents us with a higher vision of ourselves and the moral life.

LOVE AND INEQUALITY

I go on to explore some themes in Kierkegaard's writings because they help bring different strains in our thinking about love and inequality to the surface. He helps illuminate structures of thought and feeling within a liberal moral culture. In particular, he brings into question a selflessness that is part of a Christian moral tradition, the idea that we somehow prove our respect and love for others by sacrificing ourselves. As Nietzsche and Scheler recognise, this self-denial produces a culture of resentment that brings into question the surface meanings and intentions.[17]

For Kant it is difficult to think of self-respect as involving the acceptance of our feelings, emotions and desires. We do not learn to respect our natures but only our capacity for reason, which is the source of our moral actions. Similarly, when we respect others we are learning to respect the moral law which we see manifested in their behaviour. So it is that we are left with an attenuated conception of self and other as we are left bereft of any understanding of the place of history and culture in the formation of our individualities. As rational selves this is all contingent for we demonstrate our freedom to make ourselves in our own image by separating from nature as well as history and culture, as forms of unfreedom and determination.

By challenging the place of reason in our lives, Kierkegaard shows us how we are estranged from our natures in a way that leaves us with an attenuated conception of self. We are not simply rational agents guiding our lives by reason alone. As long as we insist that reason is defined in opposition to nature, so it is that we will be left with an external relationship to self and with limited self-knowledge.

Kierkegaard appreciates that only if we have learnt to love ourselves can we learn to love others. Love is not something that can be commanded or acted upon as an act of will. Though Kant recognises this, he thinks he can avoid the issues it presents us with by thinking of it as a rational feeling. Kierkegaard understands the centrality of the *relationship* that individuals have with themselves and his moral theory remains crucially significant because it opens up a space for investigation of the way that this relationship can be transformed and the different shapes it can take. We cannot separate out the respect that we have for ourselves from the kind of relationships we have with others. These are not independent processes but they have a bearing upon each other. We cannot learn to respect others before we have learnt how to respect ourselves.

A Kantian moral theory yields no space to considerations of the *quality* of the relationships that people have. For Kant what matters is the right-fulness of our moral actions, whether we have been able to act out of a sense of duty alone. For Kierkegaard we cannot separate intentions from the qualities of the person and we have to be able to consider qualitative changes in people themselves. Moral theory has to go beyond the morality of individual acts. It needs to move beyond a framework that is provided by Kant or Aristotle – between a rational calculation of individual moral acts or a consideration of particular virtues and characters. Kierkegaard draws us on to different ground, where it is possible to challenge a framework that can only see Aristotelian ethics as a form of egoism, since the polarity between egoism and altruism is taken to set the terms of philosophical ethics since Kant.

Kierkegaard draws on a Christian tradition to break the hold of an Enlightenment modernism that argues that the natural and social worlds are themselves bereft of meaning and value and that the freedom and dignity of people has its source in individuals as the creators of values. Too often within a modernist tradition we learn to think in a dualistic mode – these values are either given *or else* they are created through reason.

A strong religious sensibility allows Kierkegaard to question this framework. He challenges the Weberian tradition that founds a modernist tradition in its idea that meaning and value are assigned as an intellectual construction.[18] For Kierkegaard values have to be worked for both in our relationships with self and with others. He begins to locate meaning within the context of relationships so that value has to be explored, investigated and discerned and somehow realised in the quality of our lives and relationships. He also recognises the difficulties that people have in facing themselves.

Along with Simone Weil he recognises that knowledge is often something we do not seek, as the Enlightenment story has it. We prefer to live in illusions and fantasies, seeking consolations rather than be brought into a deeper contact with ourselves. It is in the tradition of existential psychoanalysis that Kierkegaard's influence on Heidegger shows itself in a therapeutic practice that is also informed by Freud. It is a tradition of thought and practice that our moral theory has still to learn from.

But Kierkegaard shares with Kant a suspicion of inequalities, status and vanities of the social world, though again the differences are instructive. Abstracting from the social relationships of power and subordination as if these are incidental to the persons themselves is for Kierkegaard a way of *restoring* a relationship of person to person. It is a matter of seeing the person for who he or she is, separated from power and social position. Kierkegaard recognises how inner and outer might be out of relation with each other so that our choices might not be made from a sure place within ourselves.

Kant comes to terms with the social world through assuming that we should respect the jobs and position individuals have as reflecting what they have freely chosen for themselves and so as reflecting an 'equal contribution' they are seeking to make to society. It is difficult for Kant within this rationalist framework to imagine that these might not be freely chosen if they flow from the free exercise of our reason. Kant's accommodation of social life has been crucial for a liberal theory that has sought to respect whatever position people have in society. It has worked implicitly to legitimate existing social relationships of power and subordination. Paradoxically Kierkegaard's refusal to engage with the 'social' opens up a space for a more radical questioning since we are otherwise left unaware that people might well be powerless and oppressed in the positions they find themselves in.

Simone Weil also recognises that people cannot respect others unless they have learnt how to respect themselves. This was not simply a question of attitude as Kant has it. Nor is it a matter of abstracting from differences for our dignity has also to rest in our activities and relationships. So it is that Weil challenges an Enlightenment vision of modernity that sees us as rational selves and which treats differences of class, ethnicity and gender as if they are incidental and secondary.

For Weil it is these differences that have to be faced if we are to recognise how respect and dignity is to be afforded people in their everyday activities and relationships. It is not simply our rationality that is a source of our dignity but 'all of us' is sacred, though she never found an adequate way of expressing this for she shared too many Christian notions which denigrated the body and emotional life.

But she profoundly challenges Kant's notion of dignity as an inner quality that can be sustained whatever the external condition. She learnt from her own crucial experience of factory work that this was not so. The 'inner' and the 'outer' could not be separated into discrete realms. Morality was in the end inseparable from both spirituality and politics. This radically redefines issues of freedom and justice.

Another aspect of modernity which Weil challenges is the notion that respect was not a matter of the meaning that people assigned to their lives. Life had to be made meaningful through the quality of the activities and relationships that people were involved in. It was a matter of the kind of work that a society made available to people and the character of the control that they could exercise over their everyday conditions of work and life.

She also challenges a modernist identification of morality with technical progress. With Marx, she recognises that the modern factory degrades working people at the same time as it creates material wealth. She was suspicious of Marx's emancipatory dreams since she felt the power of his analysis of capitalism as a machine to crush human lives. She was wary that the oppressed would resist rather than be beaten into the ground.

She refused to identify history with justice and forces us to forsake consolations by facing up to the injustices of society that history cannot be relied upon to redress. It might be better to name injustice for what it is, rather than to find consolation in a future always uncertain. She refused to think, with Marx, that the present might have to be sacrificed to bring a decent future nearer. Weil, like Benjamin, refused to justify present misery on the grounds that it might bring future happiness. The challenge to an identification of history and progress gives a striking resonance with some post-structuralist writing.[19]

Weil refuses to accept a utilitarian language of pain and pleasure as adequate to illuminate the injuries done to people through inequality and oppression. Inequalities could not be justified because of the general welfare that they promoted. It was not a matter, as Rawls' *A Theory of Justice* has it, that the least wealthy are not made worse off, but of judging a society by the way that its institutions and relationships sustain the dignity and self-respect of those who are least well off in the community. This goes right against the grain of a libertarian conservatism that would underpin the moral values of the market. For Weil inequalities can never be legitimated by the market for the market is not a moral mechanism.

Similarly Weil insists that a liberal language of rights, forged in the French Revolution, is inadequate to stand in a central place within a liberal moral culture. It tempts us into thinking that as long as no right has been infringed then no injury or damage has been done to a person. It also fosters a false notion that an injury that is caused can be understood as an infringement of rights. This only helps us grasp the most superficial of the indignities and humiliations that people endure. It leaves us without a moral language within which to render visible the injustices and indecencies of social life. I show the way that Simone Weil takes on this task as her own.

Respect becomes an issue of dignity for Weil, and love has to do with more than an attitude. It has to be joined with a conviction to raise people in their own eyes while refusing to give people false hopes that all the sources of their misery and unhappiness will come to an end. Necessities will not all give way and it is partly in the struggle against necessities that we define our dignity and self-respect. Theoretical work has to illuminate the reality of people's situation while giving people the strength to change the material and emotional conditions of their lives. It must not create false hopes and illusions so it must ground itself in transforming present conditions so that they genuinely affirm human dignity and self-respect.

We cannot assume, as Kant does, in a language of right that individuals are free and equally able to make their own lives. Independence and autonomy cannot be guaranteed as a condition of moral life but have to be struggled for in the everyday material world. Nor can they be brought into existence by abstracting ourselves from the inequalities of the social world. Rather they have to be struggled for partly through transforming these conditions and relationships.

But Weil's vision remains profoundly contradictory. Though she does not see spirituality in a realm of its own but as something that has to be realised within everyday material life, her vision remains Platonic and rationalist. If she seeks to draw these higher energies into deepening the quality of contact with self and others, she remains trapped by the form of her Christianity, which would reduce herself to an object to be used at God's will, and by her antagonistic responses towards the body and emotions.

In many ways this makes it hard to sustain a sense of the importance of her work, and to elucidate the character of abuse, violation and affliction that, at another level, she had learnt to name. Weil knows that often these are injuries to both the body and the soul. It also makes it hard to identify our emotions and feelings as sources of dignity and self-respect. She wants to recognise that everything about a human being is sacred, but it is difficult for her to do this.

Though she did so much to extend our sense of 'self-acceptance', including in her later work a sense of the importance of being rooted within a particular history and culture, it was impossible for her to have this for herself.[20] She knew that in people learning to despise and feel shame for who they are and for where they come from, they are learning to undermine important sources of dignity and self-respect. Freed from a sense that there are simple answers to be reached by reason alone, we can learn to treasure insights that help us face up to the difficulties of love in an unequal world.

Simone Weil crucially helps us question the Kantian notion of the autonomy of morality which is organised around the question of 'what ought I to do?', as if morality is always something I can fulfil on my own. For Weil Christianity is powerful precisely in so far as it operates against the kind of abstraction we find in Kant. She challenges the partial compromise that Kant makes with social life in his giving equal respect to people for the ends they have individually chosen to pursue, as bus driver as much as lawyer, as factory worker as much as bank manager.

If this prepared crucial ground for liberal moral and political theory, it is something Kant himself came to question, as I have shown, in his reflections upon the relations between rich and poor. Weil helps us understand that respecting others as equals is not simply a question of taking up a certain attitude towards them, but of organising social relations so that respect can be expressed in the institutions of society.

Weil also places a discussion of human needs, rather than a language of individual rights, at the centre of her moral and political theory, knowing that these needs have somehow to be satisfied if people are to live meaningful lives. She leaves us with a way of talking about social justice not simply as a matter of the distribution of resources. She also considers social relations of power and subordination which help form people's everyday experience and which have an effect upon the development of individuality and personal identity.

She helps transcend the boundaries of liberal moral theory and questions the autonomy of morality in her recognition that human dignity is not something that can be assumed in our relations with others, but has to be continually affirmed and struggled for through a transformation of social relations of power and dependency. She helps us grasp the misleading and confusing terms in which liberal theory is often contrasted with socialist theory. Different questions come into focus as we begin to face some of the difficulties and promise of personal and political transformation.

The class, gender and ethnic relations of power and subordination that have been so central to the organisation of social life within a capitalist mode of production have rarely led to a challenge to inherited traditions of moral thought. Marxism has often implicitly sustained aspects of the universalism we take so much for granted within a Kantian moral tradition. In facing up to the class relations of power and subordination Simone Weil recognises 'that humanity is divided into two categories – the people who count for something and the people who count for nothing'. We require a moral language which can fully appreciate these differences.

It was part of Weil's critique of the universal appropriateness of the language of rights, partly fostered through Kant's notion of respect as non-interference, that it falsely assimilated different situations. This involved discovering a conception of moral psychology that could appreciate the hurt and injuries done to people through the processes of social life. This in turn involved understanding that people's trust and confidence in their capacities and abilities as well as these capacities and abilities themselves, can be damaged.

People are much more vulnerable to the processes of social life than an individualistic moral theory often allows. This is not something Kierkegaard could grasp, since he assumed that people's integrity was protected in their individual relationships to God. If he reminds us that we remain human beings whatever the social distinctions which separate us, he constantly minimises the damage and suffering caused to people in the everyday conditions of their lives.

In invoking a notion of moral culture I am not simply talking about the ideas and values we are brought up to assume. I am also talking about the social relations of power and subordination and their part in the formation of people's characters and sense of identity. Sometimes we take our moral culture so much for granted, in our thinking and feeling, that it is difficult to grasp the different traditions which nourish and support it. Marxist critiques of ideology have too often assumed an abstract form, continually misunderstanding the different ways morality influences our sense of self, our identities and our understanding of a meaningful life. They have also made it difficult to address contradictions within our moral culture, tending to treat it very much as a single unity.

In drawing attention to different ways of conceiving love and inequality I have attempted to define emancipatory elements at work. I have also argued that the ways we are encouraged to show our respect for others, through abstracting from the social relations of power and dependency, has made it increasingly difficult to understand the power of social relations in forming individuals' lives and experience. If it is important for us to learn not to *reduce* individual experience, it is also important to recognise the significance of class, gender and ethnic relations of power within our moral theory.

Rather than assuming that individuals come together with given needs and wants, we have to recognise how our very existence as individuals *with control over our lives* has been attacked, undermined and become 'fictitious' through what Simone Weil calls 'the modern forms of social oppression'. This also involves recognising how our needs are distorted and redefined, as our individualities are formed within competitive and hierarchical institutions.

I have also argued for a more critical approach to liberal moral culture. I have argued against the formal and ahistorical ways it sets the 'individual' against the 'society' and implicitly assumes conceptions of self-denial while continuing to talk about individual happiness. Its inherited conception of individual freedom does not give individuals the kind of control it promises them over their lives. Liberal theory also places the responsibility for the mistreatment and indignity people suffer in unequal relations on our personal relationships with others. This creates the popular liberal notion that if only individuals could learn to relate to others with more respect and consideration, the world would become decent and just.

If this can help us assume more responsibility in our relations with others, it can blind us to the moral issues reproduced in the social relations of power and subordination. It makes it seem as if it is enough for individuals to learn to treat others differently. Simone Weil felt that only once we fully appreciate the ways our prevailing moral traditions blind us to people's suffering, will things have a chance of changing. This gives a way of validating the experience of those who are oppressed and powerless in the ways social life is organised.

At the same time it is crucially important to learn from liberalism, even as we recognise the ways it mystifies class relations of power and subordination. We have to explore the truths it voices, even if it involves a different context of personal and social relationships to develop them. So, for instance, the notion of respect as non-interference can help us become aware of the need people have for space and time in which to discover what kind of lives they want for themselves, even if it does not help us understand the broader social relationships in which such an exploration of self takes place.

So it is important for a critical socialist tradition to recognise the kind of decisions individuals have to make for themselves and the kind of learning and discovery this involves. This can help us strengthen our sense that the social world has to be organised around the fulfilment of people's lives. It is not simply something individuals have to subordinate themselves to. But this also involves recognising ourselves as involved in a broader collectivity within which we can learn to clarify our history and needs.

A sense of collectivity has long been an integral aspect of the history of the working-class movement and has been given new meaning in the experience of the revitalised women's movement in which many individual women have recovered a sense of the social and historical experience they share with other women. This has supported individual women and women collectively in the discovery and redefinition of what it means to be a woman. The women's movement has challenged the prevailing patriarchal definitions of femininity as it involves transforming the social relations and institutions which sustain these definitions.

This brings to the centre the moral issues of how to live as an individual in a society characterised by social inequality and social injustice. It is not simply a question of acting correctly as an individual towards others, without also recognising the need to transform social relations of power and subordination. It is not simply a question of treating people with love or respect, but of bringing into existence a social world in which people can live fully human lives.

We need to bring into existence relationships in which we can meaningfully relate to others with respect and love. If this involves recognising a deeper relationship between morality and politics, it is something we learn more about as we change ourselves, as we change the social world we live in. An integral aspect of this has to be a critical approach to the moral and political traditions we take for granted.

We need to question traditions of moral and political thought that have wanted to separate issues of social justice from an exploration of the needs and wants of individuals. This is not to assume a conception of the bourgeois individual who is identified with individual achievement and success, nor is it to reduce our consideration of individuality through thinking solely in terms of class, race and gender relations, however important it is for us to come to terms with our class, ethnic and sexual histories and experience.

This should not be allowed to foreclose the moral and political issues of individuality, or leave us to assume that the individual has to find fulfilment in subordinating and adapting to the needs of the larger society. This has been a feature of Durkheim's social theory as it has of moments of scientific Marxism. Perhaps this is why Marx stressed, even if he could never properly illuminate this, that: 'We must above all avoid setting up "the society" as an abstraction opposed to the individual. The individual *is* the social entity. The expression of his life . . . is therefore the expression and verification of the life of society.'[21]

2 Respect and Love

When Kant attempts to give some kind of definition of respect it is striking that he draws his bearings through relating himself to legal thought on the one hand and Christian ideas on the other. These different comparisons are brought together in his sense of respect as a negative duty:

> The duty of free respect to others, since it is actually only negative (Not to exalt oneself over others) and is thus analogous to the juridical duty (Not to encroach upon their rights), can, although it is merely a duty of virtue, be regarded as a strict duty in comparison with the broad duty to love one's fellow men.   (*The Doctrine of Virtue*, Section 25, p. 448)[1]

The universalism of Christian thought was a great and lasting influence upon Kant's thought. When he formulated his sense of our moral duties the broader conceptions of Christianity were never far from his mind. Often it seems as if this presents a perfection that we cannot expect from ordinary people. This is why it becomes so important to develop a clear sense of what people can expect from each other. This is partly why Kant thinks of our moral duty to respect others as 'analogous' to the juridical duty 'not to encroach upon their rights'. Since these duties are taken to have a perfectly clear definition within the law, they can provide a reliable bench mark against which to think about the meaning of respect.

The idea that we should not encroach upon the rights of others is central within Kant's moral and political universe. There seems little need for a discussion of the nature and character of 'rights' which are implicitly taken to be fundamental. If Kant does not say much to explain the meaning of the notion 'Not to exalt oneself over others', it seems as if reference to the juridical duty stands as some kind of explanation in itself. It is as if we have to understand the juridical duty, if we want to be able to understand the nature of our moral duty.

Our duty to respect others is explained as the negative duty 'Not to exalt oneself over others'. How is this like the juridical duty of not encroaching upon another's possessions? They are both 'negative' in the sense that they tell us what we should not do, not what we should do, towards others. Do we show our respect for others by not making them feel we are better than them, so they do not have to subordinate themselves to us? Does Kant assume social relations in which we are encouraged to define our sense of self or 'identity' in comparing ourselves with others, in proving ourselves against others? If Kant does not really clarify the kind of social relations that make it more difficult to show respect to others, this is partly because he assumes this is something we have to do, regardless of the difficulties we are presented with.

So it makes little difference to Kant to recognise that within a society organised around competitive social institutions we are inevitably asking more of people, especially when we are implicitly encouraged to define our sense of individual identity in terms of doing better or worse than others. This is a relevant consideration, since there is a significant difference between learning not to exalt yourself above others when this means not letting them feel you are better than they are (when all the time you deeply know that you are), and wanting to feel genuinely equal to others. This is a difference we will have to explore. It is important to recognise these issues since otherwise we slip into assuming we can relate to others in any ways we *choose*, regardless of the social relations through which we relate to others. Often Kant seems to assume that this is simply a matter of individual decision. But at the same time he insists that our respect has to be taken in a practical sense:

> . . . the respect to be shown to others: it is not to be taken merely as the *feeling* that comes from comparing one's own *worth* with another's (such as mere habit causes a child to feel toward his parents, a pupil towards his teacher, a subordinate in general towards his superior). Respect is rather to be taken in a practical sense (*observantia aliis praestanda*), as a *maxim* of limiting our self-esteem by the dignity of humanity in another person.   (*Doctrine of Virtue*, Section 25, p. 448)

In its own way this shows the democratic impulses within Kant's thought as he challenges the *hierarchical* sense of respect. The respect Kant talks about has to be more than the feeling of respect generated through habit of 'comparing one's worth with another's'. This does not mean that, for Kant, children should not respect their parents and pupils should not respect their teachers. But it does say something about the grounds for this respect, that it is not enough for this to be a feeling based upon habit. They have to seek their own forms of rational legitimation. Rather we respect others by adopting and acting upon the maxim 'of limiting our self-esteem by the dignity of humanity in another person'. This works to restore and sustain a child's or pupil's sense of his own worth and dignity since he knows he can share in this conception of 'humanity'.

It tends to be one of the presuppositions of Kant's thought that we have to wage a struggle within ourselves against our inclinations, to be able to do what we have decided to do. Moral struggle has this quality of being an essentially inner struggle.

An example can help illuminate the issues involved here. Kant's conception of respect as distance and his conception of moral struggle as essentially inner, can make it difficult to grasp the nature of the difficulty that, for instance, John might face in challenging the authoritarian ways of his father. His father felt he was owed respect and obedience and that he should not have to explain the orders he gives in the family. He felt that John's requests for explanations showed a 'cheek' and 'insubordination' he could not tolerate.

Against this John felt his father did not recognise that he has a mind of his own and that he is owed explanations when he is asked to do things. John was angry that his father had told his friend that he could not talk to him on the phone, because he thought he should be getting on with his homework. His father may have felt he was doing this in the best interests of his son, whilst John felt he could make his own decisions about his homework and that his father had no right saying that he could not talk on the phone.

John thought it was quite wrong of his father to think he was superior just because he was older. John felt his father had to earn his respect, not simply assume it. And John felt his father could not simply issue commands in the family without being ready to explain and talk through with people what he wanted them to do. John very much wanted to be able to respect his father, but he also wanted his father to have some kind of respect for him. This was not something he could achieve on his own, since it also called for his father to relate differently to him.

Nor can we simply say that as long as John relates towards his father in a way which limits his 'self-esteem by the dignity of humanity in another person', then he will at least be giving his father the respect owed to him. This might help set certain limits within the relationship but it *won't* guarantee that his father begins to relate differently to him. The point is that it is not simply up to us individually to decide to relate to someone in a particular way. Others have to be ready to change the ways they relate to us, if the character of the relationship is to change. The truth is that John wants to have a different *kind* of relationship with his father, while his father thinks this very desire on John's part *shows* he has a 'lack of respect for him as his father'.

At another level there remains within Kant the notion that our respect for others involves limiting the kind of comparisons we make with others. It is almost as if our respect for others sets certain limits upon the kind of comparison we can make in comparing our own 'worth with another's'. It is not to be identified with the feeling that comes with such a comparison, but is to be 'taken in a practical sense' as a 'maxim of limiting our self-esteem by the dignity of humanity in another person'. This is directly related to the sense in which we respect others by 'not exalting oneself above others'.

At some level this is to accept as a presupposition the ways we constantly compare ourselves with others, even the ways we can be expected to establish our sense of identity through these kinds of comparisons. Kant takes this to be more or less 'natural', rather than seeing it as a feature of a particular order of social relations. He is concerned to place certain limits upon the comparisons we make, rather than to challenge the very *basis* for these comparisons.

So when John wants his father to respect him as a person, he is deeply disappointed to hear from him that 'I'll respect you when you've proved yourself at school'. John does not want to have to prove himself any more, though he is aware that when he was young he took this way of relating very much for granted. He always felt his father was implicitly comparing him with his cousins who always seemed to do very well at school. He always felt he was disappointing his father because he did not do well enough.

It was hard for him not to judge himself by these standards and to find himself wanting. He was plagued by feelings of inadequacy and worthlessness. He was often left feeling ashamed for letting his father down. At some level John could be reassured by Kant's notions, feeling that there had to be certain limits set on judgments his father made 'in order to detract nothing from the worth that the other, as a man, is entitled to posit in himself'.

At the same time, the deeper presupposition which draws our 'worth' and 'dignity' from the ways we respond to the moral law can make us feel we are always trying to prove ourselves through living up to certain standards. If Kant sets certain limits to the ways we compare our 'own worth with another's', since we always have to be aware of 'the dignity of humanity in another person', this can so easily become empty rhetoric, since it has already been severed from any connection with our needs, wants and desires which have already been subordinated and disdained as part of an 'animal nature'.

As long as we identify the meaning and worth of our lives with the struggle for salvation and thereby with proving ourselves in terms of the moral law, little tension is produced, particularly if we have already been able to repress and subordinate our needs, desires and feelings. In this situation it becomes easier for us not to exalt ourselves above others, since we are each working out our individual relationships with God. This is the source of whatever has significance in our lives. In a moral culture which has become more secularised it is harder to see the continuing influence of these moral traditions upon the ways we think and feel about ourselves. If we no longer feel we have to prove ourselves to God, we live within a moral culture in which we still have to prove ourselves to others as well as to ourselves. This is basic to a fundamentally competitive ethos.[2]

'Life', as Samuel Morley the 19th-century Liberal hosiery king pronounced, 'is really a continued competitive examination'. Kant's discussion of 'human worth' and 'self-esteem' prepares the deeper ground and legitimation for this sense of life, if it also limits the extent to which we can feel superior to others. In learning not to exalt ourselves above others, we are learning not to remind others continually of what we have achieved. We must learn to keep those feelings to ourselves, and not make others feel worse than they can already feel at their own lack of esteem. But sometimes this only serves to give people compensation for the misery and hardship they endure in the everyday realities of a class society, through referring them to a different realm. The ideology of self-denial which is already embedded in the ways we are to deny our wants, desires, feelings and emotions can prepare people to think and feel that the more they have to endure and suffer, the closer they are to salvation. People learn to prove themselves through the very sacrifices they are forced to make.

John is challenging the deeper assumptions of this ethic in his feeling that he does not want to have to prove himself to his father. He wants his father to accept him as he is, not to make him feel he has to prove himself before he is to be respected. In its own way the moral law, even if it is supposed to be self-legislation for Kant, comes to exist as an external standard against which we have to prove ourselves. We are educated into accepting this since it is the only source we have of our 'worth' and 'dignity'. In a secularised form, this relates to the ways John can feel he has to prove himself to his father, for him to be respected. This reveals a deeper tension in Kant's writing.

At one level we are assured of 'the worth that the other, as a man, is entitled to posit in himself' (*Doctrine of Virtue*, p. 449), but, at another level, as we have already argued, our natures, our wants, needs, desires and feelings are not taken as having any 'worth'. This can make John feel he can only be respected by his father if he does well at school, while at another level feeling his father cannot really recognise him as a person in his own right at all, because he cannot consider his individual feelings or what he wants and needs for himself. John might feel he just is not interested in doing well at school. He wants to be a dancer. This is the way he feels he can express himself most fully and deeply. But this is not something Kant acknowledges, since he tends to assume that wants and desires have to do with furthering our individual ends and purposes. This is one reason why it is only morality that can give us 'dignity'.

John's father thinks his dancing is just a matter of self-indulgence. Kantian morality can help his father feel John should apply himself to his studies, even if he does not want to. This is the very way he can prove himself. Otherwise his father thinks he is a 'lazy good for nothing'. He thinks John can do better for himself in his studies than he could ever do with his dancing. This leaves John feeling he has to become someone he isn't, in order to win the respect of his father. His father won't respect the choices he has made for himself. Kant can be enormously strengthening to John in his notion that he knows what he wants to do with his life and that his father cannot know better than he does. But he is also *undermining* of this *very process of self-affirmation* in the way he brings us up systematically to *distrust* our wants, desires, emotions and feelings.

It becomes easy for John to feel he is only satisfying his 'animal nature' and that this kind of decision can have no 'moral worth', since John is simply following his inclinations. Rather a Kantian tradition in ethics works to separate us from our very emotions, desires and needs. Rather than help us recognise the ways they are integral to a clarification and expression of identity and self, we learn to subordinate them in our search to identify ourselves with what we 'ought to do'. Life can become very much a matter of proving ourselves. At a deeper level Kantian morality prepares the moral ground for the very 'estrangement' that Marx was to begin to analyse in his *Economic and Philosophical Manuscripts* in 1844.[3]

Sometimes it is possible to read Kant as arguing for the kind of attitude people should take up towards others. It becomes very much a 'personal decision' for people to decide not to exalt themselves above others, not to contrast themselves invidiously with others. Within this situation Kant only recognises the struggles that are going on within ourselves, with our inclinations, that would make it difficult for us to respect others. This very much presupposes that it is a 'personal decision' how we treat others.

I have already argued that it is not simply up to John to decide how to treat has father, since this very much depends upon the ways his father treats John. This is not simply a 'personal relation' that solely depends upon the individual qualities of John and his father; it is also a social relation of power that is situated as a relation between father and child. In this way it is very much mediated by the organisation of the family and broader patriarchal social relations. In a society in which children are supposed to give automatic respect to their parents and where it is a sign of disobedience to question a parent, John will find himself up against a whole set of patriarchal relationships that exist to support the ways his father wants to relate to him.

A competitive society is not simply a society with competitive individuals in it. This is important to recognise if we are to be aware of the nature of the difficulties people face in learning not to 'exalt themselves above others', when they are living in a society in which they are encouraged and assumed implicitly to draw their very sense of identity from comparison with the abilities and achievements of others.

Kant's moral theory tends to *individualise* our experience in a way that makes it difficult to appreciate *how* the very social relations we are brought up to assume within a competitive society encourage us to exalt ourselves above others. Kant is asking us to work against much *more* than our inclinations, since he is sometimes asking us to challenge the existing organisation of social relations in the ways we relate to others. This is not simply a matter of adopting a different attitude towards others but of struggling to create different kinds of relations with them. Otherwise we are in danger of simply paying lip service in 'not exalting oneself above others'.

When our identities are so closely related to a sense of 'individual achievement', it becomes almost second nature for us to take up an instrumental attitude towards others. There is a general assumption that 'if you don't look after your own interests, nobody is going to look after them for you'. So it becomes easy to treat our relationships in terms of 'what we are going to get out of them'. But it is not even something we have to be consciously aware of. This might well be the reason Kant discerns a need in his discussion of respecting people, to warn us against using people as if they were only means towards our own ends. Possibly this is why we very much *need to be reminded* that people are ends in themselves.

But Kant tends to assume that we always have a choice in the ways we relate to people, having less sense of the ways we are brought up *within* certain class and sexual relations of power. It is not simply a matter of the conscious acceptance of certain ethical maxims to regulate our behaviour, though this can help us become aware of the *difficulties* of realising these maxims in our everyday lives and relationships. Weber appreciates these issues when he says that:

> Still less, naturally do we maintain that a conscious acceptance of these ethical maxims on the part of individuals, entrepreneurs or labourers, in

modern capitalistic enterprises, is a condition of the further existence of present-day capitalism. The capitalist economy of the present day is an immense cosmos into which the individual is born, and which presents itself to him, at least as an individual, as an unalterable order of things in which he must live. It forces the individual, in so far as he is involved in the system of market relationships, to conform to capitalistic rules of action. The manufacturer who in the long turn acts counter to these norms, will just as inevitably be eliminated from the economic scene as the worker who cannot or will not adapt himself to them will be thrown into the streets without a job. (*The Protestant Ethic and The Spirit of Capitalism*, p. 54)[4]

Weber's insight has to be threatening because it challenges the kind of 'independence' people can be assumed to have in the self-awareness of liberal culture. Kant did not have to acknowledge this kind of challenge in his earlier writings since he could more easily abstract from the 'empirical world', believing individuals were guaranteed their 'independence' in their relationships with the moral law. If Kant comes nearer to acknowledging the force of this challenge in *The Doctrine of Virtue*, it has been difficult for our moral theory fully to accept a challenge to its individualistic assumptions and to the autonomy of morality which they sustain. Taking these issues seriously involves reworking the liberal relationship of morality to politics.[5]

LOVE AND RESPECT

Kant did tend to think that the social world was very much governed by laws in the way the natural world is. He was endeavouring to discover the laws which govern people's 'external relations with one another'. This is the way notions of love and respect become fundamentally related principles of social life. There are not simply different 'attitudes' people can take up towards each other.

Kant makes this clear in *The Doctrine of Virtue*:

When we are speaking of laws of duty (not laws of nature) and, among these, of laws governing men's external relations with one another, we are considering a moral (intelligible) world where, by analogy with the physical world, *attraction* and *repulsion* bind together rational beings (on earth). The principle of *mutual love* admonishes men constantly to *come nearer* to each other; that of *respect* which they owe each other, to keep themselves at a *distance* from one another. (*The Doctrine of Virtue*, p. 448)

Love and respect are 'great moral forces' which are fundamentally related to each other. They help us understand the nature of human relationships as fundamental conceptions of a moral science.

This notion of respect has had a deep influence upon liberal moral culture. It builds some kind of recognisable tension into our relations with others, since we do not want to be thought of as interfering in their lives. It tends to make us wary in approaching others, lest our intentions be misinterpreted. In many ways this throws us back upon ourselves and makes us feel it is best to live without needing the help and support of others.[6] What is more, we can be assured this is the way to maximise our moral worth.

So it becomes harder even to acknowledge whatever needs we have for others, since this is so easily taken as a sign of 'weakness'. We easily absorb an ideal of self-sufficiency and independence, priding ourselves on being able to live without the help and support of others. This will inevitably have an influence upon the form and character of our friendships.

Generally we will discover ourselves to be quite tentative in our approaches towards others. It will not be easy for us to share our pain and sorrow with them, especially if we assume we will be burdening them. It will be difficult to accept this kind of sharing as an integral part of our relationships with others, especially if we are brought up to disdain these emotions and feelings as a sign of weakness, of lack of control over our 'animal natures', which show we have not yet become the fully rational beings we aspire to be.

If I grow up to take for granted the need to show respect for others through keeping a certain distance from them, then this is simply a matter of doing my duty towards others. I will tend to see keeping my distance as a matter of fulfilling my individual duties, rather than recognising it as an aspect of social relations I grow up to take very much for granted. This will make it harder for instance for me to relate my feelings of loneliness and isolation to these social relations, thinking this just happens to be the way I feel, while assuming others feel very different.[7] I will tend to develop little sense and understanding of the ways my feelings develop in relation to the competitive social relations I am brought up to take very much for granted.

But Kant is also aware of the ways love and respect relate to each other. If respect keeps us at a distance from others there is always love which 'admonishes men constantly to come nearer to each other'. But the difference remains that in respecting someone we are only rendering to the other 'what is due to him':

> The first division of duties of virtue to others can be the division into duties by fulfilling which we also obligate the other, and duties whose observance does not result in obligation on the other part. – To fulfil the first is meritorious (in relation to the other person); but to fulfil the second is to render the other only what is *due* to him. – *Love* and *respect* are the feelings that accompany the practice of these duties. They can be considered separately (each by itself) and can also exist separately (we can *love* our neighbour though he might deserve but little respect, and we can show him *respect* necessary for every person though we might not think him very loveable). But in their ground in the law love and respect are always joined together in a duty, only in such a way that now one duty and now the other is the subject's principle, with the other joined to it as an accessory.   (*The Doctrine of Virtue*, p. 448)

This partly echoes the ways Kant sometimes thinks about the relationship of duty and inclination 'which of the two incentives he makes the condition of the other' (*Religion Within the Limits of Reason Alone*, 36 g 31 e). This seems to indicate that, though 'love and respect are always joined together in a duty', at any one time one of them 'is the subject's principle'. The clear difference, which becomes very significant in the ways Kant talks about the relationship between rich and poor, is that love obligates the other while respect simply gives to another what is due to him or her.

In this context Kant talks about the respect due to someone, but he does not invoke the same sense of distance. What is more, he also seems to be trading on what I have called a *hierarchical* sense of respect, when he says 'we can love our neighbour though he might deserve but little respect'. This seems to be a matter of respecting someone as looking up to someone, because of what he or she has been able to accomplish morally or because of moral qualities they have displayed. This is different from the more *egalitarian* sense of respect which is due to every person, though we have already shown how this trades upon a particular relationship we have as 'intelligible beings' to the moral law. The relationship to the moral law remains fundamental to Kant and influences the ways he thinks about both love and respect.[8]

Every duty involves an immediate obligation to do something, and to do it with respect to a particular person. Kant is very aware that we cannot be obligated to have particular feelings and desires, as we can be obligated to do something. For Kant, the love which comes into the morality of loving one's neighbour cannot, in any sense, be thought of as emotional love. Our feelings cannot be depended upon, nor can we have particular feelings for others, just because we want to have them. I cannot just start loving someone because I feel I ought to. It is with this realisation in mind that Kant thinks about love. It also becomes the basis for his identification of morality with what we can be obligated to do. But as Scheler has realised, 'his *conclusion* that an act of love has no moral value *because* it cannot be commanded is totally *erroneous*' (*Formalism in Ethics*, p. 221).[9]

For Kant it is only what can be obligated that can have moral worth. He puts all his emphasis upon what we are ready to do for people, knowing we cannot be obligated to feel about them in a particular way. So what becomes important is not the feelings people have for each other, but what they are prepared to do for each other. We have to be ready to do things for people, whatever we might feel about them:

> In this context, however, is not to be taken as a *feeling* (aesthetic love), i.e. a pleasure in the perfection of other men; it does not mean *emotional* love (for others cannot oblige us to have feelings). It must rather be taken as a maxim of *benevolence* (practical love), which has beneficence as its consequence. (*Doctrine of Virtue*, p. 448)

In this way Kant thinks of love as a feeling in terms of the pleasure we get 'in the perfection of other men'. This is to see it very much in terms of our individual pleasure, since, as Scheler recognises, Kant does not draw on any distinction between 'striving for one's own and striving for someone else's pleasure':

> But it is clear that in his view striving for someone else's pleasure (mediated through feelings of sympathy) can be genetically reduced to striving for one's own pleasure in someone else's pleasure. This is a clear consequence of his assumption that all pleasures and displeasures as feelings – irrespective of what they are 'in' – are *qualitatively* of the same kind and not different in *depth*, i.e. that from which all pleasure and displeasure is derived, is *sensible* pleasure . . . Since Kant considers all feelings relevant to ethics to be *sensible* feelings – with the sole exception of the feeling of respect, which he calls a spiritual feeling, 'effected by the moral law' – all feelings of sympathy, under which he also subsumes love and hate, are excluded as morally relevant determining grounds of willing and acting and as bearers of moral values. Kant's presupposition that all feelings except 'respect' are of sensible origin is the reason why he does not draw any ethical distinction

in terms of quality or depth between sensible pleasure, joy, happiness, and bliss. (*Formalism in Ethics and Non-Formal Ethics of Values*, p. 240)

Kant does not acknowledge the importance of changes in the quality and depth of our feelings and emotions. He does not develop any sense of the ways our lives come to have more meaning and our relationships more depth, as we learn to feel more deeply and more truthfully. This notion tends to be alien to Kant, who assumes our emotions and feelings have to relate to our individual pleasures. At some level people are implicitly assumed to be egoists exclusively concerned with their sensual hedonism, were it not for morality which under the force of obligation and duty constrains us to control our inclinations so we can live up to a higher idea of ourselves. This is a deeply pervasive conception of morality. It is because at some fundamental level we could never rely upon our natures, upon our emotions and feelings, that we require a conception of morality.[10]

At one level Kant conceives of morality in terms of obligation, so he wants to think of a 'principle' that 'demands reverence for a law that *commands* and does not leave it up to just any kind of choice' (*Critique of Practical Reason*, Part 1, Book 1, Ch. 3). For Kant, unless something can be commanded it means it is left 'up to just any kind of choice'. In this way our loving others has to be subordinated to the moral law, if we are to be able to depend upon it. But such a principle cannot be considered as giving an order for it does not make any sense, as Kant subsequently says, to want to 'order' or 'command' love:

[Love] is indeed possible with regard to men, but it cannot be commanded for no man can love another simply as an order. Hence it is only *practical love* which can be understood in the core of all laws. In this sense to love God means to *like* to follow his commandments; to love one's neighbour, to *like* to do all the duties with regard to him. (*Critique of Practical Reason*, Part 1, Book 1, Ch. 3)

If Kant holds that 'only what can be commanded is of moral value', and also that the good is what is commanded by a law, then he has to conclude that love has no moral value. But Kant does not want to conclude that this principle is a 'commandment that orders love' so he is forced to reinterpret the meaning of love. This is something Scheler realises:

He says that although love cannot be commanded, '*practical love*' can . . . There is no 'practical love' as a special quality of love, only love that leads to practical ways of comportment. But the *latter* cannot be commanded either. On the other hand, things other than love can lead to practical ways of comportment, too, e.g. 'goodwill' as well as 'good-doing'. The latter can be commanded. But both are basically different from the act of loving and they can exist without being consequences of love. We have 'goodwill' e.g. towards men who serve us or are useful to us. (*Formalism in Ethics and Non-Formal Ethics of Values*, p. 225)

At some level it can seem as if it is always possible for us to respect others, since it is always possible for us to keep ourselves at a distance from others, while it is not possible for us to love others if we do not feel like coming nearer to them. This relates to the particular status Kant gives to our respect. It is the moral law which can obligate us to respect others. But if respect means more than simply maintaining a distance from others, but also involves giving some kind of recognition to the humanity of another person, then this has its own difficulties.

At one level I might think that I am already giving this acknowledge-ment, through maintaining a certain distance from others. At another level I might recognise that it is quite hard for me genuinely to respect others, even when this is a matter of recognising that others have lives of their own. I might find myself always thinking about what I can get out of people. Kant warns us against this, again through drawing a contrast between love and respect:

The duty of love for one's neighbour can also be expressed as the duty of making others' *ends* my own (in so far as these ends are only not immoral). The duty of respect for my neighbour is contained in the maxim of not abasing any other man to a mere means to my end (not demanding that the other not degrade himself in order to slave for my end). (*The Doctrine of Virtue*, p. 448)

Sometimes it seems as if 'making others' *ends* my own' simply means acknowledging that others have ends of their own, which need to be care-fully protected. This kind of minimal interpretation is in line with the recognition that individuals have to be free to pursue their own ends. But this is also in line with the way Kant interprets the Christian idea of 'love thy neighbour as yourself' as 'every man has a duty to others of adopting the maxim of benevolence'. This is how Kant explains this in the section entitled 'On Duties of Love in Particular' in *The Doctrine of Virtue*:

Now the benevolence present in the love of all men as such is indeed the greatest in its *extent*, but the smallest in its *degree*; and when I say: I take an interest in this man's welfare only in keeping with my universal love for man, the interest I take is as slight as an interest can be. I am only not indifferent with regard to him.   (*The Doctrine of Virtue*, p. 450)

When Kant says that 'the interest I take is as slight as an interest can be', he is acknowledging how limited my 'universal love for man' can be. At the same time he is bringing out that what matters is not what our wishes for others are, but what we are prepared to do for them. This expresses something important, even if it allows Kant to escape difficult issues about the meaning of such notions as concern, caring, sympathy, compassion and liking, which he takes to be feelings of no moral worth.[11]

Kant does not want to provide an interpretation of our 'universal love' for others which would compromise in any way the 'independence' people have. It can seem that he talks about taking an interest in others, so he does not have to talk about developing our feelings of concern and care for others. At the same time this 'interest' is given such a minimal content that it means 'I am only not indifferent with regard to him'. But this is to say very little about the nature of our concern and caring for others. But if this is difficult for Kant since these are understood as unreliable inclinations, it says little about our sense of the needs others have and our concern for the quality of the lives others live.

In the same passage Kant acknowledges that we are closer to some people than to others, though he avoids talking about this in terms of caring for some people more than others. He acknowledges that if I am closer to someone then I will want to help that person more:

Yet one man is closer to me than another, and in benevolence I am the closest to myself. Now how does this fit with the precept 'love your neighbour (your fellow-man) as yourself'? When (in the duty of benevolence) one man is closer to me than another, I am obligated to greater benevolence to him than to the other; but I am admittedly closer to myself (even according to duty) than any other. So it would seem that I cannot, without contradicting myself, say that I ought to love every man as myself; for the standard of self-love would allow of no difference in degree. – But it is quite obvious that what is meant, in this case, is not a mere benevolence in *wishes*, which is really only a satisfaction in the well-being of all others and does not even require me to contribute to their well-being (every man for himself: God for us all). It refers, rather, to active, practical benevolence (beneficence), which consists in making another's well-being and happiness my *end*. For in wishing I can be *equally* benevolent to everyone, whereas in acting I can, without violating the universality of my maxim, vary the degree greatly according to the different objects of my love (one of whom concerns me more closely than the other). (*Doctrine of Virtue*, p. 451; Gregor translation)

So Kant builds upon his significant recognition that what we do for others matters so much more than what we feel about them. But in saying this he subordinates our caring, concern, kindness, sympathy as a 'mere benevolence in *wishes*'. In this way he severs any possible connection between the ways we feel about others and what we are prepared to do for them. This is related to a much deeper point about the connection of 'moral worth' to the sacrifices we are prepared to make in proving ourselves.

Kant seems to imply that we cannot expect to love others like ourselves since 'I am the closest to myself' and so can be expected to love myself more than others. At one level Kant acknowledges that 'the standard of self-love would allow of no difference in degree', while it is clear to him that we want to help those we are closer to more than others. This leaves an important space for friendships in which we are more committed to helping others. But the very universalism of his maxims makes it difficult to think about friendship as a particular kind of relationship. Kant has few ways of thinking about the moral significance of personal relationships in our lives, since these relations are so easily put under pressure and dissolve as they are subordinated to individuals' proving themselves in the face of the moral law.

Even though Kant talks about 'the standard of self-love' against which we cannot be expected to compare our relations with others, this remains a deeply ambiguous notion, since Kant is always warning us against the inherent selfishness of our wants and desires. It is only the somewhat external intervention of the moral law and our sense of duty which can 'save us' from this selfish nature of ours. This is one of the reasons Kantian tradition remains so deeply grateful for the moral law. In this sense it is the moral law that allows us to 'rise above' the essentially selfish natures we would otherwise be trapped in.

This is partly why our sense of morality has to be fundamentally separated from our emotions and feelings, which are taken to be inherently about indvidual pleasure and satisfaction, even when they are feelings of caring, concern, sympathy and love. Acting out of these feelings cannot have any 'moral worth' since, for Kant, we would be doing what we wanted to do, not what we ought to be doing. But this is also part of the deep ambiguity in Kant's notion of 'self-love', since this can have little to do with caring, accepting or appreciating ourselves. Rather we grow up within a Kantian tradition very much despising our natures, our desires and needs, our emotions and feelings, since we are taught to see these feelings as inherently 'selfish' and self-seeking temptations and distractions from the real meaning and goals of life. Little can be gained by dwelling upon our individual needs and wants. They offer us little understanding of our duties towards others. Very easily 'self-love' becomes a form of *self-denial* as we learn to think of our desires and emotions as temptations taking us away from the true path which moves closer to a moral ideal of selflessness.

In its own way this helps create a kind of fear of our individual pleasure which is deeply embedded within the moral culture. We grow up feeling that there is something almost sinful in pleasuring ourselves. In a strange and unspoken way this can make it easier for many people to give to others than to give to themselves. Of course this exists in a much more extreme form in moral cultures deeply influenced by Calvinism, but it remains broadly significant, even if generally unacknowledged, within more hedonistic self-conceptions of twentieth-century liberal moral culture. This is the same contradiction that allows Kant to talk about 'self-love', while being involved in developing a morality which inherently involves self-denial. But it is also why it is so difficult to recognise such processes at work.

So for Kant, the idea of loving your neighbour as yourself has little to do with learning to feel and care for others in a particular way. This might be part of a more socialist moral tradition which encouraged us to recognise ourselves in our 'neighbours' so that we become aware we share the same needs and desires, even if we also want different things out of life. Kant gives moral weight to the differences between people, tending to think that what we share with others is simply part of our 'animal natures' which cannot give our lives any worth or dignity.

He helps us avoid the issues around the needs we share with others in the way that he interprets 'love your neighbour as yourself' as a matter of adopting the 'maxim of benevolence'. It is only through accepting this duty that we can avoid being 'self-seeking'. In this way loving your neighbour becomes subordinated to the moral law, rather than in any way being a challenge to the moral law:

> According to the ethical law of perfection 'love your neighbour as yourself', every man has a duty to others of adopting the maxim of benevolence (practical love of man), whether or not he finds them loveable. – For every morally practical relation to men is a relation

of men in the thought of pure reason, i.e. a relation of free actions according to maxims which qualify for giving universal law and which, therefore, cannot be self-seeking (*ex solipsmo prodeuntes*). I want every other man to be benevolent to me (*benevolentiam*); hence I should also be benevolent to every other man. (*The Doctrine of Virtue*, p. 450)

This rests upon the important conviction that we have to act morally towards others, whether or not we find them 'lovable'. So for instance I might help the person down the street because she needs help fixing her car, even though I do not like her very much as a person. I might help her knowing that I might need her help someday. I might not like feeling this way. This is still different from helping her so that she will have to help me if my car breaks down. Kant thinks that we can only guarantee against such 'self-seeking' if we are acting 'according to maxims which qualify for giving universal law'. This is the only way we can guarantee we are not being 'self-seeking'.

In doing this we are always abstracting from the feelings we have for particular people. Feelings of sympathy, caring, kindness are seen as having less 'moral worth' because they are seen as essentially partial. We care for some people but we do not care for others. This helps Kant to the conclusion that they can have no moral worth, especially since they often mean we are doing things for people because we want to, which is taken as a form of 'self-seeking'. This is what makes it easy for Kant to conclude that 'only what can be commanded is of moral value'.

If Kant acknowledges that we act out of kindness and sympathy for others and that sometimes this leads us to do the same things for others as we would if we were acting out of a sense of duty, this makes little difference to the moral worth of our actions. It is not simply that our emotions and feelings are unreliable guides in our behaviour. But Kant thinks that our emotions and feelings have no connection with our knowing and understanding, which have their independent source in our reason. Kant thinks that if we act because of the influence of an emotion or feeling then this inevitably detracts from the rationality of the choice we have made. Our choice can no longer be as 'free' as it would otherwise be, since it would be made under the influence of an external influence.

Kant has little sense of the *development* of our emotions and feelings, but thinks within a tradition which fundamentally opposes our emotions, sensibility and desires to our rationality. Kant tends to assume a theory that implies that through struggling against our inclinations, they will inevitably come to have less influence upon our lives. This is sometimes conceived of as a process of attrition through which the influence of our emotions and feelings is first weakened and then reduced. This is supposed to make us freer to act out of a sense of duty. It was Freud who helped us understand that if we subordinate our emotions and desires they do not cease to have an influence upon our behaviour, even if we become less aware of the influence they continue to have. A rationalist theory of ethics finds it difficult to come to terms with this discovery.[12]

There is little space within Kant for a discussion of the 'rationality' or 'appropriateness' of our emotions and desires. There is little sense of the significance and meaning which our emotions and feelings have within our relationships. Rather our feelings are assumed to have no bearing upon the 'moral worth' of what we do. For Kant it can be no part of morality for us to develop certain kinds of caring and loving relationships with others. These relationships can give no more meaning to our lives than other relationships. Rather there is a deeper presupposition which works to *subordinate* the meaningfulness of relationships within our lives. Kant is concerned with how people come to do what they ought to do. This is essentially an individual decision that has bearing upon the 'moral worth' of an individual.

At a deep level Kant prepares us for a moral culture in which we are continually having to *prove* our worth, since this can never be assumed. What is more, we always have to prove ourselves *individually*, which means our moral energies have to go into affirming the moral worth of what we do individually. At a fundamental level, what matters to us cannot be the relationships we have with others, but the opportunities which these relationships have afforded to us to prove ourselves individually. We can expect to find little 'meaning' and 'worth' within these relationships themselves. This tends to encourage the very kind of instrumental attitude towards others, where we are naturally focussed upon what we can 'get out of others', that Kant warns us about. The deeper presuppositions of Kant's moral theory seem to encourage us into the very relationships with others he is careful to warn us about. This is one of the deeper contradictions we unwittingly inherit within our liberal moral culture.[13]

This is related to the ways Kant seems to make the moral value of an action depend on its *cost*, on the *sacrifices* we are ready to make. So in the *Critique of Practical Reason* Kant reminds us that 'Virtue is worth so much here only because it costs so much, not because it brings us something'. This notion is deeply embedded within Kant's moral theory and is something we inherit in a taken-for-granted way in our liberal moral culture. So it is easy to think that our actions are bound to be more worthy because of the sacrifices we had to make in doing them. We can feel that we have shown how much we love someone by the sacrifices we have been ready to make for them.

It is almost as if we can *prove* the love we have through showing the sacrifices we have been prepared to make. Not only can we make someone feel guilty when a person thinks about the sacrifices others have been ready to make, but it is easy to fall into accepting such sacrifices as proof of someone's love. This can involve the acceptance of a certain kind of cruelty towards oneself and one's feelings, though this might be barely experienced as such. Such notions have profound implications for our moral psychology, since they often mean we unwittingly feel easier in denying ourselves as a proof of our devotion to others, than giving ourselves emotionally to them. This can make us identify with the very sacrifices we make, as a way of proving ourselves.[14]

At another level it remains important to think about the kind of effort which a certain action has taken. It can also be important to think about the kinds of things I am prepared to do for others. It makes a difference to what I think about someone if he continually talks about wanting to help me out, but never seems to have much time for me. But this is different from the ways we can identify with the sacrifices we make in our own wants and desires, thinking that in this way we prove our moral worth. In this process it becomes easy to devalue our very wants and desires, rather than think this is a genuine sacrifice we have chosen to make because it is important for us to help others.

This involves a very different attitude towards our wants, desires, needs and emotions. It is not simply that we are more ready to sacrifice our needs and desires than we should be. Rather we tend to devalue our wants and needs as 'animal', in contrast to something 'higher' which we are brought up to identify ourselves with. This tendency in our thinking and feeling is encouraged through the ways we are brought up to assume that the satisfaction of our individual wants and needs has to be 'self-seeking'.

In this way we can think we prove our moral worth through showing we are ready to make greater sacrifices than others. In its own way this prepares the way for a morality of individual achievement and success. We are ready to make whatever sacrifices are necessary as long as we secure our individual achievement. Here we are talking about identifying similarities in the formation of what we can think of as our moral characters. Whether we are proving ourselves in terms of our moral worth, or whether we are proving ourselves through fulfilling the goals we have set for ourselves, there is a similar acceptance of the need to deny our desires, needs, emotions and wants to fulfil a 'higher purpose'. The meaning of our lives is given in a sphere radically demarcated from the fulfilment of our human wants and needs.

Kant is suggesting it is possible to live our lives with a supreme awareness of our 'sublime moral disposition'. Not only does this assume people are 'free' to set their own ends, but it assumes people can pursue their own ends, without becoming dependent upon others. This is necessary if it is granted that each individual has to work out his or her own moral destiny in working out a relationship to the moral law. This is why Kant needs to think so fundamentally of respect in terms of distance. Kant wanted to guarantee the independence of people to prove their individual moral worth. People are to subordinate themselves to a moral law they legislate for themselves. Subordination relates to each person individually. The fact that we are to give this law to ourselves is supposed to make the subordination more bearable. It is consciousness of our 'moral disposition' that should be enough for us to assume a position of equality with others, regardless of the situation of power and domination we are living in. Kant wants to protect us from a subordination to other people, while making us aware of the nature of our subordination to the moral law. There is a deep assumption of 'independence' that is supposedly guaranteed to each of us individually, through the respect due to us.

The fact that we are people with duties laid upon us by our reason is supposed to give us a way of feeling equal to whoever we come across in our lives. This puts limits on the ways others can treat us and means we must adopt the maxim 'of not abasing any other man to a mere means to my end'. This seems to guarantee our freedom and equality with others. What is more the ways Kant thinks of 'dignity' in terms of 'inner worth' make it seem as if this is invulnerable to the social relations of power and dominance in everyday social life. Kant tends to think of 'living a moral life' as an individual venture in which the highest value is placed upon 'being able to represent oneself as good' and on 'being able to esteem oneself'. He makes us think and feel we have to be continually proving ourselves. This helps Kant think of our moral lives as very much about the moral worth of individual actions and needs. The individual proves himself or herself through the number of good deeds he or she does.

This relation to the moral law remains untouched by the character of the society people are living in. Rather Kant can be largely unaware of the character of the assumptions he makes about social life and the social relations of power and subordination, because of the ways he conceives individuals' being able to abstract themselves from the responsibilities of social life to be able to listen to the higher voice of the moral law. So morality is about a particular aspect of our lives, our relation to the moral law. The issues then focus upon whether we have the strength of character and will to do what is required of us by the moral law. There is little sense of the ways in which moral issues are presented to us through the social relations of power and dominance we are obliged to live in, in our everyday social lives. There is also little sense of the ways people change and transform themselves as moral beings, other than by proving themselves in terms of the moral law.

It is only later when Kant is forced to think about the moral relations between rich and poor that he is forced to rethink the assumption of 'independence' that he assumed to be guaranteed by his notion of respect. It was no longer enough for Kant to warn us against exalting ourselves over others or of treating others as means to our own ends. It could no longer simply be a question of individual conviction and individual personal decision. Rather the very assumptions which guaranteed the autonomy of morals would have to be rethought. Kant withdrew from this difficult edge. This is something I have discussed in *Kant, Respect and Injustice*; the tension in Kant that seems crucial to mention here is that he wants to invest the individual with some sort of worth, but he achieves it at the cost of seeing social phenomena as contingent. In the following chapters I shall move to consider how far Kierkegaard, with a different sense of what is at issue in relationship, meets this difficulty. This issue, as I go on to explore it, has to do with the particular quality of capitalist society as a competitive society. I have already shown how Kant presupposes these particular kinds of relations; now I am going to consider Kierkegaard's understanding of them.

Kierkegaard's philosophy is challenging to Kant at different levels. He offers us a way of bringing duty and love into a different relation, so that we are led to consider the relationship between our substantive capacities to love and the kind of persons we are. Through this connection Kierkegaard helps us to think about the quality of our relationships in ways that are undercut by the radical fragmentations we have seen to be built into Kant's rationalism. Yet if Kierkegaard helps us to fill out a conception of love as a practice, he does it within the context of a vision limited by its grounding in a particular form of Christianity. It is a vision which is nevertheless arrested at a point which defines structures of power as beyond the sphere of morality and thereby leaves the structural dimensions of oppression untouched.

3 Love and Equality

LEARNING TO LOVE OTHERS

Following Kant, Søren Kierkegaard's *Works of Love* illustrates a conception of Christian equality which essentially *abstracts* from the everyday conditions of power and subordination within social life. He offers us a picture of social life that would systematically deny the moral significance of social inequality. For Kierkegaard, however, it is through the duty to love others that I am to learn to recognise others as 'neighbours'. This is to create a connection between us as human beings that is supposed to be more important than whatever divides us in the social world. This is the importance of Christian love:

> It is the Christian love which discovers and knows that the neighbour exists, and what amounts to the same thing, that everyone is a neighbour. If it were not a duty to love, then the concept of neighbour would not exist; but only when one loves one's neighbour, only then is the selfish partiality eradicated, and the equality of the eternal preserved. (*Works of Love*, p. 37)

Kierkegaard tells us that: 'If it were not a duty to love, then the concept of neighbour would not exist.' It is not simply a question of being made aware of what it means to be a 'neighbour' in our everyday language. Often analytical procedures seem to presume a fundamentally contemplative relationship towards the rules of language. We are to be made aware of how certain concepts are used through being made aware of the rules of usage. This can be to see language as a set of rules to which we have to conform. Such a vision is a widespread misinterpretation of Wittgenstein's ideas which never comes to terms with what he learnt from Kierkegaard.[1]

Kierkegaard is suggesting a more active and involved sense of ourselves in relationship to the language we speak.[2] It is only through the experience of *learning to love* one's neighbour that one can learn the meaning of 'the concept of neighbour'. This is not something we can hope to understand if we have not begun to learn *how* to love our neighbour. It is not simply a question of taking this injunction to heart. This makes it different from the relationship between respect, love and the moral law we find in Kant. It is not like reminding myself that if I make a promise then I have to keep it.

Nor is it something solely within our individual control that we can simply make an individual decision of will about. I have also got to be ready and open to learn to love my neighbour.

Christianity makes it our duty to love others. It is only when we have learnt to love that our 'selfish partiality' is 'eradicated' and 'the equality of the eternal preserved'. In this way our 'selfish partiality' is understood to be in direct conflict with 'the equality of the eternal'. In this way Kierkegaard also seems to challenge the kind of moral psychology of liberalism that we find in Rawls of 'free and rational persons concerned to further their own interests'.[3] This would be part of the 'selfish partiality' he wants to challenge. This is the way Kierkegaard's Christianity is essentially critical of the kinds of social and personal relationships which liberal moral and political theory takes so much for granted in its vision of the relationship between individual and society.

Partiality and selfishness are not taken to be features of relationships within particular societies, but of human relationships more generally. It is only through learning to love others as neighbours that we can hope for some kind of *transformation* to take place in our sense of ourselves in relation to others. This seems to involve much more than simply taking up a different attitude towards others. It also involves developing *different kinds of relationships* with others. This is the way we can challenge our 'selfish partiality'. Such a view also contrasts with Kant. It is not simply through an act of will and individual determination that we can hope to change ourselves. It is not like cutting out the part of an apple which is rotten. This is not simply a matter of subordinating aspects of our natures which would make it harder for us to act out of a sense of duty.

This challenges a very powerful conception within our moral culture. It is very easy to feel that my selfishness just proves what a worthless person I am. Without recognising the cultural and historical sources of these feelings it is also easy to feel that I have to repress my selfish inclinations if I want to have a chance of becoming less selfish. Without being aware of the moral psychology we are tacitly committing ourselves to, this is often the way we implicitly assume that people change.[4]

The conception that Kierkegaard offers us is very different. It is only through learning to love others that we will discover that our 'selfish partiality' has been eradicated. We do not have to focus upon challenging these feelings directly. Rather we have to learn *how* to love others as neighbours. This is the way we will contact a deeper sense of equality with others. Kierkegaard helps us learn how to love others through helping us become more aware of what is involved in loving ourselves. This involves appreciating a very different kind of moral and political psychology from that which we find in Kant. It is not simply a question of obeying the moral law and remembering each time we meet someone that we have to love him or her as a 'neighbour'. Nor is this a matter of gradually extending the circle of people we love.[5]

For Kierkegaard it is very much a matter of the *quality* of our relationships which will be connected with the quality of our relationships with ourselves.[6] This is something we can learn through the transformations taking place as we learn to love others as our neighbours. But this is to recognise the *difficulty* of relating to even a single person as a 'neighbour':

> 'Neighbour' is itself a multitude, for 'neighbour' implies 'all men', and yet in another sense one man is enough to enable you to obey the commandment. In a selfish sense it is an impossibility to be two in being a self; self-love demands that it be one. Nor are three needed, for if there are two, that is, if there is one other human being whom, in the Christian sense, you love 'as yourself', or in whom you love the 'neighbour', then you love all men . . .
>
> 'Neighbour' presses as closely as possible upon the selfishness in life. If there are only two men, the other man is the neighbour, if there are two millions, each one of these is the neighbour, who is again closer to one than 'the friend' and 'the beloved', insofar as they, in being objects of preferential love, gradually become analogous to the self-love in one . . .   (*Works of Love*, p. 18)

Kierkegaard thinks that the difficulties in learning to love someone as a 'neighbour' are akin to the difficulties of loving someone 'as yourself'. We have to learn to challenge the 'selfish partiality' which is an aspect of our 'self-love'. Kierkegaard makes us aware of the ways we so easily make friends and lovers 'the objects of preferential love' which 'gradually becomes analogous to the self-love in one'.

Kierkegaard questions some of the liberal assumptions we make about human relationships. He questions the moral psychology implicit in Kant's writings and which we so often assume within our moral culture. This encourages us to feel that we respect others by making sure we have the correct attitude towards them. This is deeply related to a rationalist tradition within moral philosophy. It becomes a matter of *deciding* to take up a certain attitude of respect or love towards others because we have been given sound reasons for doing so. Because we have been convinced that this is the correct attitude, we do our best to relate to others in this way. This is related to our sense of the importance of living up to the moral law regardless of our individual feelings and wants. We inherit a Kantian sense of our 'moral worth' through being prepared to obey the dictates of the moral law. In a similar way we learn that we have certain duties towards ourselves.

So it is no surprise that Kant has separate and distinct discussions which talk of our duty to ourselves and our duties to others.[7] The focus in each situation is upon doing what our reason has discerned to be required by the moral law. In its own way this can unwittingly encourage us to objectify ourselves in very much the same ways as we can learn to objectify others. Kant unwittingly prepares the ground for this *impersonalisation* of our moral experience in a morality largely defined in terms of universal principles, in his conception that all respect for people is really respect for the moral law.

The moral psychology that Kierkegaard offers us is very different and implies that our relations with others are connected with the quality of the relationship with ourselves. This is a dialectical conception which is deeply challenging to our inherited Kantian sense that relating to others with equal respect is centrally a matter of taking up the correct attitude towards them. This involves more than will. It involves more than making an intellectual decision and then having the determination to put it into practice. We have to challenge the inherited rationalism to learn the nature of the *difficulties* we meet in changing the ways we relate to others. This challenges our common-sense conceptions as we learn we have to work on ourselves and on our relationship with ourselves, if we want our relationship with others to change. It can no longer simply be a matter of deciding to relate to others in a certain way.

There is a deeper psychological and moral understanding in Kierkegaard's recognition that we have to learn to love ourselves in a different way, if we want to learn to love others as neighbours. This involves a process of personal and moral transformation. This is not a matter of placing a different ideal before ourselves that we want to aspire to. It is not a question of setting a different goal or end for ourselves, as we would tend to assume within Kant's moral theory. It involves a different kind of awareness of our changing experience. It is only *as we learn* to love others that we discover we ourselves are going through a process of change and transformation in which our 'selfish partiality' will be 'eradicated'. Now we also learn, somewhat paradoxically, that this involves learning to love ourselves in the right way:

> when the commandment is rightly understood, it also says the converse, *'Thou shalt love thyself in the right way'*. If anyone therefore, will not

learn from Christianity to love *himself* in the right way, then neither can he love his neighbour; he may perhaps, as we say, 'for life and death' – cling to one or several other human beings, but this is by no means loving one's neighbour. To love one's self in the right way and to love one's neighbour are absolutely analogous concepts, are at the bottom one and the same. (*Works of Love*, p. 19)

In learning to love ourselves in the right way, we are already challenging the ways we are brought up to think and feel about ourselves. This partly involves challenging a Kantian inheritance if we are to grasp what is involved. Learning to love ourselves in the right way is not simply a matter of living up to a law we know to be correct. There are other issues which do not seem so visible or significant within a rationalist tradition. How do we know that we are learning to love ourselves in the right way? This is not just a matter of appealing to some standard or ideal that exists outside our experience, against which our experience is to be judged. There is a different kind of epistemology at work here.

We learn *through our experience* that loving oneself in the right way is 'absolutely analogous' to loving one's neighbour. This is not something we can learn intellectually and *then* try to make true for us. Rather it is something we learn the truth of *through* the changes in our experience. This is very different from the empiricist idea that we validate the truth of this notion through our own experience. Such a view retains an essentially external relation between our ideas and our experience. It is part of what is being challenged as we learn the truth of this connection through our experience of it. In a very real sense we have to *experience the truth* that they 'are absolutely analogous concepts'. This helps us develop a more phenomenological understanding.[8]

Kierkegaard is critical of the 'selfish partiality' which he takes to be a feature endemic to earthly life. He is also critical of the ways we tend to 'cling to one or several other human beings' and the ways people become 'the objects of preferential love' for us. This is all related for Kierkegaard to the ease with which we 'confuse love with the possession of the beloved'. Our relationships become possessive and we cannot help feeling that others belong to us, though we would hardly want to recognise this about ourselves. Often we take for granted the pattern of social relations within our society so that we barely realize their possessive character.[9]

Just think for a moment of the difficulty which a married woman could have within conventional society asking a man to go to the cinema with her. They might both share an interest in the cinema and she might just want to share this experience with him. Her husband might discover all kinds of possessive feelings he did not think he had. The person she asks might feel equally uneasy about the suggestion. He might feel uneasy at the fact she had taken the initiative, which in some masculine sense should be his. Kierkegaard recognises the *ease* with which we relate to others possessively. We might even find ourselves becoming anxious as a friend of ours is getting close to someone else, because we fear they will not want to be so friendly with us.

This is not anything we might feel rationally. At one level we might feel quite easy about our friends developing new friendships. But at another level we can discover ourselves feeling anxious, lest they turn out to like this new person better than they like us. At some level this can relate to a deep and unexplored feeling we have that we are not really lovable ourselves and we do not really deserve the friendships we have.

Kierkegaard has the psychological understanding that can help us grasp this. He is also aware of the need to work on the ways we feel about ourselves, if we are to feel more secure and less anxious in our friendships. But this involves being prepared to recognise and acknowledge the anxieties and fears we feel, even if we cannot make sense of them rationally.

For Kierkegaard, the ways our love is possessive is connected with the notion of dependency:

> He in whom love is a necessity certainly feels free in his love . . . on one condition, that he does not confuse love with the possession of the beloved . . . When love does not make the same demands upon itself as it makes upon the object of its love, which is still dependent on that love, then it is still dependent in a false sense; that law of existence lies outside itself, and hence it is dependent in the corruptible, earthly, temporal sense. But the love which underwent the change of eternity becomes duty, and loves because it must love, it is independent . . . This love can never become in a false sense dependent, for the only one it is dependent upon is duty, and duty is the only emancipatory power. (*Works of Love*, p. 32)

Our love is dependent 'in a false sense' when it remains conditional upon what others are ready to do for us. So we find that we love others because of what they are ready to do for us. Our love has to be deserved. This is telling of a moral culture in which we are brought up to think of love as a scarce commodity that can easily be exhausted. This means we have to be careful to distribute it only to the deserving.

So children might experience their parents making them feel their love has to be worked for and will be withdrawn if they misbehave. At another level they might be left feeling they do not deserve love because they are wicked and unlovable. In this way love can be used as a form of control. It will have an effect upon the ways these children grow up to give and receive love. Kierkegaard is less helpful in illuminating how the form and character of this love has to do with the relationship of power and dependency between adults and children. It is partly an expression of the ways children are dependent upon their parents that love can be used as a means of control in this way.[10]

This is also related to the ease with which people can 'confuse love with the possession of the beloved' when they demand that their children carry out their wishes and commands.[11] Often it is hard to see others as independent human beings who need to make their own decisions about the lives they want to live, when they are economically dependent. This seems as true of relationships between the sexes as it is true of the relationships between the generations.

Kierkegaard thinks it is essentially through our relation with Christian conceptions of love that we can hope to transform the ways we think and feel about ourselves and our relationships with others. This gives people a deep source of strength to question the ways we are brought up to think and feel within our moral culture. It is not simply a question of replacing secular ideals with Christian ideals and goals. There is a deeper issue of epistemology and moral psychology involved. This is involved in grasping through our experience that 'To love one's self in the right way and to love one's neighbour . . . are at bottom one and the same'.

Such a notion challenges the deeply held cultural idea that to love ourselves is a form of selfishness and self-indulgence, as if the more we love ourselves the less love we have for others. Kierkegaard understood this as an opposition created within our moral culture. Learning to love ourselves does not withdraw our love from others, if we challenge our conception of love as a scarce commodity. Christianity had taught Kierkegaard the ways it can deepen our love for others. Even if Kierkegaard thought he was making a critique of earthly life in general, rather than of a particular form of social relations, he shows the radically different conceptions of love and inequality which can be available.

Christianity helps Kierkegaard recover a sense of the centrality of morality. It helps him challenge the conventional ways love and friendships are interpreted in a way that deprives them of their moral dimensions. This is to challenge the ways a liberal moral culture has sought to isolate morality, following Kant, in a discrete and autonomous realm. We are forced to confront moral issues where we are no longer taught to expect them:

Christian love teaches love of all men, unconditionally all. Just as unconditionally and strongly as earthly love tends towards the idea of there being one single object of love . . . Earthly love and friendship . . . as the poet understands them, involve no moral problems. Love and friendship are a matter of chance; it is fortunate, poetically understood . . . to fall in love, to find the one and only beloved . . . At most, the moral task lies only in being duly thankful for one's good fortune. On the other hand, the task is never that one must love the beloved, or find the friend; this cannot be done, as the poet very well understood. The problem consequently depends on whether fortune will furnish one with a task; but this is precisely the same as saying that morally understood there is no task.

If, on the other hand, one *must* love his neighbour, then the task *is* the moral task, which is again the source of all tasks. (*Works of Love*, p. 42)

This contains a critique of earthly love and friendship. It does not simply juxtapose a different conception to it. I think Kierkegaard also wants us to learn that love and friendship are not simply a matter of chance, even if we are brought up to think and feel they are. This is not to say that chance is not important too. At some level he recognises that if we do not know how to love ourselves, or if we have been brought up unconsciously to feel we are not lovable, then it is not going to be easy to love others. In the same way as we have to *learn* how to love ourselves we also have to learn to love others. These are not two separate and independent processes but they are part of the same process. The process is dialectical. It is also something we have to *experience for ourselves* as we learn how to *work* on ourselves. It is no accident that Kierkegaard has been so important in the development of modern existential psychotherapy.[12]

It is also important to realise that women are often depended upon in heterosexual relationships to do this kind of emotional work, if we take seriously the difficulties we have grasping what is at issue. The very conceptions of 'love', 'masculinity' and 'friendship' which prevail in the culture can make men despise this emotionality at the very moment they depend upon it to give them more understanding of themselves and grasp of their experience. Forms of emotional dependency are also an integral aspect of relationships of power.[13]

Liberal moral theory can make it difficult to recognise responsibilities within relationships. Relationships have to be given time and nourished. It is not simply a contingent fact that some people get on while others do not. This suggests there is little to learn and that everything can be left to chance. When Kierkegaard says one must love the beloved or must love his neighbour he is not talking about the duty of instruction and command. He does not think this is something we can do simply because we have been given instructions to do it. Rather he is recognising the possibility that we can change ourselves so that we love others because we *must* love. This has become an integral aspect of our natures. This becomes something we want to do as much as something we feel we ought to do. He also knows this is something difficult for us to learn, because of the ways we are brought up to think and feel about ourselves. This insight also resonates with aspects of feminist theory. It involves learning to love ourselves in a different way. It involves recognising we have certain moral tasks that we have to take responsibility for in our relationships with others. We have to learn to make ourselves open and responsive and ready to give and receive in our relationships. This gives us the chance of deeper and more meaningful relationships, which in turn involves accepting moral tasks our patriarchal culture too easily blinds us to.

LOVE, INEQUALITY AND DIFFERENCE

For Kierkegaard, learning to love someone as our neighbour is learning to relate to someone as an equal. In a passage that can remind us of Kant, he helps us understand how we are challenging our 'passionate partiality' when we learn to love someone as a neighbour. Sometimes Kierkegaard insists upon our abstracting ourselves from the distinctions and relations of social life, so that we can recognise others as neighbours. We will explore this later.

Sometimes he is more ready to come to terms with social life. In this situation loving others as neighbours seems to have a moderating effect upon social life itself.

> . . . The neighbour is your equal. The neighbour is not your beloved for whom you have a passionate partiality, nor your friend for whom you have a passionate partiality. Nor, if you are an educated man, is your neighbour the one who is educated, with whom you are equal in education – for with your neighbour you have equality before God. Nor is the neighbour the one who is more distinguished than yourself, for loving him because he is more distinguished can easily become partiality, and insofar selfishness. Nor is your neighbour one who is inferior to you, that is, insofar as he is humbler than yourself he is not your neighbour, for to love one because he is inferior to yourself can

readily become the condescension of partiality, and insofar selfishness. No, loving your neighbour is a matter of equality. It is encouraging to your relationship to a distinguished man, that in him you *must love* your neighbour; it is humbling in relation to the inferior that you do not have to love the inferior in him, but you must love your neighbour; it is a saving grace if you do it, for you must do it. The neighbour is every man; for he is not your neighbour through the difference, or through the equality with you as in your difference from other men. He is your neighbour through equality with you before God, but every man unconditionally has this equality, and has it unconditionally.   (*Works of Love*, p. 50)

Kierkegaard stresses that 'with your neighbour you have human equality before God'. He is not concerned with the kind of equality that two people might feel because they have received a similar education. A recognition of this kind of equality 'in your difference with other men' can distract you from the moral task of learning to love others as your neighbour. So, for instance, you might enjoy the equality in the intellectual relationship but be unable to talk more personally and directly to someone.

Identifying qualities we might share with others in order to form the basis for our feelings of equality with others is of no interest to Kierkegaard. In this he is different from Kant, who draws attention to the equality that exists between us as moral beings who have an equal capacity for morality and are equally subject to the moral law. But this can make it more difficult to give meaning to the 'human equality before God' which we share with our neighbour, even if we are told 'every man unconditionally has this equality, and has it unconditionally'.

This is made a little clearer in Kierkegaard's discussion of relations between unequals, where he says that loving your neighbour has to be distinguished from particular ways of relating to others. If we think of this for a moment in terms of the relations between rich and poor it can help connect with a crucial discussion in Kant. Kierkegaard shares with Kant the sense that loving someone because he is rich often allows people to feel self-important and better than others. This can be a way of feeling better about ourselves as well as a way of seeking favours. In a similar way loving someone who is poorer can make us feel how morally worthy we are. It can also give us a false sense of importance.

Kierkegaard recognises that it makes a difference to the quality and character of these relations, so for instance he says, 'it is humbling in relation to the inferior, that you do not have to love the inferior in him, but you *must* love your neighbour'. It is 'humbling' because it challenges the ease with which we can feel superior to someone who is poorer than ourselves. It is 'encouraging in your relation to a distinguished man' because it does not mean that you have to see someone as superior to you just because he happens to be richer. In this way learning to love your neighbour can have a moderating effect upon what the inequalities of wealth and power within social life lead people to think and feel about themselves.

Possibly it is because of the ways Kierkegaard thinks we can abstract ourselves from the inequalities of earthly life through being reminded of our 'human equality before God', that he does not have to focus upon the difficulties of relating equally within these unequal relationships. He does not have to come to terms with the moral tasks presented within these unequal relationships in the way Kant is sometimes forced to do in his later writings. It becomes possible to think that if some people are richer than others or more educated than others, this has to reflect individual abilities and determination, or else is a matter of chance where 'the moral task lies only in being duly thankful for one's good fortune'.

At the same time Kierkegaard realised both the difficulties of learning how to love our neighbour as well as the deep challenge this presented to the nations of respect and equality that existed within the Copenhagen society he knew:

> For consider the most cultured man you know, about whom we all admir-ingly say, 'He is so cultured', and then consider Christianity which says to him, 'Thou shalt love thy neighbour!' Moreover, a certain urbanity in all relations, a courtesy towards all men, a friendly condescension toward inferiors, a confident bearing toward the influential, an admirably controlled freedom of spirit: truly that is culture – do you believe that it is also loving your neighbour?   (*Works of Love*, p. 50)

Learning to love others as our neighbours challenges the ways we can be condescending and patronising to others while we think we are treating them with respect. But Kierkegaard tends to think of differences of skill, strength, ability, education, wealth, power in very much the same terms. It is partly because Christian equality is not concerned to focus upon any of these differences within the earthly sphere, that he can think about them in the same terms. As long as we realise that 'one *must* love his neighbour' then other moral tasks seem to fall into insignificance.

Kierkegaard was aware of the different forms of social inequality which were developing in society while people talked of equality. Simone Weil was also to recognise the new forms of inequality sanctioned by the French Revolution of 1789. She was aware of 'A mobile fluid inequality' which 'produces a desire to better oneself' and so substitutes one form of inequality for another (*The Need for Roots*, p. 10). Kierkegaard recognised how education, rather than being something that makes people more alike, becomes another way of asserting differences between people, making us feel we have to prove ourselves to be better than others. He asks a critical question:

> . . . has your education, or do you believe that any man's enthusiasm for an education, has taught him to love his neighbour? Alas, has not education and the zeal for acquiring it rather developed a new kind of difference, the difference between the educated and the uneducated? Only listen to what is said among the educated about earthly love and friendship, what equality in education a friend must have, how a girl must be educated and just in that way. (*Works of Love*, p. 49)

So we have to be suspicious of the kinds of equality promised in earthly life. Even when we think we are approaching a situation of equality through education, inequalities are often being reproduced. So we become trapped into proving we are better, more educated than others, so we can feel good about ourselves. This tends to confirm Kierkegaard in his belief that we need the help of Christian equality to challenge the prevailing inequalities of social life.

For Kierkegaard the duty to love our neighbour goes against the temptation that seems endemic in the bourgeois society he knew, to prove ourselves through comparing ourselves with others. It stands firmly in opposition to the tendencies of competitive individualism. Christianity, through reminding us of the equality we share before God, helps us recognise others as equal neighbours. It is almost as if this is supposed to help us 'see through' the distinctions we become so attached to and identified with in earthly life.

So the duty to love our neighbour goes against the constant temptation we feel to judge people and to test ourselves against the qualities they have, or against the power, authority and wealth they have within the larger society. Kierkegaard retained a strong critical eye. His Christianity seemed to give him a strength to question what were presented as the progressive ideals of bourgeois society. He was critical of the ways we establish our very sense of individual identity through proving ourselves against the qualities and performances of others. He was ready to question the pretensions of social life as well as the self-images we often have of ourselves.

Kierkegaard recognises the ways in which earthly life can make us 'blind' because of the kinds of distinctions it encourages us to make between people. It tends to focus upon the differences that exist between people, because this is what makes them special and what comes to justify our love for them. It is easy to believe that our friends have to have particular qualities to deserve the friendship which we are ready to give. We so easily pride ourselves on the special qualities our friends have. We do not want to give our love too easily or to those who are not deserving of it, since this would seem to devalue it. This kind of possessive individualism can make it difficult to appreciate what we share with others.[14]

It can also distort our understanding of individuals because of the ways we focus upon their particular qualities. In this way Kierkegaard provides us with a deep critique of the particular form of possessive individualism we are brought up to take for granted within bourgeois society. We give the earthly differences a kind of significance they do not have:

> And it is true . . . that one sees the neighbour only with the eye closed, or by looking *away from* the differences. The sensual eye always looks at the differences. Therefore earthly prudence always cries early and late: 'Look out, whom you love!' Alas, if one truly loves his neighbour, then it is better not to look out for everything; for this prudence, when it comes to testing the object, will actually bring it about so that you never get to see your neighbour because he is every man, any man taken quite blindly . . . earthly love makes a man blind, but it also makes him very particular not to confuse any other man with this one beloved; hence it makes him blind as regards the beloved, by teaching him to make a tremendous distinction between this one beloved and all other men. But love for one's neighbour makes a man blind in the deepest and noblest and most blessed sense, so that he blindly loves every man as the lover loves the beloved.   (*Works of Love*, p. 57)

Kierkegaard helps us think of different kinds of individualism. He makes us aware that we are not faced with a simple choice between the recognition of individual qualities and the assertion that people are all the same. This is a crude opposition that does not do justice either to liberal or socialist moral writings. Even if Kierkegaard tends to focus a distinction between earthly love which makes a person blind 'by teaching him to make a tremendous distinction between this one beloved and all other men' and the Christian love which 'sees the neighbour only with the eye closed, or by looking *away from* the differences', he does make us aware of the possibility of different kinds of human relations with people. He also makes us acutely aware of the kind of blindness that is created when we only focus upon the particular qualities someone has.

If we are always anxious to prove we are as clever as others, this will often be determining in the way we relate to others. We might discover ourselves automatically making some kind of judgment to show we are cleverer. This might make it difficult to appreciate the sensitivity and understanding someone has. We might never have fully learnt to value these qualities. We might have a friend we value because of her intelligence. We might be so focussed upon her intelligence, for instance, that we are unable to realise how sad and lonely she has been feeling since her father died. It is almost as if we do not expect her to have these kind of feelings, because this questions the image we have of her. This is part of the 'blindness' of earthly love. It can make it difficult for us to appreciate, for instance, that others have human feelings and emotions as we do.

If Christian notions of love of your neighbour can help us question the notion that our love is a precious commodity that has to be earned, or that our friends have to be loved for the particular qualities they have, or that we have to be continually proving ourselves to show we deserve the love of others, it can also create its own form of blindness. It can make it difficult for us to appreciate the particular qualities people have. It can make it difficult to value the individuality people want to express as well as the particular needs and wants they have. If Kierkegaard makes it easier for us to acknowledge that we share an equality in the eyes of God, he does not say enough about the kinds of needs and wants we share with each other. Rather he tends to think that any attention at this level is bound to be a distraction from listening to the voice of God.

If we learn of the ways we can put too much emphasis upon individual qualities and how these can be used to establish a false sense of ourselves in competition with others, there is also the danger that we will not be able to *acknowledge* and *validate* the kind of effort and qualities individuals have been developing. If the 'sensual eye' always looks at the differences, then the only alternative is not to look away from the differences. It can also be a matter of *how* these differences are to be understood and what kind of place they are to have in our understanding and appreciation of people. Sometimes it seems as if Kierkegaard is presenting us with a false alternative.

If Kierkegaard wants to understand all kinds of personal and social differences in the same way, because they can all be used as aspects of a possessive individualism, he risks failing to draw important distinctions. If we close our eyes it may help us to listen to the voice of God, but we can also learn to think about these differences in different ways. It is almost as if Kierkegaard sometimes wishes that we could not see these differences at all. The deepest form of blindness is still a form of blindness. It does not help us to see differently:

Oh, well, then close your eyes – then the enemy absolutely resembles your neighbour; close your eyes and remember the commandment *thou shalt love*, then you love – your enemy? No, then you love your neighbour, for you do not see that he is your enemy. That is, if you close your eyes, then you do not see the earthly difference; but enmity is also one of the earthly differences. And when you close your eyes, then your mind is not distracted and diverted at the very moment when you should listen to the word of the commandment. Then when your mind is not distracted and diverted by looking at the object of your love and the difference in the object, then you become merely an ear for hearing the word of the commandment which said to you, and you alone, that 'thou' shalt love thy neighbour.   (*Works of Love*, p. 56)

All earthly differences are treated by Kierkegaard in very much the same way. This is also a deeply rooted tendency in our thinking about equality. We often think of differences in strength, imagination, intelligence, wealth and power in the same terms. Such a tendency is partly made plausible in the ways we see social distinctions of wealth and power in society as the expression and consequence of these individual differences of talent and ability. This makes it difficult to think seriously about the ways class relations of power in society make it difficult for people to develop a sense of their individuality, which has not been limited and distorted through possessive and competitive considerations.

Kierkegaard closes his eyes to these issues. He tends to reassure us that 'when you close your eyes, then your mind is not distracted and diverted by looking at the object of your love and at the difference in the object'. Since he shares with Kant the deeply Protestant conception that sees individuals working out their individual relationship with God, he is most concerned that we are not distracted from hearing the word of the commandment. This gives us a particular interpretation of what it means to love our enemy. Such notions can too easily disarm people in the face of those who would exploit and oppress them. We can be encouraged to believe in the good intentions of others at the very moment that they threaten us. It can make it harder for people to defend themselves if they are simply told that 'enmity is also one of the earthly differences'. It can too easily encourage people to accept their suffering willingly, and not to seek to understand its causes so that they can struggle against them.

Visual imagery is very powerfully invoked in Kierkegaard's writings. It can encourage us to treat earthly differences in very much the same way without understanding that these differences can have very different sources. The strongest tendency within his writing is for a denial of the significance for people of these earthly differences. This seems to be the only way people can restore a sense of a shared human equality in the eyes of God, which seems constantly threatened by the false significance that seems to be given to the distinctions of earthly life. This leaves no room for the transformation of social relations of power and dominance within our earthly lives.

4   Morality and Inequality

DIGNITY, INEQUALITY AND DIFFERENCE

The Christian tradition is often characterised by a deep division between the earthly and the spiritual realms. Often people are conceived of as locked into the earthly realm with all the needs, wants and desires of earthly life while aspiring to live in the different realm of the spiritual. So the kinship and human equality people are to recognise before God is something that has meaning and significance within the spiritual realm. It is as if the very recognition of others as 'neighbours' is already to situate our relationship with others within this spiritual realm.

This can fragment our experience of ourselves, as we become used to living within these different realms of experience. This can reflect deep divisions we feel within ourselves between our animal natures which seem focussed upon our selfish wants, needs and desires, and our moral selves which are more concerned with doing what is right and what is morally demanded of us. We found this articulated in Kant's writings.

Kierkegaard is very much within the Christian tradition that thinks we can deny the significance of the distinctions of earthly life by 'emphasising the kinship between man and man'. As long as we are ready to listen to the voice of God's commandments then we can find our salvation in our individual relationship with God. This inevitably turns our attention away from thinking of the discriminations and oppressions of earthly injustice since the only justice that matters is established in our individual relationships with God.

It is almost as if Christianity sets each individual so high that it is almost beneath us to be taken up with these concerns. We have to accept the inequalities of social life knowing they make little difference to the possibility of living a moral life in the eyes of God, which is the only guarantee we can have of our salvation. Such a view throws into sharp relief the kind of compromises with social life Kant was prepared to make in discovering a way of giving equal respect to people whatever their job or goal. This accounts for his particular importance within the formation of a liberal moral culture.

Kierkegaard emphasises the role of Christianity in teaching people the kinship they have with others. This is something we learn to acknowledge

despite the very different conditions of people's lives. It also helps
Christianity to a sense of its moral superiority:

> . . . discriminations of earthly life, of how the caste system inhumanely
> separates man from man; how this ungodly wickedness inhumanly
> teaches one man to disavow kinship with another; teaches him pre-
> sumptiously and madly to say about another man that he does not
> exist, that he is 'not born'. Then even that man praises Christianity
> which has saved men from this evil by deeply and forever unforgettably
> emphasising the kinship between man and man, unconditionally every
> man – for before Christ, as little as before the face of God, there is
> no number, no multitude, the innumerable are numbered to him, the
> multitude is made up of individuals; so high has Christianity set every
> man, so that he may not harm his soul by becoming arrogant, or by
> groaning over the discrimination of the earthly life. For Christianity has
> not *taken away* the *differences*, any more than Christ himself would, or
> would ask God to *take the disciples out of the world* – and this amounts
> to one and the same thing.   (*Works of Love*, p. 52)

So Christianity could establish its sense of moral superiority through
knowing it alone fully acknowledges 'the kinship between man and man'
and establishes a sense of human equality in the eyes of God. Since it brings
this very sense of equality into the world, it becomes more difficult to say
it does not fully acknowledge the significance of the inequalities of power
and wealth within earthly life. It seems invulnerable to this charge, because
it is so obviously something taken into consideration in establishing its own
higher sense of human equality. We just show we have not really understood
how 'high Christianity set every man'.

It is partly because we can be reassured within the Protestant tradition
that we each have our own individual relationship with to God, that we do
not have to be so concerned with the interests of others. We can know they
are working out their own relationship and that we each have our lives to
live, even if it seems difficult to grasp the injustices of the social world.
We can know we are each individually recognised and acknowledged by
God. This is something we should be so grateful for that it seems wrong
to complain about anything in the organisation of the social world.

This is confirmed for us when we are also told 'that he may not harm
his soul by becoming arrogant, or by groaning over the discrimination of
the earthly life'. It is as if our soul can be protected whatever we are made
to suffer in our everyday social lives. Our souls remain untouched. This
is something Simone Weil could not accept. It remains a fundamental

aspect of Kierkegaard's understanding. He shares with Kant the sense that the dignity of the individual can be sustained in his or her relationship with God.

So Christianity gives people a way of believing in themselves regardless of the indignities, suffering, oppression and humiliations of subordination they have to endure in their everyday lives. Christianity 'has not taken away the differences', nor could we expect it to. In some way it matters less that these distinctions exist, if we are also assured they cannot hurt us or damage our souls. It also makes a difference if we know they do not compromise the equality that exists between us as human beings when we stand before God. This inevitably undermines whatever significance and meaning we would have otherwise given to our earthly sufferings. Since the meaning of life was to be sought in eternal salvation, rather than in the trials and tribulations of earthly life, we should learn to bear this suffering and pain in silence.

Christian equality can make us feel that however unimportant and insignificant we are made to feel in the subordination and oppression of everyday social life, we continue to matter equally in the eyes of God. We can know that we are acknowledged as individuals in the eyes of God at the very moment when we are denied this confirmation and recognition in our everyday lives. We can be made to accept our position in earthly life knowing that this is all part of a greater design we cannot hope to make sense of ourselves. In this sense Christianity's conception that we are all members of one body prepares the cultural ground within which we can accept prevailing functionalist explanations of social inequality.[1]

We do not have to concern ourselves with how others treat us in our everyday relations of subordination, knowing that what matters to us is the recognition that we have in the eyes of God. In being made aware of the individuality of our relationship with God, it becomes difficult to grasp the class relations of power that exist within society. It becomes difficult to recognise both the individuality of our experience and the class relations of power that influence and determine so much of our lives.

Christianity so often works to individualise our understanding of social life and so makes it more difficult to develop a social and historical consciousness. This has had a deep effect upon the formation of liberal moral culture. Some of these themes were captured in a letter written by C. S. Lewis:

> I would prefer to combat the 'I'm special' feeling not by the thought 'I'm no more special than anyone else', but by the feeling 'Everyone is as special as me'. In one way there is no difference, I grant, for both

remove the speciality. But there is a difference in another way. The first might lead you to think, 'I'm only one of the crowd like everyone else'. But the second leads to the truth that there isn't any crowd. No-one is like anyone else. All the 'members' (organs) in the Body of Christ are different and necessary to the whole and to one another; each loved by God individually, as if it were the only creature in existence.   (20 June, 1952)[2]

Kierkegaard seemed to think that people show themselves to be worthy of living a Christian life by resisting the temptation to compete for the prestige and power of the social world. As long as we think of the hardships and distinctions of social life as 'temptations', it becomes difficult to focus on the power they have to undermine people's sense of themselves. At one level this can make people feel they simply are not struggling hard enough against these temptations, rather than that they should struggle against the injustices of these relations of power and domination. In its own way this conception can simply make people feel inadequate, unworthy and undeserving of 'the blessed equality of the Christian life'. If people cannot help 'groaning over the discrimination of the earthly life' this can simply add further to feelings of inadequacy and ingratitude.

The social world becomes very much the kind of testing ground we can discover implicitly in Kant. It gives people a chance to prove themselves worthy of salvation. It educates people into thinking and feeling they cannot hope to find fulfilment and realisation within earthly life. Rather people have to be focussed upon proving themselves in the eyes of God. If Kierkegaard helps us question some of the notions of competitive individualism, this can have the effect of freeing people from invidious comparisons with others in which we are continually trying to prove ourselves better than others, so we can be open to the confirmation and acknowledgement that awaits us in our individual relationship with God.

The structures of power and domination within social life can almost be justified by Kierkegaard as temptations that people need in order to prove themselves as true Christians:

These must continue as long as temporal existence continues, and must continue to tempt every man who comes into the world. For by being a Christian he is not exempt from the differences, but by triumphing over the temptation of the differences, he becomes a Christian . . . for if the poor and the impotent man merely defiantly aspire to the advantages denied him in the earthly life, instead of humbly aspiring to the blessed equality of the Christian life, then he also harms his own soul.   (*Works of Love*, p. 57)

It is as if the struggle of the poor to better their material and social conditions is to be radically contrasted with aspiring to the 'blessed equality of the Christian life'. We have a clear choice of which path to follow. What is more, we are warned that a struggle against the structures of power and subordination within earthly life threatens to harm our own souls. It shows this struggle to be radically misconceived. It is to fail to grasp that the meaning of life and human fulfilment can only be discovered within the spiritual realm. This makes clear that recognising others as 'neighbours' does not question the character of the social relations of power and subordination. This is systematically to deny the significance of the social world, establishing whatever sense of human equality we can trust solely within the spiritual realm.

Such a view makes it difficult fully to understand how hard it is for people to believe in themselves and sustain a sense of the value of their own experience, when they are forced to endure social relations of subordination and oppression. It makes it difficult to grasp the power of these structures of dominance to undermine people's very sense of themselves. It can make people turn in on themselves to blame themselves for whatever feelings of failure, inadequacy and worthlessness they are made to experience in their everyday lives, say on a factory assembly line or working in the laundry of a large hospital or cleaning the floor in the local bank.[3]

Such notions help us grasp the essentially asocial character of this tradition of Christian thought. It becomes difficult to identify the moral problems we are confronted with in the inequalities and social relations of power within social life, because we are already assured of the only equality that matters, which is the equality before God. The struggle for earthly equality becomes presented as the aspiration for 'advantages' that have been denied to some. It cannot easily be experienced as a struggle for a certain ordering of human relationships that would allow people to express the human equality in the everyday organisation of social life.

It is partly because of the deep individualism of this tradition that sees individuals finding meaning only in their individual relationships with God, that it is difficult to give weight and meaning to the relationships people can have with each other. It becomes difficult to focus upon our difficulties within these relationships, since so much in the culture teaches us to minimise what we can receive from them. More precisely, we can feel split between the single loving relationship we are supposed to enjoy and our relationships with others. These different relationships will be affected in different ways through the ways we have been brought up to identify ourselves very much with our individual achievements. In a similar way that proving our moral worth makes it possible to gain salvation, so proving ourselves in our earthly lives can make us feel that we deserve whatever happiness we discover. These tensions are deeply embedded within our liberal moral culture.

Kierkegaard presents the struggle for equality and social justice not as a way in which people might want or need to express the human equality they have become aware of in their everyday lives, but as taking us away from the real search for Christian equality. The very search for Christian equality abstracts us from our everyday experiences and relationships as the question of equality is firmly placed within a different realm. The dangers of people thinking more about the differences that exist between them, rather than what they share as neighbours become 'temptations' that have to be overcome. It becomes increasingly difficult to restore this to a living critique of the possessiveness and selfishness that Kierkegaard identified in the social relations of the society he knew. Because these are taken to be features of earthly life in general, the only solution becomes one of how to escape from this earthly life, or at least minimise its significance for us.

Kierkegaard's Christianity does not take sides in the struggles of social life, or so it presents itself. It takes a position outside and beyond social life, choosing to see social life itself as a struggle for positions that it wants to distance itself from. This resonates with the position of objectivity that we are familiar with in positivistic conceptions of the social sciences.[4] Both in their different ways tend to see the earthly sphere, or social life, as lacking any morality since they make us feel that it is a continuing struggle for positions. Morality can only be brought into this sphere if it is brought from outside.

This is bound to undermine our sense of the morality in the struggles against domination and oppression. These will simply be construed as attempts to replace one set of authorities by another, and it will be seen as simply motivated by envy because people want to have the positions of authority occupied by others. This makes people think that the struggle to realise equality in their everyday relationships has little to do with restoring human dignity and more equal human relationships. For one thing, this dignity is always ready for people in their relationship with God if they are only open to it.

So Kierkegaard's Christianity minimizes the moral dimensions of a struggle for social justice. He resolutely takes a position of neutrality, wanting to defend himself against a challenge of being blind or one-sided:

Christianity is not blind, nor is it one-sided; with the calm of eternity it looks dispassionately at all the differences of the earthly life, but it does not contentiously take sides; it sees, and certainly with sadness, that earthly busyness and the false prophets of worldliness will conjure up this appearance of equality in the name of Christianity – as if it were only the powerful who are tempted by worldly differences, as if the poor would be justified in doing anything to gain equality – not merely by becoming Christian in deed and truth. I wonder if by that way one could come any nearer to the Christian likeness and the Christian equality . . .   (*Works of Love*, p. 59)

In this way Kierkegaard presents the structures of power and subordination within social life as if they are 'differences' of strength and ability. This makes it difficult to think about the kinds of inequalities in power and wealth, say, that could be justified. There is no room for the kind of rational reconstruction that we find, for instance, in John Rawls' *A Theory of Justice*, wherein a point of commonality, albeit a hypothetical one, is identified from which a standard of social justice can be derived. For Kierkegaard these differences are 'given' and moral behaviour has to do with how we relate to them.

Nor is there room for Kierkegaard to recognise that the genuine differences that might exist between people, say in their wants, desires, aspirations and needs, might be distorted because of the form in which they have to be expressed and realised within a particular culture. This is something Kierkegaard can help us glimpse though he would not draw these kinds of inferences. So he is very aware of the ways our love becomes possessive and takes on a particular form within a particular kind of society.

This might relate to the ways we feel we have to prove ourselves in our loving relationships, feeling threatened we might be compared with others. Similarly, it can be true that some people are more interested in ideas than others, but rather than this being accepted, all kinds of judgments are placed upon these differences as they are given a particular form as another arena in which people have to prove themselves to be better than others. These differences come to assume a different significance for people.

Kierkegaard warns us against the illusion 'as if it were only the powerful who are tempted by worldly differences'. We are to acknowledge that people are equally subject to these temptations, so that if everyone is guilty no problem of morality arises. This undermines the struggle against social injustice so that Kierkegaard does not have to say what the poor would be justified in doing to gain equality. This question no longer has significance or meaning. We simply have to accept that earthly life is a struggle for power and position. This can have little to do with morality. It becomes difficult to uncover the moral issues of power, dependency and subordination as the social relations of power are presented to us as 'worldly differences', as if it were simply a matter of some people having more wealth than others without this carrying any implications for the relationships of power and subordination.

It is partly because of the ways human equality is already promised to us within the spiritual realm, that it is made difficult for us to think critically about the importance of people having equal relationships with each other. It becomes difficult to relate these to issues of self-respect and dignity, personal identity and sense of self, since these are all guaranteed to us in a different realm. These are not things that we have to struggle for against the social relations of power and dependency.

In a similar way within liberal society these become guaranteed within our notions of citizenship and democratic rights, which make it so much harder to identify the workings of relations of power and subordination within a factory or within the domestic relations of the family. These are imagined to be areas in which contracts are made between 'equal partners'. It becomes difficult even to grasp the relevance of a language of power and subordination.

This is why it becomes important to develop a moral language which can identify and recognize the damage done to people's sense of themselves and to their capacities and confidence, within these relationships of power and subordination.[5] As with Kant, this is not simply a question of the power one individual has in relation to another, but also concerns the character of class and institutional power within the larger society. This is a need which Simone Weil responds to.

It is partly through the very power of these Christian notions within secularised liberal society that we find it easier to see others as 'neighbours' and to recognize that we share an equality before God, than to theorize meaningfully about what it would mean to have equal relationships with others and live in a genuinely equal society. There is some continuity between the ways people think of themselves as equal before God and the ways we think of ourselves as being equal before the law.

So we are equally accountable to the law whatever our position in society. This encourages us to see the law as a neutral institution above the struggles of social life. It becomes much harder for our thinking to grasp the ways in which it confirms and even legitimates and reinforces certain relations of power in society.[6] This is only one reason why it is important to become aware of the source of some of these ideas within a Christian tradition.

EQUALITY, DIFFERENCE AND INJUSTICE

Kierkegaard thinks that people can recognise themselves as equals without having to challenge the inequalities of earthly life. Christianity offers us a 'short cut' which can help us rise above these earthly distinctions. He sees the possibility of establishing a meaningful equality between people without having to transform social relationships. Christian equality is to reduce to insignificance whatever distinctions are drawn between people in social life. Sometimes it seems as if seeking equal relationships within the social world is a goal impossible to achieve, while at other moments it is presented as unnecessary because Christianity 'is immediately at the goal'.

There is little sense that struggling against these inequalities can be a matter of struggling against the relationships of subordination and oppression which work to undermine people's sense of themselves, or that this can be a struggle for human dignity and self-respect which is systematically denied within, say, the social relations of imperialist domination or within the social relations of capitalist production. Somehow Kierkegaard tends to think of this 'common equality' as if it has to be thought of as some kind of abstract goal people want to realise. If there have been times when equality has become a goal separated from a consideration of meaningful human relationships, there is no reason to think it has to be.

Kierkegaard's conception of 'common equality' relates directly to his conception of social inequality in terms of 'difference'. He tends to see all differences of social power, wealth and status as if they are individual differences like differences of individual strength. This makes it difficult for him to appreciate how individual qualities become formed in a particular way within particular relations of power. It becomes difficult to recognise the nature of individual differences if, for instance, differences are always seen in terms of being better or worse then others. This competitive formation can make it difficult for us to develop qualities in which we are not likely to excel, so that rather than learning to draw I become uneasy because I am aware that others draw so much better than me. I fear making myself vulnerable to being put down by others. I find it hard not to think of myself as a failure in this area.

It is largely because of the ways in which these 'differences' are conceptualised, that it becomes easy to think of making people equal as if it means making people the same. This has deep sources. It becomes difficult to make sense of the idea that more equal relations of social power are important because they can allow for the full development of individuality and individual differences. This involves taking to heart Kierkegaard's critique of possessive relations, while also acknowledging the needs people have for love, recognition and confirmation in relationship with others. This is something people can receive more fully from others in the context of developing more equal relationships. Kierkegaard's individualism is built upon the realisation that this is what individuals are already assured of in their individual relationships with God.

Kierkegaard insists upon a sharp distinction between Christianity and worldliness. He draws a sharp distinction between worldly equality and Christian equality. It is as if it is impossible for them to learn from each other:

> Christianity and worldliness can never come to understand each other, even if for a moment – to a lesser scrupulousness, they may delusively seem to. To secure an equal place in the world with other men, to make temporal conditions as similar as possible for all men, those are certainly things which worldliness considers of extreme importance. But even in this respect, what we may venture to call intentioned worldly effort never completely understands Christianity. The well-intentioned worldliness holds itself piously – if one wishes to call it that – convinced that there must be one temporal condition, one earthly difference – which one may find by the help of calculations and surveys, or in any other preferred manner – where there is equality. If this condition were to become the only one for all men, then equality would be brought about. But partly, this cannot be done, and partly, this common equality of all arising from having the same temporal differences, is not at all Christian equality; worldly equality, even if it were possible, is not Christian equality. And to bring about a perfect worldly equality is an impossibility Christianity, on the contrary, by the help of the short cut of eternity, is immediately at the goal: it allows all the differences to continue, but it teaches the equality of eternity. (*Works of Love*, pp. 59–60)

It is partly because the conception of worldly equality as people becoming the same flows from Kierkegaard's conception of 'differences', that he can say that 'even if this endeavour were carried on for a thousand years, it would never attain its goal'. He does not allow the possibility of there being *different* conceptions of worldly equality. His difficulty in acknowledging this possibility is also related to his conception of inequality in terms of 'differences'. It is partly because he sees all distinctions between people in very much the same way that equality has to mean the end of these differences. This is what Christianity can offer in teaching us to rise above all these earthly distinctions.

Because of these considerations Kierkegaard can draw such a sharp distinction between worldly and Christian equality, and then go on to say that Christian equality offers a 'short cut' to what seems to be the same goal. Christianity just teaches people 'to rise above the earthly distinctions'. What is more, because it demands that both rich and poor are to rise above earthly distinctions it takes itself to be dealing 'equitably'. It assumes that because it is asking the same of people whatever their social position of power and wealth it cannot be accused of taking sides. In this way he confirms and legitimates a conception of equality which involves demanding the same effort from people regardless of the situation they are in. This is a conception that Simone Weil directly challenges. It remains fundamental to Kierkegaard:

> Christianity . . . teaches the equality of eternity. It teaches everyone to *rise above* the earthly distinctions. Pay close attention to how equitably it speaks; it does not say that it is the humble who should lift himself up, while the mighty man should perhaps descend from this exalted position; ah, no, such a speech is not equitable. And the equality which is brought about by the mighty descending and the humble ascending, is not Christian equality, it is worldly equality. No, whether it was the one who stood highest, even if it were the king, he must *lift himself above* the differences of high place, and the beggar must *lift himself above* the differences of insignificance. Christianity always allows the differences of earthly life to persist, but this equality in rising above earthly differences is implicit in the commandment of love, in the loving one's neighbour.   (*Works of Love*, p. 60)

If we do as Kierkegaard asks us and 'Pay close attention to how equitably it speaks' we realise how Kierkegaard's Christianity fosters this particular notion of equality. In this sense it would not be 'equitable' to ask people to fulfil different demands, even if they have very different positions of power and wealth in society. So it is only 'equitable' if we ask people to do the same things. This assumes that we are asking the mighty and the humble to make much the same effort when we ask them to rise above earthly distinctions. Our concern is not with explaining how it is that some people have power and wealth while others are relatively powerless and poor. Somehow it is unquestionably assumed that these social positions have an independence, so that the wealth of the few is not built upon the dispossession of the many. This was the difficult issue that Kant came to the edge of confronting.

The conception that Kierkegaard has of the 'differences' within social life allows him to assume that we are asking people to do the 'same thing' when we ask them to 'rise above earthly distinctions'. It is as if we can assume that we demonstrate our sense of 'equity' through being oblivious to the fact of whether someone is rich or poor, mighty or humble. It is as if these differences are no concern of ours. This is something we can prove through asking people to 'rise above earthly distinctions' whatever their position in society happens to be. It does not matter whether this involves people lifting themselves up from 'the differences of high place' or 'the differences of insignificance', since the same 'lifting' is being asked of people.

This notion is supported by the realisation that the mighty person is likely to be as identified with his wealth and sense of superiority over others, as the poor person is identified with a feeling of being less worthy and successful than others. If a notion like this seems to support Kierkegaard's sense of 'equity' it is not clearly argued. It is very much assumed in the picture he has of the differences of social life. It remains a powerful image within liberal moral culture.

Can we ask whether it is more difficult for a beggar to lift himself 'above the difference of insignificance' than it is for a king to lift himself above the 'differences of high place'? Is it simply a question of considering the kind of effort involved? Even if we acknowledge that it can take great effort on the part of the rich and powerful person not to feel superior to others, this is because society is often organised to support these feelings of arrogance and superiority, making someone feel better than others. If wealth is taken as an indication of success in society, then a rich person is going against the very grain of social relations in treating a beggar as his equal. Talking about 'differences' in the way Kierkegaard does, makes it difficult to realise the social power which the rich person has over the beggar. It makes it difficult to realise how much of social life is organised in the interests of those who have wealth and power in society.

This can also help us understand that a different kind of effort has to be made by the beggar, because society is organised against their interests if wealth involves having power over the ways society is organised. The beggar is fundamentally made to suffer because they do not have the means to satisfy their needs. They cannot afford enough food to eat, let alone the kind of housing they need. Without a job and forced to beg, everything in society makes them feel that they are failures. It can make them think that they personally lack will and determination since otherwise they would have found decent employment.[7] The market ethic of a capitalist society makes a poor person feel that he or she only has himself or herself to blame. The poor should be grateful for whatever help they receive. They should never feel entitled to the good things the world has to offer.

Because Kierkegaard's Christianity gives such primacy to an individual's relationship with God, he does not have to face the moral and political questions in people's relationships with each other in the social world. It is also because it is assumed people can abstract from these social relations of power and subordination that the suffering and hurt, humiliations and deprivations people endure do not have to be given moral significance. It becomes easier to think of them as tests which can help people prove themselves in the eyes of God. It is almost as if the more people are made to suffer and sacrifice in their earthly lives, the more confident they can be of salvation. This shows the depths of a morality of self-denial.

The Christian tradition takes a moral vantage point outside the social world in a realm of its own, which allows it to declare its opposition to all discriminations. As long as we discriminate between people we are taking up a 'worldly point of view'. This can tempt us into thinking and feeling that it makes little difference whether we judge people according to wealth, property, family background, individual merit or intelligence. Christianity sees these as different ways of 'judging people', against which it sets out the idea of loving others as 'neighbours', where we are blind to whatever position or qualities individuals have. no. distinction is made between the social relations of power and wealth and the individual qualities of intelligence, kindness, sensitivity, warmth, so that we cannot think of the ways these qualities are given a particular form and meaning within a particular culture and organisation of social relations of power and subordination.

Some recognition is given to this within a liberal tradition when it is acknowledged that a rich person might be stupid and insensitive while a poor person might be wise and imaginative. This supports our sense that if one person is a king while another is a beggar this does not have to make a difference to the 'personal relationship' they have. It is assumed possible for them to develop a relationship which grows out of whatever individual qualities they have as people. On the other hand this liberal conception which would separate the possibility of personal relationships from the social relations of power and subordination, does not prepare us for the very real difficulties encountered within such relationships.

Christianity makes us blind to the particular qualities and positions people have. People do not have to prove themselves to us to earn our love. We love others as a duty. The Christian vision maintains part of its force for us, because it is possible to see these different 'distinctions' between people, as different ways of grading them.[8] The Christian idea helps us reject the idea that people need to be graded or compared with each other to prove themselves as individuals. This helps us feel that a person does not have to be more intelligent, active, creative or sensitive, to feel that he or she has worth as a human being.

At the same time this can deeply mystify us about the actual practices of a society that is so deeply organised around such judgments. In its own way this can fragment our consciousness, as we develop this awareness within our personal relationships and our sense that others should be given equal respect whatever power and wealth they have. This becomes radically separated from our social and historical consciousness and our sense of social relations. It is as if we can make individual moral choices in our personal relationships to relate to others as equals, while we remain outside the social world which we take to be organised positivistically around certain laws of social behaviour to which we have to adapt ourselves.

Christianity can prepare us for a particular conception of objectivity as it takes a vantage point outside earthly life. It can make us feel that it is only fair of us to make the effort. This is echoed in writings such as Bernard Williams', where our respect for others means 'that each man is owed the effort of understanding, and that in achieving it, each man is to be (as it were) abstracted from certain conspicuous structures of inequality in which we find him' (*Problems of the Self*, p. 237).[9] This is supported by the sense that the discriminations of social life and so the structures of power and subordination remain 'superficial', when contrasted with the deeper level of Christian equality.

This goes along with a sense that when we struggle to transform the social relations of power and subordination within the social world, we are simply working to replace one set of discriminations by another. For Kierkegaard this means that we are fighting 'to maintain discrimination':

> . . . everyone who contends against discrimination in such a way that he wishes to abolish one definite discrimination in order to substitute another, he indeed fights to maintain discrimination. Whoever, then, wishes to love his neighbour, consequently does not concern himself in abolishing this or that discrimination, or, from a worldly point of view, in doing away with all of them, but is devoutly concerned in interpreting his own difference with the saving thought of Christian equality: he easily becomes as one who does not fit into the earthly life . . . he becomes like a sheep among the ravening wolves . . . (*Works of Love*, p. 61)

Such notions leave no room for struggling to transform the inequalities of the social world. These struggles are doomed before they begin. Our hopes are bound to be dashed as we inevitably replace one set of discriminations by another. It is only through Christian equality that we seem to have a chance of realising the hopes we have. But since 'Christianity always allows the differences of the earthly life to persist' this seems to leave us powerless to challenge the sufferings, oppression and injustices of earthly life. It is as if these sufferings and injustices have to be endured, since whatever we replace them with has no chance of making lives more human and the society more just. In this way whatever energy and commitment we put into struggling against the inequalities and injustices of the social world is undermined.

Christian equality is not something that has to be realised and expressed in the everyday organisation of the social world. It is something that gets defined very much *in opposition* to the everyday conditions of the social world. It tempts us into accepting and legitimating the social world as it is, thinking it makes little difference to the quality of people's lives or to the meaning we give them, what the manner and basis of the discriminations of social life happen to be. These changes are bound to be superficial when we contrast them with the possibilities of Christian equality. It does not encourage us to think very deeply about the differences between discriminating between people on the basis of family background or on the basis of merit, since these differences are bound to be superficial and therefore of little real consequence.

If we are concerned with what is pictured as the much deeper concern of loving our neighbour, then we cannot be concerned with 'abolishing this or that discrimination'. In this way Christian equality is directly posed against a transformation of social relationships of power and subordination. We generally have to learn to abstract from the everyday realities of misery and suffering, joy and difficulty, so that we can acknowledge the equality that exists before God. In its own way this builds a tension in our experience of ourselves and our relationships with others. This makes it difficult to recognise our individual experience as also a social experience formed within particular relationships of power and subordination, since we have to abstract ourselves and our sense of others from these relationships to recognise ourselves as 'neighbours'.

This might help us touch a deeper truth, that for all the differences in power and wealth that separate us within social life, we remain human beings with very much the same needs and wants. Kierkegaard is right to acknowledge the ways that the inequalities of social life threaten our grasp of this truth. But the very picture Kierkegaard has of the 'differences' within social life, means that we can only acknowledge this truth at the expense of denying how deeply people are influenced by the social relationships of power and subordination. Not only does Kierkegaard deny that a recognition of this equality as neighbours has any profound implications for the organisation of social relationships, but he denies the significance of the social world in the formation of people's identities and everyday experience.

EQUALITY, RESPECT, AND SUBORDINATION

Notions of Christian equality have made a difference to the ideals which inspire liberal society, even guiding the relations people want to have with each other. The idea of existing equally for all people, regardless of the inequalities of power and wealth that divide us, has a powerful influence within liberal moral culture. This can help us to a sense that we can individually choose what kind of relationship to have with others, since it makes us confident we can always abstract from the social relations of power and subordination that threaten to separate people.

So it makes us feel that the fact that someone is a factory owner and someone else is a factory worker does not have to make a difference to the relationship they have with each other. This relationship simply depends upon the qualities we have as individuals. If this makes it difficult to understand how issues of class relations of power enter into the tensions, anxieties and unspoken fears of this relationship, it does give people the strength and confidence to know they can struggle against power or wealth, making any difference to the equal relationship they want to have. This can help us relate equally to others whatever their situation in life happens to be.

Liberalism encourages the belief that if people live differently, or are engaged in different kinds of work, or are poor, this should not have to make a difference to the ways we relate to them. It can help us recognise the wrongness of breaking off our conversation with the woman who brings round the tea in the office because the director has walked into the room. It helps us feel we should be ready to give equal time and attention to people, and should be careful not to patronise and condescend towards them. This can help us become conscious of the ways we might exist differently with different people. We might realise how anxious we are to make a good impression with those who have authority over us while we are more relaxed with our equals.

It is very much the influence of notions of Christian equality which helps us abstract from the relations of power and subordination in our personal relations. At the same time it encourages a break in our understanding of personal relations, which seem to be very much a matter of individual choice and decision, while our social relations exist within a social world taken to be governed by laws of social behaviour. In this way a voluntaristic conception of personal relations is connected with a much more deterministic conception of social relations.[10]

Kierkegaard's Christianity does carry with it a critique of social relationships and also of certain conceptions of social life. Even if Kierkegaard tends to separate his ethics of personal relationships from what he says about the 'distinctions of earthly life', he does question the way social life might encourage us to relate. He is critical of the ways we might spend time with others according to the advantage we get from them. If he does not say much about the ways this can be encouraged within a particular pattern of social relations, he does make clear that this is not what it means to love your neighbour, even if this is what people think they are doing. In this way he is also critical of those who would use liberal ideas of respect as non-interference, so that they will not have to engage with others:

> To love thy neighbour, while allowing the earthly differences to continue, is, as was pointed out, essentially to wish equally for every man unconditionally. Manifestly, merely wishing to exist for other men in proportion to the advantages provided by earthly distinctions, is pride and presumption; but the clever idea of not being willing to exist at all for others, in order secretly to enjoy the advantage of distinction in union with equals, is cowardly pride. In both cases there is dissention; but he who loves his neighbour is calm. He is calm through being satisfied with the conditions of earthly life assigned to him, be they those of distinction or poverty, and for the rest, he allows every distinction to retain its power and to pass for what it is and ought to be here in this life.   (*Works of Love*, p. 69)

Christianity can strengthen our resolve to exist equally for every person. It is because it instils a sense that we remain equal before God, that it so easily legitimates the 'conditions of earthly life'. Because the distinctions of earthly life cannot matter so much when meaning in our lives is given in the spiritual realm, it somehow becomes admirable to accept the world as it is. Since there is no longer a contradiction between treating others equally and 'allowing the earthly differences to continue' since this equality is guaranteed in the spiritual realm, these can now become complementary goals.

This prepares important ground for liberal moral and political theory, since even if we no longer speak so easily of a spiritual realm, our sense of moral worth has been deeply influenced by Kant's notion of rationality as an independent and autonomous faculty. This makes it easier to think we can choose to have whatever personal relationships we want to have with people and that these do not have to be mediated by class, racial and sexual relations of power. It is as if our personal relations can exist in an autonomous sphere of their own.[11]

Kierkegaard is unsatisfied with the adequacy of the notion of respect for persons as non-interference which Kant has so crucially prepared for liberalism. Respect is not a sufficient guide in our relations with others. A person focussed upon pursuing his own ends, even though he does his best to relate to others as equals whenever they happen to cross his path, does not love his neighbour. Kierkegaard would want people to learn to relate differently. This prepares the ground for a critique of liberal moral relations:

> But the one who in cowardice would only exist within the partition walls of association where he would accomplish so very much and gain so many advantages; the one who in cowardice dared not attract the attention of men, the poor, or the rich, because he suspected that the attention of men was a dubious good – if one has something true to communicate; the one who in cowardice carried out his favoured activities within the security of the respect for persons: – he bears the responsibility – that he does not love his neighbour. (*Works of Love*, p. 70)

People have to be concerned with the wellbeing of others, not simply with their own advantage. Kierkegaard is suspicious of 'the security of the respect for persons'. He recognises how it is possible for people to hide themselves behind the morality of earthly life, thinking that this is all that is required of them. So Kierkegaard does make demands upon us to challenge the ways we are encouraged to relate to others within earthly life. At the same time it is important for him to think you can relate to others in a more Christian way without thereby questioning the 'distinctions of earthly life'.

Kierkegaard recognised that living a Christian life would bring you into conflict with earthly morality. It is in this way that Christian morality remains as a potential challenge:

> ... However ridiculous, however backward, however inexpedient loving one's neighbour may seem in the world, it is still the highest a man is capable of doing. But *the highest* has never quite fitted into the relationships of earthly life ... (*Works of Love*, p. 74)

Kierkegaard does not make the same kind of compromises with earthly life that Kant helped prepare. This makes it harder to acknowledge in our respect for others the kind of goals individuals have set themselves, say, as bankers, butchers or boilermakers. Kierkegaard does not prepare us to think and feel that we have to respect the kinds of earthly lives people have chosen for themselves. This is not his concern. He wants to teach people to love their neighbour even if this brings people into conflict with earthly morality. This helps him develop a very sharp critical eye for the hypocrisies of conventional morality. He thinks the deeper meaning of life lies elsewhere.

5 Inequality and Subordination

IDENTITIES, DIFFERENCE AND SUBORDINATION

Christianity reminds us that despite the distinctions in the everyday conditions and relations of people's lives, people share a fundamental humanity. In Kierkegaard's Christianity this shared humanity is something that we come to recognise in our individual relationship with God. It is in the spiritual realm that our sense of human dignity is confirmed. Kierkegaard's Protestant conception too easily sees earthly life as a trial and as a source of sacrifice, which helps us prove ourselves in the eyes of God. Whatever fulfilment we can hope to achieve is going to have its source in our individual relationship with God. It is not going to come from the satisfactions of earthly life.

Kierkegaard can systematically deny the reality of our everyday lived experience within earthly life because he always assumes we can abstract ourselves from the demands and structures of power and subordination. This goes along with the powerful image Kierkegaard has of social life as a play in which we are all actors. It has deep resonances with the ways we are brought up to think and feel about our social lives within a liberal moral culture.

It also produces a powerful picture of the ways we are to make sense of the distinctions of social life. The conceptions of role theory within contemporary social theory show how this image comes to be given a theoretical formulation.[1] In questioning the validity and implications of this picture we are also questioning strands in the self-understanding of liberal society that have been developed within social theory. We can also become aware of the ways in which we implicitly invoke this picture to make sense of the distinctions we meet in the everyday relations of power and subordination.

For Kierkegaard the social world is a world of appearances. People are other than what they present themselves to be in social life. If people identify themselves too closely with the positions they have within social life they are in danger of missing the reality of human life.

> . . . Consider for a moment the world which lies before you in all its variegated multiplicity; it is like looking at a play, only the plot

81

is vastly complicated. Every individual in this innumerable throng is by his difference a particular something; he exhibits a definiteness but essentially he is something other than this – but this we do not get to see here in life. Here we see only what role the individual plays and how he does it. It is like a play. But when the curtain falls, the one who played the king, and the one who played the beggar, all the others – they are all quite alike, all one and the same: actors.   (*Works of Love*, p. 72)

This vision retains a critique of the forms of social life. Kierkegaard does not accept the social world as it is, nor the ways that people present themselves in the social world. The distinctions of social life allow a person to 'exhibit a definiteness but essentially he is something other than this'. In social life we can only see that someone is a king and someone else is a beggar, but we are mistaken if we think that this is what someone *is*. Someone is always more than being a beggar, as someone is always more than being a king. These are simply the roles that people play and we have to be careful not to identify people with the particular roles they have. He makes us aware that everyone has a part to play so that 'when the curtain falls' 'they are all quite alike, all one and the same: actors'.

The social world as a play that people are acting in is profoundly rejected by Kierkegaard's Christianity. This helps us grasp the superficiality of social life and the self-conceptions we often develop of ourselves, when we identify ourselves too closely with the positions of power or subordination we occupy. In this way Kierkegaard remains a powerful critic of the ways of the social world. He does not prepare for the kind of accommodations of the social world that Kant offers in his moral theory. This has made him a much more marginal figure in liberal moral and political theory.

He does not say that we have to respect people equally whether they are 'kings' or 'beggars', because these reflect goals individuals have chosen for themselves and because they offer equally important contributions to the ongoing society. This is the kind of vision which Kant helps prepare. But at the same time Kierkegaard does not offer hopes for the transformations of the social relations of inequality and injustice, so that the critical significance of his writings has often been missed.

In Kierkegaard's Christianity our equality is guaranteed in our spiritual relationship with God, not in any recognition that we share human needs. It is generally assumed that however the social relations of power and subordination are organised, this does not compromise the equality we have before God. The social world is almost legitimated through default, as our concern is moved to the deeper issues involved in our individual relationships with God. At the same time Kierkegaard makes us critical of the social relations we take very much for granted. We learn how the processes of social life almost inevitably encourage us to exaggerate the differences between people. We can easily be taken in by the appearances of social life and the differences these establish between people.

In society we are all 'actors' who are equally capable of identifying ourselves with the roles we play. This can encourage us to feel we are superior and more important than others, or else inferior and inadequate because we are powerless within society. Kierkegaard seems to be more concerned with making us aware that we are all 'actors' than with bringing out that we are all human beings who share the same earthly and spiritual needs. It is because in social life we are all 'actors', that we are all equally capable of identifying ourselves with the positions we have. If this minimises the very different consequences of living your life in society as a king or a beggar, it can help us remain aware that people are human beings whatever lives they have.

Social life encourages us to identify ourselves with the particular position we have in society, so we tend to gain a sense of individual identity in our differences with others. It becomes easy to identify ourselves with what we do to earn a living. We identify ourselves with the externalities of social life and tend to judge others in this way. This can even make us blind to qualities we have as individuals and the ways we could grow and develop ourselves as individuals.

So, for instance, the fact that John is a lawyer and can draw considerable prestige from this position does not mean that he is a sensitive or imaginative person. Our respect for his position might blind us to the truth of what kind of person he is. Kierkegaard helps us understand that there is much more to a person than the position he or she has, even if they closely identify with it.

> . . . Alas, but in actual life one fastens the upper garment of his difference so tightly that it completely conceals the fact that this difference is an outer garment, because the inner glory of its likeness to others never or so very infrequently shines through, as it nevertheless should or ought to do . . . the reality of life, even if it is not, like eternity, the truth, ought to be truthful, and therefore the other man, who everyone essentially is, ought always to be glimpsed through the disguise . . . (*Works of Love*, p. 72)

Social life is not truthful because it tends to exaggerate the differences that exist between people. For 'the reality of life' to be truthful we have to see through the distinctions of social life. This means recognising the kinship we have with others and the equality that exists before God.

Kierkegaard draws a distinction between the social differences between people which is an 'outer garment' and the likeness we share with others which is an 'inner glory'. Social life is untruthful because it makes us focus upon the differences that exist between people in the social lives they have, not in the individual qualities they have. Our lives and our relationships with others cannot be truthful because the social distinctions prevent 'the inner glory of its likeness to others never or so very infrequently shines through'. It is only if we are in touch with 'the inner glory of its likeness', that our relations with others can hope to be truthful. This should help us identify with the lives other people live as 'the other man, who everyone essentially is' is 'glimpsed through the disguise'.

Social life is essentially a disguise. We hide behind the differences and distinctions that social life maintains. This encourages us to feel superior to people we have power over. It can also make us feel inferior and inadequate when we compare ourselves with those who have been more successful. So, for instance, this can make John the lawyer feel superior to Dave who is a baker. It will be easy for John to feel that his position could only have been achieved because of the superior qualities he has as a person. John might think that he has so little in common with Dave that he cannot expect to get very much from spending any time with him. John has become so identified with himself as a lawyer that he can hardly listen to what Dave has to say. He easily assumes that he has little to learn or receive from Dave. Even if John recognises that Dave has his own thoughts and opinions and that they share similar rights in the larger society, it is easy for him to pay lip service to these democratic notions. He is too identified with his own position of superiority and status.

We need to become aware of the ways we become more identified with these social differences as we grow. This profoundly affects the growth and development of people. Kierkegaard recognises that this identification with social distinction and the ways we identify ourselves constantly in relation to others has a profoundly damaging effect. Kierkegaard seems to be challenging our utilitarian language which would talk in terms of the satisfactions of different ways of living.

In drawing a contrast between what he calls 'temporal growth' and 'the growth of eternity' he shows that we are not simply taking the appearances of social life too seriously, but we are bound to be damaged in our growth as human beings. This will be a central theme in our discussion of Simone Weil. She helps us develop this kind of language, as she makes us aware of the inadequacy of the language of rights to identify and express the ways in which people are affected by the social relations of power and dominance in society. It is not simply that people are less happy and fulfilled than they could be. Social life has the power to damage and cripple us as human beings.

Kierkegaard is caught between seeing social life as a play in which we are acting different parts and his partial recognition that people can be deeply hurt and crippled through the processes of social life.[2] At one level it seems as if social life is bound to be superficial, while at another moment it seems to carry deep consequences. There is a sense in which people can grow or be prevented from growing in their social lives, that is often absent when we are trapped into thinking of social life as a play.

This also reflects more general contradictions within liberal culture, since it is often difficult to develop our insights into the ways in which we can grow and develop as human beings when we are so dominated by utilitarian conceptions of social life. Kierkegaard finds it hard to develop some of his own insights within his more general conception of social life as a play:

> Alas, but in actual life, the individual in his temporal growth grows together with the temporal differences; this is the opposite of the growth of eternity which grows away from the differences; every such individual is crippled, is in the sense of eternity a deformity. Alas, in real life the individual grows fast to his differences, so that at last death must use force to tear them away from him.
>
> Nevertheless, if one is truly to love his neighbour, he must remember every moment that the difference between them is only a disguise. For, as was said, Christianity has not wished to storm forth to abolish the differences, neither those of distinction nor of humbleness, nor has it wished in a worldly sense to effect a worldly agreement between the differences; but it wants the difference to hang loosely about the individual, loosely, like the cape a king casts off to reveal himself; loosely, like the ragged cloak in which a supernatural being has concealed itself. When the difference hangs thus loosely, then that essential other is always glimpsed in every individual, that common to all, that eternal resemblance, the equality. If it were this way, if every individual lived in this way, then would the temporal existence have attained its highest point. (*Works of Love*, pp. 72–3)

When Kierkegaard acknowledges the consequences of the realisation that 'the individual in his temporal growth grows together with the temporal differences' he seems more concerned to affect our earthly lives, rather than simply to abstract from them. While reassuring us that his basic intention has not changed, he wants 'the difference to hang loosely about the individual', so that we can more easily glimpse the other person through the 'disguise'. This would make it easier for earthly life to 'be the reflection of eternity' and for it to 'save its soul from the difference in which it still continues'. Here Kierkegaard seems to be acknowledging real difficulties in abstracting from the structures of power and dependency within social life. He recognises the very real consequences our social lives can have for the growth of our individualities. This is not something that can always be safely secured in our individual relationships with God.

At the same time the general distinction Kierkegaard makes between the external character of our social lives seen as 'an outer garment' and 'the inner glory' makes it difficult for him to acknowledge the ways people are going to be more identified and 'grow together with the temporal differences' in societies where the institutions are organised around people developing a sense of personal identity in constantly proving themselves to be better, more intelligent, more humorous, more attractive, stronger, more lovable, than others. This is to perpetuate the strong cultural theme of the 'inner' and the 'outer' being as two separate and autonomous realms that have very little bearing and influence upon each other. If social theories have often given too little recognition to the importance of our inner lives and our relationship to ourselves, psychological theories can often focus exclusively upon these 'inner processes'.

Some of Wittgenstein's writings, particularly in the *Philosophical Investigations*, can help us question this distinction between the 'inner' and the 'outer'.[3] He can help us think about how it might be important to express 'the inner glory of its likeness' in the ways we live our everyday lives. Such an expression could help this 'inner glory' become more of a reality for us. It will not simply be a question of glimpsing something that remains essentially 'inner' but of experiencing this quality more and more in our relationships with others. But Kierkegaard finds it difficult to acknowledge that if this equality were more realised in our everyday social relations, people would be less likely to identify themselves so strongly with the differences. Even if he glimpses how damaging this identification can be for our growth as human beings, he remains with the recognition that 'Christianity has not wished to storm forth to abolish the differences'.

The distinctions and inequalities of social life conceal deeper truths of human equality. Social life confuses us because it encourages us to focus upon the differences between people. At the same time it is possible to remain aware of this equality if we make sure that the differences 'hang loosely about the individual'. Kierkegaard thinks that this would make it easier to pay the homage and respect to those in power and authority, since these differences are no longer all important if we are aware of the 'equality of glory':

> . . . this would be the reflection of eternity. Then you would indeed see the ruler in real life, gladly and respectfully offer him your homage; but you would nevertheless, see in him the inner glory, the equality of glory which his magnificence merely conceals. You would indeed see the beggar, perhaps in your sorrow for him suffering more than he, but you would still see in him the inner glory, the equality of glory, which his shabby cloak conceals. Moreover, wherever you turned your eyes, you would see your neighbour . . . In being king, beggar, scholar, rich, poor, man, woman and so on, we do not resemble one another, for just therein lie our differences; but in being a neighbour we all unconditionally resemble one another. The difference is the confusion of the temporal existence which marks every person differently, but the neighbour is the mark of the eternal – on every person.   (*Works of Love*, p. 73)

Kierkegaard can help us think that this 'inner glory' remains untouched by the everyday realities of power and subordination. When we acknowledge others as 'neighbours' we are aware of the 'equality of glory' which tends to get concealed by the differences of social life. This involves a deeper way of relating to others as we refuse to be impressed by the distinctions of social life. The way Kierkegaard mentions that in our relationship with a beggar 'perhaps in your sorrow for him suffering more than he' can help us deny the everyday weight of suffering a beggar has to endure in a society so clearly organised around individual achievement. It makes it easier for us to assume that people simply adapt to whatever position they find themselves in, in social life.

This finds resonance in the ways we think about social inequality within liberal society. We are less aware of the relations of power and subordination that connect the experience of people with each other and more aware of people carrying out different roles or functions in the larger society. We tend to see these different roles as more or less independent of each other.

DIFFERENCE, POWER AND SUFFERING

Within liberal moral and political theory we tend to think of social classes not in terms of social relations of power and subordination, but in terms of income groups or in terms of life-style differences.[4] Even Marxist theory, which recognises the reality of class relations, often finds it difficult to connect this understanding with the lived experience of individuals. This can easily become a scientific discourse which takes itself to be giving a purely descriptive account of the relations between social classes. It is almost as if the language and understanding of individual lives and experience can be *replaced* by a discussion of class relations. This can easily involve a mystifying reductionism.

It becomes equally difficult to investigate the power and influence of the social relations of power and subordination over the formation of individual experience. The crucial mediations between the social relations of power and subordination and the lived experience of individuals are missing. This has sometimes been recognised in the discussions about the problematic relationship between Marxism and morality.[5]

Kierkegaard helps foster an image of social life and social differences that makes it difficult to grasp the powerful influence of class and sexual relations of power and subordination in people's experience. It is as if we have to recognise social life as essentially superficial, if we also want to acknowledge that 'in being a neighbour we all unconditionally resemble one another'. This becomes the 'reality' we can discover to exist beneath the 'appearances' of social life. This very sense of the 'equality of glory' can help us sustain the essential individualism of liberal moral culture. It becomes easier to think that individuals are more or less free to pursue their own individual lives.

The question of power rarely enters our understanding of the relations between individuals and the ways they are mediated by relations of class, sex and race. Rather it confirms our sense that as long as we have the will and determination, we do not have to make discriminations in our relations with others if we treat them as individuals with particular abilities and qualities. The issue of power is very much reserved for defining the limits of state power so that some kind of framework of non-interference can be provided for individuals to pursue the goals they have set themselves. Kant's moral theory has been significant in presenting this understanding of social life.

Kierkegaard tends to think that if we recognise the 'equality of glory' this goes some way to proving the superficiality of social life. As far as he is concerned it is always possible to treat others as neighbours and so to minimise the social relations of power that separate people. This makes it harder for a baker, say, to understand what makes him feel so small and inadequate in his relations with a lawyer. He finds it so easy to assume he has nothing to say that could possibly interest the lawyer. He has a sense that they almost live in different worlds, so that lawyers are not ordinary people like other working people. This common experience of class relations can be muted by the realisation that 'in being a neighbour we all unconditionally resemble one another'.

At the same time as this can make the baker feel better about himself, it does not necessarily affect the sense the baker has that the lawyer counts for something in society. He can be so conscious and aware of the social power a lawyer has, to experience the equality that exists in the personal relationship they have. It may help the baker feel better about himself, but it may not help him understand what makes him feel so anxious and inadequate when he thinks he is going to meet the lawyer. Rather it can make him blame himself as he internalises this sense of inadequacy without developing much grasp of what is making him feel this way.

Even if Kierkegaard readily admits that the processes of social life 'confuse' because they make people feel different from each other, he also acknowledges that the 'inner glory' can be 'glimpsed through the disguise'. Since he sees the social relations of power and subordination very much as 'outer garments' it is particularly difficult to understand what it means to be powerless and oppressed within society. It is difficult to appreciate how much energy and strength people need to believe in themselves, and in the validity of their own experience, if the daily conditions of subordination and oppression continually reproduce a sense of impotence and insignificance.

The structures of power and subordination will be continually undermining people's sense of themselves and fragmenting people's sense of their own experience, since whatever sense of equality is guaranteed exists in another realm. Often people will be left to reconcile the daily experience of subordination at work or in domesticity, while somehow being assured of a sense of equality with others in the public realm of the voting booth or before the law.

In Kierkegaard's way of thinking, people's different social positions accords with the idea of actors playing different parts. Since this is a 'part' someone is playing it should not be taken too seriously, nor could it have profound effects upon a person's character or personality. It is easy to slip into thinking that a person's character or personality is to be identified with something essentially 'inner' that remains untouched by the particular part someone happens to be playing. Social life becomes almost a contingent matter.

If this is combined with Kierkegaard's awareness that we are equal before God, it becomes hard to acknowledge the ways people can be made to suffer and be damaged by the social relations they live out in their everyday lives. It is as if people have to learn not to take the parts they play too seriously, or to identify too closely with them. This can suggest that people only have themselves to blame if they get hurt, undermined, or damaged through playing the particular parts they have. It is up to people themselves to learn the ways they can be nourished in their individual relationships with God.

If this encourages us to see a beggar as acting out a particular part, this can encourage us to invalidate the experience of suffering and affliction. This makes it harder to be sensitive to the everyday conditions of a person's life. It can make us feel there is little to understand in why someone is made to beg in a society which is so technologically advanced. It will be easy to think this is a role someone has chosen so they are somehow responsible for the conditions of their lives. Or else it can foster a kind of fatalism in which a person has simply been assigned this role in life.

All the time it will be easy to minimise the suffering and hardship involved, since we know little of this matters when compared to the equality people are assured in the spiritual realm. Do we acknowledge someone as a 'neighbour' only through denying the reality of a person's hardship and suffering as a beggar? What does it mean to validate someone's experience as a beggar? This is not simply a matter of having sympathy with the details of a person's suffering.

Some of the processes at work might become clearer if we imagine for a moment Rita's anger and resentment at those who seem so well provided for when she has so little. The possibilities of *validating* Rita's experience will partly depend upon accepting the appropriateness of her anger and resentment. This will depend on our sense of the justice of her anger, which will itself depend upon our understanding of the sources of inequality within society. So our validating someone's experience depends upon our understanding of their experience.

Kierkegaard can help Rita feel better about herself, as he helps us recognise her as a neighbour. This can make people critical of the ways they are brought up to patronise and condescend to people less fortunate than themselves. But this recognition can be given at the cost of making Rita feel that her anger is not appropriate in the situation, either because her hardships are a particular test, or else because it is simply the part she has been given. This would not then be considered a question of justice. Rather, Rita should learn to rise above these distinctions of earthly life to find true meaning in her relationship with God.

As long as we learn to focus upon the 'equality of glory', we can see through the structures of domination and subordination, or at least rise above them. This is to reject the connection between the human and the social, to maintain a connection between the human and the spiritual. A consequence is to abstract the individual's understanding of their experience from the social and the historical. I have been endeavouring to show the strength of Christian traditions which inform liberal moral culture's resistance to the social and historical understanding of our experience.

Such a notion is illuminated in a different way, in a remark Cavell makes about Wittgenstein's and Austin's attempt to put us back in touch with our language, and so return us to our experience:

> Wittgenstein's motive (and this much is shared with Austin) is to put the human animal back into language and therewith back into philosophy. But he never, I think, underestimated the power of the motive to reject the human: nothing could be more human. He undertook, as I read him, to trace the mechanisms of this rejection in the ways in which, in investigating ourselves, we are led to speak 'outside language games', consider expressions apart from, and in opposition to, the natural forms of life which give those expressions the force they have. (*The Claim of Reason*, p. 207)[6]

I would say that our human experience also has to be understood as a social and historical experience. If it is important for us to find ways of reminding ourselves of the equality we share with others in our common humanity, this does not have to be done through withdrawing us from the social world. This very escape from the social and historical world in which our experience is formed and our lives are lived is another attempt to 'reject the human'.[7]

A conception of the social world as a play moves the structures of power and inequality in society beyond moral criticism. People have to learn to define morality in terms of their individual relationship with God and their search for salvation. Kierkegaard too easily assumes that a concern with earthly equality means that people will have to identify fulfilment and happiness with the individual search for wealth and power. Even if this critique of earthly life is well-taken, it is deeply mystifying if it works to undermine our sense of the importance of everyone in the society having decent food, clothing and housing as well as meaningful work and caring and loving relationships with others.

Kierkegaard encourages us to deny the central importance of the material conditions of people's lives, because we are warned of the dangers of dedicating ourselves too narrowly and hopefully to the equalisations of people's living conditions. At the same time the ways Kierkegaard thinks of people playing different roles make it difficult for him to grasp how our relationships with others are deeply mediated by the social relations of power, such as those of class, gender, race and ethnicity. The relationship between the baker and the lawyer is not simply a personal relationship that can be separated from the social power the lawyer has. This is not simply an 'interference' the effects of which can be minimised if people acknowledge each other as 'neighbours'. This does not mean it is not possible to *work through* some of the difficult feelings they have about each other. This can help people feel better about each other, but it will not dissolve the relationship of power.

In a similar vein the personal relationship between a man and a woman cannot be abstracted from the gender relations of power that exist between men and women in the larger society.[8] Nor would an attempt to abstract this relationship give people more understanding of it. It would be through more fully appreciating how a woman's individual experience has been affected by a particular social and historical experience of femininity, that a woman night learn how difficult it has been for her to value her time, ideas and understanding within the relationship.

IDENTITIES, ABSTRACTION AND JUSTICE

Kierkegaard helps foster a moral culture in which we discover the equality that exists between people through abstracting from the distinctions of social life. This encourages us to remove ourselves from our social and historical experience. Not only does this encourage a particular sense of ourselves as individuals, but it also protects our individualities from damage and hurt. We do not have to struggle to feel secure and confident in our individualities.

Nor are equal relationships with others something we must struggle for against the social relations of power and subordination. In these different ways we are encouraged to find ourselves through abstracting ourselves from the social world. This is the way we can acknowledge others as neighbours and discover the equality that exists between us.

At the same time Kierkegaard insists that relating to others as neighbours has to change our relations with others. He acknowledges the ease with which people can pay lip service to the idea of equality as an abstract notion. He demands that people recognise what this means for their immediate relationships:

From the height of his superior condescension, the great man under-stands equality between man and man. From the height of their mys-terious superiority the scholar and the educated man understand equality between man and man . . . at a distance the neighbour is recognised by everyone: God alone knows how many really recognise him, that is, close by. And yet at a distance the neighbour is merely a figment of the imagination; he who is neighbour by virtue of being near by, is any man, unconditionally every man. At a distance the neighbour is a shadow who in imagination passes through every man's thought – but, alas, perhaps he did not discover that the man who at that very moment really did pass by him, was his neighbour . . . if you do not see him so close at hand, that, before God, you see him unconditionally in every man, then you do not see him at all. (*Works of Love*, p. 66)

The ease with which our sense of equality with others can become 'a figment of the imagination' is recognised by Kierkegaard, but he assumes it does not have to be so. He knows it is not simply an abstract principle we can subscribe to with little connection with our everyday experience. In this way we can also read him as critical of a morality of principles which somehow come to exist over and above social life. He would be critical of aspects of Kant's conception of our relation to the moral law. Morality is not a matter of living up to abstract principles that we come to know as correct because of the workings of our reason. It very much concerns the quality of our human relationships with others. He wanted our sense of human equality to change the *quality* of our relationships.

At the same time Kierkegaard realised how the very social situation we are in can actively question the meaning of what we say. This seems to highlight a moment of tension. It is not simply a question of what we argue for, since the situation we are in can reproduce the very distinctions we are questioning:

. . . To defend an opposing view within the partition wall of the differences, to defend behind this wall a view which, in the Christian sense (not in the sense of raising a rebellion), wishes to take the differences away, that is simply to preserve the differences. In the company of the learned, or within a circle of associates which assures and emphasizes his distinction as such, the scholar might perhaps be willing to deliver an inspired lecture on the equality of all men; but that is simply maintaining the differences. In the company of the wealthy, in surroundings which simply make the advantages of wealth obvious, a rich man might perhaps be willing to make every concession about equality between men; but this also means preserving the differences. (*Works of Love*, p. 64)

'Surroundings which simply make the advantages of wealth obvious' are acknowledged by Kierkegaard, but it is unclear whether someone has to leave these surroundings if he or she is not to preserve the differences. Certainly Kierkegaard thinks that an important measure of a person's disposition is 'how great a distance there is between his understanding and his actions'. What matters is the ways we relate to others in our relationships with them. Kierkegaard's Christianity wants us to understand 'the human equality'. He thinks this is an understanding that we share since:

> At bottom we all understand the highest things; a child, the simplest man, the wisest man, they all understand the highest things, and all understand the same things; for it is, if I dare say so, a lesson set for us all. But that which makes the difference is whether we understand it only remotely – so that we do not act accordingly; or near at hand – so that we do act accordingly, and 'cannot do otherwise', cannot refrain from doing it . . .   (*Works of Love*, p. 65)

How do we learn to take these understandings to heart so we 'cannot do otherwise' but practice them in our relations with others? This is not simply a matter of will and determination.

Kierkegaard has a real sense of the difficulties of learning to love our neighbour. Somehow this is closely connected in his mind with accepting the distinctions of earthly life. It is as if we could not want to transform the social relations of earthly life as an aspect of our learning to love our neighbour. Kierkegaard even shows his powerful psychological understanding of the workings of relations of subordination, while not wanting to question the basis of these relationships.

This is deeply contradictory, since we might have expected his own understanding of loving your neighbour to bring him to question his own characterisation of 'the lower classes'. He does not shrink from these contradictions but is ready to express them clearly. This is a mark of his greatness as a thinker. He recognises how people are forced to make certain compromises with the relations of power:

> Let us now consider the differences in the lower classes. The times are past when what one calls the lower classes had no conception of themselves, or only the conception of being slaves, not merely poor men, but actually not even men. The wild rebellions, the horror which followed on horror, are perhaps past; but I wonder if viciousness cannot therefore lie hidden in a man. If so, then the vicious inferiority complex will make the poor man imagine that he sees an enemy in the powerful

and the rich, in everyone who is favoured by some advantage. But caution, it says, for these enemies still have so much power that it might easily become dangerous to break with them. Therefore the hidden viciousness will not teach the poor man to raise a rebellion, or absolutely refuse every expression of deference, or let his secret become manifest; but it will teach him that the deference shall be expressed and still not expressed, expressed and yet expressed in such a way that the powerful will find no pleasure in it, while he is still not able to say that this homage is refused him. Therefore in this submission there must be a cunning defiance which secretly embitters, a reluctance which secretly says 'no' to what the tongue affirms; a dissonance of suppressed envy in the jubilation which honours the powerful. (*Works of Love*, p. 66)

In all this there is a definite rationality, given the unequal relations of power. There is a real understanding of the workings of 'submission'. It is the very relations of power and subordination that can help us understand the 'viciousness' and the 'vicious inferiority complex' that 'lie hidden in a man'. It is partly because Kierkegaard assumes there is an alternative path of Christian equality which gives 'every advantage of the earthly life its due', that he can blame people themselves for this 'secret envy' and for letting this viciousness 'get this power over him'. This means he can firmly place the responsibility for these feelings upon the shoulders of the poor themselves, even if they cannot be held responsible for their situation of poverty and subordination.[9]

Kierkegaard shows how the social relations between the powerful and the poor are bound to become untruthful as people learn 'that the deference shall be expressed and still not expressed'. Kierkegaard realises that 'therein lies exactly the art and the secret of the resistance'. He also knows that the poor and the powerless are forced to resist in these ways, because they do not have the power to make an open challenge. He is also aware of the workings of submission in which there 'must be a cunning defiance which secretly embitters, a reluctance which secretly says "no" to what the tongue affirms'. In a very real sense people cannot be truthful to themselves. The relations of power and subordination force people to betray themselves and their understandings of the world.

This is in deep tension with Kierkegaard's general conception of the social world as a play in which we are all acting our parts. The idea that we can see through the masks of social life to a deeper level of human equality encourages us to think and feel that the relations of power and subordination can only have incidental consequences for the relations people have with each other. Then it was relatively easy to think of human equality guaranteed to us in the spiritual realm, since we had such a clear picture of the superficiality of relations of inequality and power within society.

As long as Kierkegaard can convince himself that the viciousness that 'lies hidden in a man' is something that the poor can have only themselves to blame for, then he can think of the inequalities of earthly life as always justified. This means the anger and resentment of the poor and the powerless against the organisation of society is never justified. The general ways Kierkegaard thinks about 'earthly life' make it difficult to distinguish between different kinds of societies. Since it is always possible for us to abstract ourselves from the social world to relate equally to others, issues of the justice and injustice of particular forms of social inequality need never be raised. In exploring this in Kierkegaard we are also exploring a deep issue within liberal moral culture. We can begin to understand some of the broader sources for the *displacement* of considerations of justice in our thinking about social inequality.

In Simone Weil's writings we have a conception which recognises the different kinds of needs we share with others as human beings and the need for this equality to be recognised and affirmed in the everyday organisation of social life. This is crucial for Weil because she understands the ease with which our respect for others can become 'fictitious' if it is not grounded in and expressed through the everyday organisation of social relationships. It is a strength of Weil's writing that she casts the relationship between the individual and the social in such a way that she can acknowledge the 'equality of glory', while also appreciating how damaging the social relations of power and subordination can be to people.

Weil does not take a person's individuality for granted, but knows how this individuality can be denied in the social relations of affliction and oppression. At the same time, because the individual is for her a category, she does not marginalise the significance of this damage but retains it as central to her grasp of the workings of power. Weil is concerned to identify the damaging effects of social life for many people and to help us develop a language in which this experience can be expressed.

Even in her later writings, which were deeply informed by Christianity, she is still convinced that the social relations of power and subordination have to be transformed if our equality with others is to be realised. Though by this stage her thinking has long broken with an orthodox tradition of Marxism,[10] this helps us question the general picture of society we often implicitly assume within liberal moral theory, which is so clearly presented in Kierkegaard, and would locate our equality outside or beyond concrete social relations, as well as simplistic and mechanistic conceptions of social change.

She helps us situate ourselves more firmly within the social world rather than abstract ourselves from it, as the search for more equal human relationships becomes more identified with a struggle for social justice. Weil's centralisation of justice leads her to formulate her discussion of respect in terms distinct from Kant and in such a way that politics and morality can be brought into a different relation.

6   Respect, Human Needs and Equality

RESPECT, DIGNITY AND SUBORDINATION

When Simone Weil talks about the respect we owe to others as human beings, she talks about it as an obligation we have towards others. She recognises that we have this obligation towards other human beings, whether or not we acknowledge it in our relations with others. This was an idea that she shared in her earlier socialist writings as well as in her later Christian writings. It was a theme which moved deeply in all her writings. She expresses this clearly in an early remark in *The Need for Roots*:

> There exists an obligation towards every human being for the sole reason that he or she is a human being, without any other condition requiring to be fulfilled and even without any recognition of such obligation on the part of the individual concerned.   (*The Need for Roots*, p. 4)[1]

Simone Weil is clear that this respect does not simply mean taking up a certain attitude towards others. She also feels the inadequacy of a notion of respect for others centred around a notion of non-interference and which assumes people are in a position to pursue ends they have chosen for themselves. She recognises how the class relations of power within a capitalist society deny this very assumption of independence. She is aware of the need to face up to the moral consequences of relations of class power and subordination. This does not mean that she does not believe individuals have to discover the meaning of their individual lives, but this has to happen in a context in which they can also learn to appreciate the needs they share with others as human beings. It is the fulfilment of human needs that Weil places at the centre of her account of the respect we owe to others.

This brings her into conflict with some of the deep assumptions of liberal moral and political theory. She questions the particular form of individualism which is embedded in Kant's notion of respect as non-interference. She can help us recognise how some of these very assumptions make it difficult for Kant to give sufficient weight to the notion of respect as not treating others as a means to our own ends. Weil shows this is not simply a question of how we choose to behave towards others in our personal relations. The very independence of people from each other, which is a deep assumption of Kant's moral theory, is questioned by the class relations of power which characterise capitalist society. It is partly this changed social and historical situation that makes it difficult to think of respect simply as a question of non-interference, if we are also aware of issues of class power and dependency.[2]

Simone Weil was anxious that our respect for others should not simply be formal and rhetorical so that she needed a way of thinking about our 'obligation towards every human being' in a way which could also come to terms with relations of power and dependency. She did not believe in Kierkegaard's option of abstracting from these social relations of power and dependency. This would easily invalidate people's own experience of these relations when Weil wanted us to learn to respect others *through* confirming and validating their everyday experience of the social world. This is very different from passively accepting this experience. In her earlier writings it was clear it meant struggling against the social relations which oppress and subordinate people.[3]

She learns to challenge the centrality which Kant gives to the notion of respect as non-interference. Kant himself became troubled by this as he thought about the moral relations of dependency between rich and poor. He could not continue with his assumption that people were essentially independent agents in their economic lives, so that people's wealth or poverty was simply a reflection of their individual qualities and abilities. The issue of class relations of power and dependency questions those individualistic theories which would argue that the poor somehow benefit from the wealth of others, or that social inequalities can be justified if the poor are somehow made better off than they would have been before. Within such a framework it is often argued that if someone has grown richer this does not harm someone who has always been poor. This is supposed to show that inequality does not do any harm to the poor. Weil questions some of the assumptions upon which these ideas are based.

Weil is struggling to understand the moral realities of the 1930s. She is aware of the ways we are made blind to the moral realities that surround us by the moral traditions that cannot, if they ever could, illuminate the moral realities of a class society. This did not mean that notions of individual dignity and respect were not a central part of her moral universe; but it did mean we had to question the assumption of individual independence and autonomy upon which they were based. This was not simply a question of realising that we live in a different society in which it has become much harder to put these values into practice. A deeper social and historical

understanding was called for. Martin Jay shows that Simone Weil was not
alone in recognising the need to question our inherited moral and political
conceptions.[4] Adorno challenged Fromm on this score:

> The revisionists . . . were also naive in their explanation of the sources
> of social disorder. To claim as they did that competitiveness was a
> major cause of conflict in bourgeois society was fatuous, especially in
> face of the acknowledgement in *Fear of Freedom* that the spontaneous
> individual had all but vanished. In fact, 'competition itself never was the
> law according to which middle-class society operated'. The true bond of
> bourgeois society had always been the threat of bodily violence, which
> Freud more clearly perceived: 'In the age of the concentration camp,
> castration is more characteristic of social reality than competitiveness.'
> (Quotations from Adorno: 'Social Science and Sociological
> Tendencies in Psychoanalysis', 27 April 1946 (unpublished);
> *The Dialectical Imagination*, pp. 104–5)

Weil realised we did not simply need to understand these social and
historical transformations. We also needed to challenge the sources of
our positivistic traditions which would deny the moral aspects of this
investigation, separating out as they do issues of values from the empirical
investigation of laws of social development. She recognised that Kant's
notion of respect as refusing to treat someone merely as a means, suggests
a critique not simply of the ways individuals relate to each other but also
of class relations of power and subordination. This involves challenging the
moral psychology Kant took for granted and developing a moral language
that has the power to illuminate what Weil identifies as 'the modern forms
of social oppression'.

This forces her to question the tradition of individual rights when this
assumes all individuals are equally protected by a circle of rights. This
makes it hard to illuminate the ways in which the social relations of
power, dependency and subordination can cripple and damage a person's
capacities and so prevent the development of a person's individuality. This
is to acknowledge that social life has a much more powerful effect upon
the form and character of individual experience and relationships.

A deep sense of justice motivated Simone Weil. This became an integral
aspect of her critique of the notion of rights which seemed connected to
distributive conceptions of justice. She was continually searching for a conception of justice which talked more directly of people's relationships with
each other. It was this deep concern which connected her early socialism
with her later understanding of Christianity. Looking back in her *Spiritual*

Autobiography it seemed to her as if she had always shared a Christian conception of love for one's neighbour:

> Whilst the very name of God had no part in my thoughts, with regard to the problems of this world and this life I shared the Christian conception in an explicit and rigorous manner, with the most specific notions it involves. Some of these notions have been part of my outlook as far back as I can remember . . . From my earliest childhood I always had also the Christian idea of love for one's neighbour, to which I gave the name of justice; a name it bears in many passages of the Gospel and which is so beautiful. (*Waiting on God*, pp. 29, 31)[5]

Her sense of justice involved her in socialist politics while she was a student at the École Normale and was part of her desire to get a job in a factory so she could have more of a direct experience of suffering and oppression. Her year's experience in working in different factories around Paris had a profound effect upon her.[6] It profoundly affected the ways in which she experienced herself and understood her relations with others.

She learnt how hard it was to maintain a sense of dignity and self-respect when working in a situation of subordination in a factory. She was forced to acknowledge the power of social life and to question moral traditions that saw dignity and respect as somehow guaranteed as 'inner qualities'. She expresses this clearly in a letter that she wrote to Albertine Thévenon:

> . . . What working in a factory meant for me personally was as follows. It meant that all the external (which I had previously thought internal) reasons upon which my sense of personal dignity, my self-respect, was based were radically destroyed within two or three weeks . . . (*Seventy Letters*, p. 19)[7]

Simone Weil's difficult experiences of factory work also profoundly affected her attraction to and understanding of Christianity. I shall give a long quotation from her *Spiritual Autobiography*, since this allows her to speak for herself about some of these crucial changes. It can also help us towards a sense of some kind of underlying unity in her development:

> After my year in the factory, before going back to teaching, I had been taken by my parents to Portugal, and while there I left them to go along to a little village. I was, as it were, in pieces, soul and body. That contact with affliction had killed my youth . . . I knew quite well that there was a great deal of affliction in the world. I was obsessed with the idea, but

I had not had prolonged and first-hand experience of it. As I worked in the factory, indistinguishable to all eyes including my own, from the anonymous mass, the affliction of others entered into my flesh and soul. Nothing separated me from it, for I had really forgotten my past and I looked forward to no future, finding it difficult to imagine the possibility of surviving all the fatigue. What I went through there marked me in so lasting a manner that still today when any human being, whoever he may be and in whatever circumstances, speaks to me without brutality, I cannot help having the impression that there must be a mistake and that unfortunately the mistake will in all probability disappear . . . There I received for ever the mark of a slave, like the branding of the red-hot iron which the Romans put on the foreheads of their most despised slaves. Since then I have always regarded myself as a slave.

In that state of mind then, in a wretched condition physically, I entered the little Portuguese village, which, alas, was very wretched too, on the day of its patronal festival. I was alone. It was the evening and there was a full moon. It was by the sea. The wives of the fishermen were going in procession to make a tour of all the ships, carrying candles and singing what must certainly be very ancient hymns of a heart-rending sadness. Nothing can give an idea of it. I have never heard anything so poignant unless it were the song of the boatmen on the Volga. There the conviction was suddenly borne in upon me that Christianity is pre-eminently the religion of slaves, that slaves cannot help belonging to it, and I among others.   (*Waiting on God* pp. 33–4)

Simone Weil's conception of Christianity as 'the religion of slaves' helped her challenge the notion of rights where this proved inadequate to express the suffering and affliction that working-class people were forced to endure in their everyday lives. She realised how the 'daily assault of poverty, subordination and dependence' makes it 'quite natural to count for nothing'. She recognised a real difference between her experience in the university where, as she says in a letter, 'I have rights and dignity and a responsibility to defend', and the experience of working-class factory workers where the language of rights serves to mystify the class relation-ship of power that exists. As Weil says in the same letter, 'What have I to defend as a factory worker, when I have to renounce all rights every morning at the moment I clock in? All I have to defend is my life.' (Letter to Monsieur B, 1936, *Seventy Letters*.)

She needed a language which would not mystify but which would illuminate the damage being done to people forced to endure these class relations of power and subordination. This was the situation she wanted to have a more detailed understanding of as she decided to get a job in the factory. It was also a task which her Christianity helped her with. It helped her develop a moral language that could illuminate these moral realities, even if it also profoundly changed her sense of the ways social conditions were to be changed.

RESPECT AND HUMAN NEEDS

When Simone Weil talks about the respect which is owed another human being she is not just talking about taking up a certain kind of attitude to others. She is aware of the ease with which the respect for others can become lip service to an idea which hardly affects our relations with others. But Weil has a very different conception from Kierkegaard's of the ways we are to guarantee that this respect be 'effectively expressed':

> The fact that a human being possesses an eternal destiny imposes only one obligation: respect. The obligation is only performed if the respect is effectively expressed in a real, not a fictitious way; and this can only be done through the medium of Man's earthly needs. (*Need for Roots*, p. 6)

This directly questions Kant's notion of respect, which is related to a sense of ourselves as moral beings radically separated from any consideration of our 'earthly needs'. If there is little explanation for why our respect for others to easily becomes 'fictitious', there is a sense that this can be prevented if our respect for others is 'effectively expressed' 'through the medium of Man's earthly needs'.

For Simone Weil learning to respect others is not tied to a recognition of people's relation to the moral law. There is an implicit critique of the rationalism of Kant's view which would separate our understanding of our moral natures from any consideration of our earthly needs. For Weil, learning to respect others involves developing an understanding of the needs which people have in their everyday lives. The book that she wrote for the regeneration of France after the Second World War, *The Need for Roots*, opens with an investigation of the needs which people share as human beings. In this way she challenges the tradition of moral thought which would grasp these needs as the 'ends' which individuals choose for themselves.[8] This tends to displace any discussion of human needs from a central position within our moral theory.

We too easily assume that this has to involve minimising important differences which exist between individuals or that somehow it has to involve telling people what they need, even if they do not recognise these needs for themselves. Weil is careful not to deny the importance of differences between people, or to recognise that people often want very different things out of life.

But at another level she is aware that it is difficult to understand the significance of individual differences of wants, desires, needs, aspirations, hopes, feelings and emotions, if we cannot also recognise needs we also share as human beings. It is partly because of the ways a liberal moral culture tends to focus upon individual differences *without understanding* the ways a capitalist patriarchal society has tended to give them a particular form, as they become ways we have to prove ourselves to be better, more intelligent, more interesting, richer, etc., than others, that we lose a sense of the needs we share with others.

An investigation of the needs which we share with others as human beings will help us question the ways we think about the differences that exist between individuals. We tend to assume a liberal conception of freedom that says people will find fulfilment if they are left alone to pursue ends they have set for themselves. This can make it difficult for us to grasp how deeply influenced we can be by the character of the society we live in, to set certain ends for ourselves. So for instance within a capitalist society it is very easy to identify ourselves with individual achievement and the need to prove ourselves to be better than others.

In our discussion of Kant we have shown how this can make it difficult for people to think about what they want for themselves, especially if this leaves them in conflict with what their parents and the larger society would admire and respect. Weil helps us to a deeper questioning, through bringing us to think about the kind of needs we are fulfilling for ourselves in our everyday lives. Happiness is not simply a question of fulfilling certain ends which we have set for ourselves. Often this notion of happiness can turn out to be illusory, as we find ourselves continually trapped into setting yet further goals to prove ourselves.

As human beings we share different kinds of needs. We show our respect for others by acknowledging the needs which they have. This is a question of distinguishing 'what is fundamental and what is fortuitous' for people, for as Weil says, 'Man requires, not rice or potatoes, but food; not wood or coal, but heating' (*The Need for Roots*, p. 9). It is analogous to the sense in which hunger can be said to express a 'vital need' which has to be met, that Weil thinks about the human needs we share. This helps her define the nature of the obligations that we have towards others:

So it is an eternal obligation towards the human being not to let him suffer from hunger when one has the chance of coming to his assistance. This obligation being the most obvious of all, it can serve as a model on which to draw up the list of eternal duties towards each human being . . .

Consequently, the list of obligations towards the human being should correspond to the list of such human needs as are vital, analogous to hunger.

Among such needs, there are some which are physical, like hunger itself. They are fairly easy to enumerate. They are concerned with protection against violence, housing, clothing, heating, hygiene and medical attention in case of illness. There are others which have no connection with the physical side of life, but are concerned with its moral side. Like the former, however, they are earthly, and are not directly related, so far as our intelligence is able to perceive, to the eternal destiny of Man. They form, like our physical needs, a necessary condition of our life on this earth. Which means to say that if they are not satisfied, we fall little by little into a state more or less resembling death, more or less akin to a purely vegetative existence.

They are much more difficult to recognise and to enumerate than are the needs of the body. But every one recognises that they exist . . . Every one knows that there are forms of cruelty which can injure a man's life without injuring his body. They are such as deprive him of a certain form of food necessary to the life of the soul. (*The Need for Roots*, pp. 6–7)

In this way Simone Weil identifies what she calls 'the vital needs of the human being'. These are needs which 'play a role analogous to food'. They are needs which have to be met if we are to be able to grow and flourish as human beings. If these needs are not met then we are bound to shrink and 'fall little by little into a state more or less resembling death, more or less akin to a purely vegetative existence'. Weil recognises both our physical needs and our moral, emotional and spiritual needs. These needs have to be nourished with the food that is appropriate to them.

This is why it is so important for her to identify these different needs that we share as human beings and to insist that 'they are earthly'. This is as true of our physical needs as it is of our 'needs of the soul'. These needs have to be met in the ways that we live our everyday lives. So when Simone Weil investigates 'those needs which are for the life of the soul what the needs in the way of food, sleep and warmth are for the life of the body', she is aware that these different needs have to be satisfied in the ways we live and the ways that our everyday lives are organised.

At the same time, Simone Weil recognises that these needs can be met in different ways. As she says, 'we must recognise the different, but equivalent, sorts of satisfaction which cater for the same requirements'. But she also warns that: 'We must also distinguish between the soul's foods and poisons which, for a time, can give the impression of occupying the place of the former' (*The Need for Roots*, p. 9). This involves a careful exploration of the different needs that we have and the ways that we satisfy them in the ways we live. This opens up the space for a powerful critique of any society which does not acknowledge and meet these different needs which we share as human beings.

THE NEED FOR EQUALITY

Equality is one of the 'vital needs of the human soul' which Simone Weil identifies in the indications she gives for a discussion of human needs in the early part of *The Need for Roots*. We need to receive the same amount of respect and consideration that is given to every human being. But it is not enough for this simply to be an attitude that is taken up towards people. It has to be expressed and embodied in the everyday organisation of social relations. Our equality is not to be expressed through abstracting ourselves from the social world. It has to be grounded in the very organisation of social life:

> Equality is a vital need of the human soul. It consists in a recognition, at once public, general, effective and genuinely expressed in institutions and customs, that the same amount of respect and consideration is due to every human being because this respect is due to the human being as such and is not a matter of degree.   (*The Need for Roots*, p. 15)

In this way she thinks about equality in terms of 'the same amount of respect and consideration (that) is due to every human being'. This is not simply something that we desire for ourselves in our relationships with others. It is something which we need to be able to sustain ourselves and grow as human beings. There is a deeply held developmental conception of our growth as human beings. She is not simply talking about what people want for themselves, as we might easily assume within a utilitarian tradition. It is not simply that people will be deprived of certain possible satisfactions if these needs are not met. It is easy for us to recognise certain physical and biological needs which have to be satisfied. So we know that people starve if they do not have sufficient food to eat.

It involves a deeper questioning of our inherited self-conceptions for us to appreciate the ways in which people are made to suffer because, for instance, they do not enjoy the same amount of respect and consideration as others. It involves acknowledging the ways in which people can literally shrink from life and withdraw into themselves, or as Simone Weil describes it, 'fall little by little into a state more or less resembling death, more or less akin to a purely vegetative existence' (*The Need for Roots*, p. 7).

Simone Weil realises that this equality has to be 'at once public, general, effective, and genuinely expressed in institutions and customs'. It does not simply relate to how individuals treat each other. If someone is deprived of this equal respect and consideration in the ways that society is organised, this is to deprive someone 'of a certain form of food necessary to the life of the soul'.

So, for instance, a teacher might ridicule a student in front of the class because of his poor spelling when he writes something up on the board. This might well undermine a student's self-confidence. It might also make him nervous about taking the risk of answering one of the questions that the teacher puts to the class. The student might shrink inside as the class is encouraged to laugh at his spelling. This kind of hurt can cause its own damage. It is a form of 'cruelty that can injure a man's life without injuring his body'. This might encourage the student to withdraw into himself. It might make it even more difficult for him to make meaningful contact with the other students than it already was.

The teacher might defend this behaviour by saying that this is the way to get people to learn, even if he acknowledges it is a little unfair to the student who is chosen for this treatment. He might be so identified with the exam performance of his students, that he does not recognise the damage that he does to the students in this way. He might console himself by saying it is all done for the students' own good anyway, since it is in their interests to do as well as they can in the exams. Simone Weil can help us challenge this kind of schooling. Not only does she question a behaviourist conception of education, she questions the social relations of schooling which embody this conception.[9] She gives us a moral language which shows the different ways that people can be hurt.

If John withdraws into himself because of the ways he was humiliated in front of the class, this can be damage that is not easy to repair. It is not simply that John will choose not to take this kind of risk again. Rather, sometimes he will lose the power to make this kind of choice as he discovers himself to be more anxious and fearful in his relationships with others. We often carry the scars to our inner lives in our relations with others, even if we do not want to show others the ways we have been hurt. Simone Weil helps us clarify and deepen our thinking as she makes us aware, though not very systematically, of the different needs we share as human beings.

In *The Need for Roots*, her thinking about equality is deeply influenced by her Christianity. She focuses less upon the transformation of social relations of power and subordination and thinks more easily in terms of a certain 'balance' between equality and inequality.[10] The focus is upon being able to guarantee the equality of respect and consideration for people:

> It follows that the inevitable differences among men ought never to imply any difference in the degree of respect. And so that these differences may not be felt to bear such an implication, a certain balance is necessary between equality and inequality . . . Equality is all the greater in proportion as different human conditions are regarded as being, not more or less than one another, but simply as other. Let us look on the professions of miner and minister simply as two different vocations, like those of poet and mathematician. And let the material hardships attaching to the miner's condition be counted in honour of those who undergo it . . . It would mean honouring each human condition with those marks of respect which are proper to it, and are not just a hollow pretence. (*The Need for Roots*, pp. 16, 18)

If this does not call us to abstract ourselves from the social world, it has a direction that is also present in Kant. It helps us acknowledge the everyday conditions of people's lives as miners or as ministers by asking us somehow to regard them 'as two different vocations, like those of poet and mathematician', but she does not talk as much about the difficulties of doing this effectively and the kind of social transformations which would make this possible. Rather we find these deep tensions between the different moments of Weil's writings, especially as she is struggling to reconcile herself with Christianity.

At other moments in her writings Simone Weil is aware of just how difficult it is within an unequal relationship of power and subordination to regard 'the professions of miner and minister simply as two different vocations'. The very structures of power and dominance almost inevitably make those who are rich and powerful in the society feel they count for so much more, even if they pay lip service to a notion of equal respect. There is a remark collected in *Gravity and Grace* which shows this awareness:

The recognition of human wretchedness is difficult for whoever is rich and powerful because he is almost invincibly led to believe that he is something. It is equally difficult for the man in miserable circumstances because he is invincibly led to believe that the rich and powerful man is something. (*Gravity and Grace*, p. 110)[11]

If this echoes a theme we discovered in Kierkegaard which wants to recognise that it is 'equally difficult' for the rich and the poor to abstract themselves from the situation they are in, Simone Weil makes us aware of how the relations of power and circumstances of life of both rich and poor lead people to believe 'that the rich and powerful man is something'. The poor have continually to work *against* the structures of power and dominance to believe in themselves. They are constantly being undermined in a way that makes it difficult to maintain a sense of themselves as counting for something in the organisation of society. If Weil came to think differently in her later writings about how people were to learn to maintain a sense of their equal worth as human beings, this was a constant task for her.

Simone Weil was aware of the crushing load of working class people's experience at work. She had experienced this for herself. This gave her an understanding of the enormous power of these relationships of subordination to both the assembly line and the demands of foremen, over people's experience of themselves. She realised what it meant to endure these relationships at work. She also knew that people did not want to talk about this experience because it was too painful and people knew they could not escape from it. This did not make her underestimate the significance of the legal and political rights people were assured in a liberal democracy, but she always felt these had to be understood within the total context of people's lives.

She appreciated the ways that this could help working class people feel that they mattered as much as anyone else in the organisation of the larger society, but she also knew the ways that this was systematically denied in the subordination people were forced to endure in their everyday conditions of work. She knew that this fragmented people's experience of themselves. It encourages people to identify themselves as voters or consumers where they feel granted some equality, and to remain silent about their everyday experience at work.[12]

Simone Weil was well aware that the vote did not give people control over their own lives. In this sense it created illusions in people, even if it helped working-class people feel they counted as much as everyone else. She valued the ways this could give confidence to working-class people in their relations with others, making them feel they are owed the same amount of respect and consideration as everyone else. It can help people challenge the ways in which those in authority might patronise and condescend towards them.

But Weil also knew that the very organisation of capitalist production continually questions the confidence working-class people can feel in themselves, through the ways they are subordinated at work. This remained a powerful understanding for her, even when she became sceptical about a direct challenge to the capitalist mode of production.

She was suspicious of a Marxism that was not developing in close contact with people's everyday experience at work. She was deeply interested in changes that could be made in the organisation of factories. She was convinced that 'nothing must be done to make it worse; that everything must be done to make it less' (*The Need for Roots*, p. 56). She was aware that very different people had defined the problem for which she wanted to find a solution. As she says:

> The subject of such investigations would be easy enough to define. A pope once said: 'Material comes out of the factory ennobled, the workers come out of it debased.' Marx made exactly the same observation in still more vigorous terms.   (*The Need for Roots*, p. 56)

Simone Weil became much less concerned in the late 1930s with a revolutionary transformation of capitalist social relations and much more concerned with changes that could be made through making the capitalist class more responsible. She tended to develop a much more organic conception of society in which different groups had a distinct role to play. She was focussing upon reforms which would give workers more control over their experience of work. She tended to believe that these reforms were possible within a fundamentally capitalist mode of production. She tended to accuse both capitalists and trade unions of criminal neglect, thinking somewhat voluntaristically that they could be brought to act differently:

> Just as the capitalists have betrayed their calling by criminally neglecting not only the interests of the people, not only those of the nation, but even their own; so the workers' trade unions have betrayed theirs by neglecting to protect the wretched ones among their ranks, in order to turn their attention to the defence of special interests . . . In actual fact, the really wretched part of the factory population – the youths, women, immigrant workers, whether foreign or colonial – was abandoned to its wretchedness . . .   (*The Need for Roots*, pp. 61, 62)

She did not seem to be convinced by Marx's argument that at least the capitalists were forced to act in this way because production had to be organised around profit, however individual capitalists would have liked to be able to behave towards their workers. Simone Weil thought that capitalist production could operate with different forms of subordination, especially if piece-work was challenged:

> . . . Nor would obedience be any longer a matter of uninterrupted submissiveness. A workman or a group of workmen could have a certain number of orders to fulfil within a given time, and be left with a completely free hand in the actual layout of the work. It would be a different thing altogether from knowing that one had to go on repeating indefinitely the same movement, in obedience to an order, until the precise second when a new command came to impose a different movement for an equally unknown length of time. There is a certain relation to time which suits inert matter, and another sort of relation which suits thinking beings. It is a mistake to confuse the two. (*The Need for Roots*, p. 57)

She was always passionately interested in the details of the organisation of work. She recognised that basic changes have to be made, but she thought they had to be made with a full appreciation of people's everyday experiences of work. She was concerned to understand the details of the labour processes so she could develop a more detailed sense of the ways the same amount of respect and consideration could be 'effective and genuinely expressed in institutions and customs'. This would involve a transformation of relationships at work, even if it did not challenge the capitalists' control of the means of production.

This involves the recognition of the centrality of people's working experience within their everyday lives.[13] It is a recognition that the equality that exists between people cannot be guaranteed in people's individual relationships with God, or in the legal and political rights people are assured of in the public sphere. The equal respect which we owe to others will constantly threaten to become 'fictitious' if it does not find expression in people's experience at work.

If capitalists were to retain the power they had in the larger society then this had to go along with greater responsibility. In its own way this was to question the assumption of equality embodied in notions of equality before the law. This was to recognise that the relations of power and subordination we find reproduced with the social relations of production of a capitalist society leave people in very different situations. The later writings of Weil argue that the different power that capitalists have in society should carry with it different responsibilities. The notions of equality before the law which we take very much for granted within bourgeois society do not acknowledge the inequality implicit in treating people in very different situations of class and individual power as if they are in similar situations.[14]

This is to take the self-conceptions of liberal society to heart even though they are based solely upon the public sphere and blind us to the inequalities reproduced within the relationships at work. Simone Weil was no longer calling for a revolutionary transformation of social relations, but she was asking for 'a certain balance' between equality and inequality:

> Applied to the maintenance of social equilibrium, it would impose on each man burdens corresponding to the power and well-being he enjoys, and corresponding risks in cases of incapacity or neglect. For instance, an employer who is incapable or guilty of an offence against his workmen ought to be made to suffer far more, both in the spirit and in the flesh, than a workman who is incapable or guilty of an offence against his employer. Furthermore, all workmen ought to know that this is so. It would imply, on the one hand, a certain rearrangement with regard to risks, on the other hand, in criminal law, a conception of punishment in which social rank, as an aggravating circumstance, would necessarily play an important part in deciding what the penalty was to be. All the more reason, therefore, why the exercise of important public functions should carry with it serious personal risks. (*The Need for Roots*, p. 17)

If her thinking about respect and equality is always influenced by her thinking about experience at work, her later writing is influenced by her faith in the supernatural virtue of justice. Yet whilst we see a shift in emphasis from the early to the later work, Weil's continuity lies in her grasp of relations of respect, power and deference as qualitative, substantive and societal in character. The relationship between the individual and society continues to be a moral relation, even if her changing sense of what it is possible to transform in society moves her to pose different questions about that relation.

7 Inequality and Justice

JUSTICE, POWER AND SUBORDINATION

In the more Christian moments of her writings Simone Weil thinks it should really be possible to treat others with equal respect and consideration. While not underestimating the influence of the social relations of power and subordination, she feels convinced that we can call upon something deeper in ourselves. The source of the strength we require is supernatural. She thinks of this as 'the supernatural virtue of justice'. In this way she places a conception of justice at the heart of our understanding of our human relationships.

She implies a deep connection between our being able to relate to others as equals and our conception of justice. In so doing she draws upon a deeply Christian conception of justice to think about the nature of our relationships with others:

> The supernatural virtue of justice consists in behaving exactly as though there were equality when one is stronger in an unequal relationship. Exactly, in every respect, including the slightest details of accent and attitude, for a detail may be enough to place the weaker party in the condition of matter, which on this occasion naturally belongs to him, just as the slightest shock causes water which has remained liquid below freezing point to solidify. (*Waiting on God*, p. 100)

Simone Weil is aware of how difficult it is to behave towards others 'exactly as though there were equality when one is stronger in an unequal relationship'. This is not a matter of abstracting ourselves from the differences that exist between us or attempting to see the world from another person's point of view. She wants us to acknowledge and recognise the relations of class power that exist between, say, a minister and a miner so that they can confirm each other in what they do and how they live. She does not want to ignore these differences or pretend they do not exist, or that they do not make real differences in the ways people can live their lives.

It seems much easier for us to abstract from these differences with the awareness that they do not have to make a difference to the personal relationship we can establish with someone. This is the liberal option which Kant encourages us to adopt and it is something Kierkegaard gives us a picture of. Weil does not believe in this option though she shares a sense of a shared humanity, regardless of the social differences that exist between people.

For Weil it was important to recognise something deeper than the inequalities which divide people, which give some people social power over others. 'Behaving exactly as though there were equality' is part of acknowledging this shared humanity. At the same time she is critical of those who would minimise the difficulties of this task. It is not simply a question of taking up a certain attitude towards others. This easily becomes a 'fictitious' way of expressing our respect for others. This means we do not have to face up to the hardships, sufferings and deprivations people endure in their everyday lives. It is not enough to acknowledge a shared humanity unless this can 'be done through the medium of Man's earthly needs'.

She recognises the need for a certain balance between equality and inequality because she knows there are clear limits to the level of inequality which are compatible with treating others with equal respect. This is something Kierkegaard does not recognise and it is something Kant barely acknowledges in his later writings. Weil knows that if the strong are powerful enough they do not have to worry about justice:

> When two human beings have to settle something and neither has the power to impose anything on the other, they have to come to an understanding. Then justice is consulted . . . But when there is a strong and a weak there is no need to unite their wills. There is only one will, that of the strong. The weak obeys. Everything happens just as it does when a man is handling matter. There are not two wills to be made to coincide. The man wills and the matter submits. The weak are like things. There is no difference between throwing a stone to get rid of a troublesome dog and saying to a slave: 'Chase that dog away.'
>
> Beyond a certain degree of inequality in the relations of men of unequal strength, the weaker passes into the state of matter and loses his personality. The men of old used to say: 'a man loses half his soul the day he becomes a slave.' (*Waiting on God*, pp. 99–100)

If Simone Weil came to acknowledge that inequalities were an inevitable aspect of social life, she always knew that there had to be a certain balance between equality and inequality. The more unequal a relationship the easier it was for the smallest aspect of accent, tone, movement, to reduce someone in a situation of inequality and dependency 'into a state of matter'.[1] Kant also came to realise how hard it was to give to others who are dependent upon you, while allowing them to maintain a sense of their respect as equal human beings. Beyond a certain degree of inequality it could no longer still be a matter of the sensitivity and tact of those with power over the lives of others. Rather, as Weil acknowledges, 'the weaker passes into a state of matter and loses his personality'. This is the moment at which the supernatural virtue of justice becomes central. This is the only way we can restore a sense of our freedom in the ways we can choose to relate to others.

The Christian influence upon Simone Weil's thinking during the late 1930s and early 1940s about the sources of social inequality encourages her to think of social inequalities as if they are akin to individual differences of strength. This helps her conception of the 'naturalness' of these inequalities, even if she also calls for a certain balance between equality and inequality. This relates to the ways she comes to think of our obligations towards others.

Her thinking is very much controlled by the picture she has of our 'eternal obligation towards the human being not to let him suffer from hunger when one has the chance of coming to his assistance'. It is partly because of the ways she takes this obligation to be 'the most obvious of all' that she thinks 'it can serve as a model on which to draw up the list of eternal duties towards each human being'. She is quite clear that this list 'ought to proceed from the example just given by way of analogy' (*The Need for Roots*, p. 6).

This shows a Christian strain that does not really question the sources of the inequalities but assumes they simply have to be accepted. The poor and the powerless have to be grateful for what they receive. This is in tension with another moment in her writing when she questions the whole conception of charity which we so easily take for granted. Both moments are alive, particularly in the period of writing collected together in *Waiting on God*. Again it is interesting to explore this tension for the ways that it reveals some of the deeper tensions and contradictions about our thinking about respect and equality within a liberal moral culture.

When Weil is thinking about the 'supernatural virtue of justice' she is clear that it is only the 'stronger in an unequal relationship' who has to behave 'exactly as though there were equality'. The poor and the powerless have to learn to be grateful for what they receive. This clearly echoes Kant's conception:

> Supernatural virtue, for the inferior thus treated, consists in not believing that there really is equality of strength, and in recognising that his treatment is due solely to the generosity of the other party. That is

what is called gratitude. For the inferior treated in a different way, the supernatural virtue of justice consists in understanding that the treatment he is undergoing, though on the one hand differing from justice, on the other is in conformity with necessity and the mechanism of human nature. He should avoid both submission and revolt.   (*Waiting on God*, p. 100)

In this vein of her writings, acting according to 'the supernatural vir-tue of justice' does not challenge the nature of the relationship which exists between rich and poor, powerful and powerless. Rather it shows the strength of Christianity in limiting our conceptions of morality to a concern with how people should behave towards each other *within* such a relationship of power and subordination. It gives different responsibil-ities to the different parties. It preserves what we have thought about as the autonomy of morality. It does not encourage us to question the moral and material basis of the relationship. It even makes clear that the poor and underprivileged cannot expect or demand to be treated with 'the supernatural virtue of justice', to be treated as though there were equality in the relationship.

People have to accept that even if they are not treated justly, this is 'in conformity with necessity and the mechanism of human nature'. This says that people cannot expect justice from others. This is why they have to be grateful for whatever they receive. It is as if anything they receive from others is a 'gift' that others need to give:

He who treats as equals those who are far below him in strength really makes them a gift of the quality of human beings, of which fate has deprived them. As far as it is possible for a creature, he reproduces the original generosity of the Creator with regard to them.   (*Waiting on God*, p. 101)

I have already mentioned how Simone Weil's conception of Christianity was marked by her experience of factory work. It made her feel that she could not expect anything from others. She mentions how years later when any person speaks to her without brutality 'I cannot help having the impression that there must be a mistake' (*Waiting on God*, p. 33). She felt she really could not expect anything from others. It is almost as if it is wrong for us to expect anything from others. This is why we should be grateful to receive anything from others, since at some level it is not anything we deserve. We should not really want things for ourselves. At this level there is a continuity between Simone Weil and Kant.

There is a shared ethic of denial. This is the way we prove ourselves to be worthy. This is one of the pervasive strains in the formation of our moral culture. It produces an ethic of restraint and renunciation. This profoundly influences Weil's conception of Christianity as well as her sense of what we can expect from others:

> On God's part creation is not an act of self-expansion but of restraint and renunciation. God and all his creatures are less than God alone. God accepted this diminution. He emptied a part of his being from himself . . . God permitted the existence of things distinct from himself and worth infinitely less than himself. By this creative act he denied himself, as Christ has told us to deny ourselves. (*Waiting on God*, p. 101)

Weil's discussion of inequality in her article 'Forms of the Implicit Love of God' is inspired by the vision of the Good Samaritan. This organises the vision she has of 'the supernatural virtue of justice'.[2] It helps her grasp the ways that giving to others is a renunciation, an acceptance of being diminished. It is partly because others are not in a position to help us feel more of ourselves but can simply take our energies. But she seems to be focussing upon an extreme situation of affliction, though it seems to illuminate something much more general in our giving to others:

> Christ taught us that the supernatural love of our neighbour is the exchange of compassion and gratitude which happens in a flash between two beings, one possessing and the other deprived of human personality. One of the two is only a little piece of flesh, naked, inert and bleeding beside a ditch; he is nameless, no one knows anything about him. Those who pass by this thing scarcely notice it, and a few minutes afterwards do not even know that they saw it. Only one stops and turns his attention towards it. The actions that follow are just the automatic effect of this moment of attention. The attention is creative. But at the moment when it is engaged it is a renunciation. This is true, at least, if it is pure. The man accepts being diminished by concentrating on an expenditure of energy, which will not extend his own power but will only give existence to a being other than himself, who will exist independently of him. Still more, to desire the existence of the other is to transport himself into him by sympathy, and, as a result, to have a share in the state of inert matter which is his. (*Waiting on God*, p. 103)

This seems to be an image for different kinds of suffering and affliction.[3] Simone Weil seems to think they are analogous with giving bread to the starving. When we give our love, compassion, understanding and caring to others who are suffering we are giving them a form of food, a way of nourishing themselves. This can be as important for them to receive as the food they need to fill their empty stomachs. We also suffer from empty hearts and from empty souls. We need different kinds of food. We do not give to receive anything ourselves.

Weil is concerned that we do not make others dependent upon us. This is very easy to do within unequal relationships. We are not trying to extend our power in relation to others. Rather we want others to exist independently of us so that they develop a sense of their own individual lives. Kant was also aware of the many different ways in which we can give to others. As Weil has it:

> It is not surprising that a man who has bread should give a piece to someone who is starving. What is surprising is that he should be capable of doing so with so different a gesture from that with which we buy an object. Almsgiving when it is not supernatural is like a sort of purchase. It buys the sufferer.   (*Waiting on God*, p. 104)

She shares with Kant an understanding of the ease with which we can come to control the lives of others, especially if they are dependent upon us for their very means of livelihood. They share a concern with the morality of giving to others. Not only was Weil aware of the ease with which almsgiving 'buys the sufferer', she also recognised the importance of not compromising the freedom of others in the ways we relate to them. This involves a particular form of denial of oneself, just because of the ease with which we can extend our power over others who are dependent upon us. She does not underestimate the difficulties. But this is partly because of the ways she comes to accept these inequalities as 'natural' so that she thinks 'the sympathy of the strong for the weak' is in some sense 'against nature'. This recognises how easy it is for people with power to extend their power over others to compromise their very freedom.

In her most Christian writings Simone Weil seems to accept the naturalness of our extending our power and control over those who are dependent upon us. We have to be ready to make this sacrifice of our own power. It is partly because Simone Weil is thinking here of the picture of the Good Samaritan, when she thinks of relations of inequality, that she is aware of the energy it costs us to restore others to a sense of their own individual freedom:

> Whatever a man wants . . . he wants above all things to be able to exercise his will freely. To wish for the existence of this free consent

in another, deprived of it by affliction, is to transport oneself into him, it is to consent to affliction oneself, that is to say to the destruction of oneself. In denying oneself, one becomes capable under God of establishing someone else by a creative affirmation. One gives oneself in ransom for the other. It is a redemptive act.

The sympathy of the weak for the strong is natural, for the weak in putting himself into the place of the other acquires an imaginary strength. The sympathy of the strong for the weak, being in the opposite direction, is against nature.

This is why the sympathy of the weak for the strong is only pure if its sole object is the sympathy received from the other, when the other is truly generous. This is supernatural gratitude, which means gladness to be the recipient of supernatural compassion. It leaves self-respect absolutely intact. The preservation of true self-respect in affliction is also something supernatural. Gratitude which is pure, like pure compassion, is essentially the acceptance of affliction. The afflicted man and his benefactor, between whom diversity of fortune places an infinite distance, are united by this acceptance. There is friendship between them in the sense of the Pythagoreans, miraculous harmony and equality. (*Waiting on God*, pp. 104–5)

This shows how Simone Weil's Christian writings of the late 1930s involved a deep acceptance of the social relations of power and dependency. She was concerned with how people should behave *within* these relations, rather than with any challenge to the basis of these relations. She does not seem to feel that these relations *have to* compromise a person's self-respect so that these relations have to be transformed. Weil tends to think of power and inequality in terms of the relations of affliction. She tends to think of poverty as a form of affliction. She focusses upon the ways in which people cease to exist within affliction. She quotes a popular Spanish song which says that 'If anyone wants to make himself invisible, there is no surer way than to become poor' (*Waiting on God*, p. 106).

This helps Simone Weil recognise something important about the consequences of social relations of dependency and subordination, even if she wants to think of these as forms of affliction. This is partly because different forms of affliction have similar consequences and demand similar responses. It is not simply a question that some people have more resources and goods than others. Social inequality also concerns deeper consequences for the ways people can exist as individuals. As Weil recognises, 'a man who is entirely at the disposal of others does not exist. A slave does not exist either in the eyes of his master or his own' (*Waiting on God*, p. 106).[4] It is this extreme situation that is supposed to convince us of the need for God's power. It is to put us in touch with a different part of ourselves:

> God alone has this power, the power really to think into being that which does not exist. Only God, present in us, can really think the human quality into the victims of affliction, can really look at them with a look differing from that we give to things, can listen to their voice as we listen to the spoken words. Then they become aware that they have a voice, otherwise they would not have occasion to notice it.   (*Waiting on God*, p. 106)

This relates to the ways in which Weil thinks of love for our neighbour as a form of 'creative attention'. As she says this 'means really giving our attention to what does not exist' (*Waiting on God*, p. 105). It is partly because of the 'ways she recognises that relations of inequality and subordination can work to undermine people's sense of themselves, that it is so important to give others this kind of 'creative attention'. This is a way of helping people to believe in themselves more. This involves encouraging people to trust their own capacities, abilities, potentialities and intuitions.

If Simone Weil focuses upon an extreme example of affliction, she can help us think about more general processes which are at work within relations of subordination. She gives us a moral language in which we can identify the ways people can be continually undermined as they lose trust and confidence in their own individuality. This suggests a far deeper critique of relations of power and subordination than we are familiar with in discussions that operate solely within a framework of distributive theories of justice.

In demonstrating some of the effects of social relations of power and subordination, Weil makes us aware of the inadequacy of thinking that we simply have to show our respect for others by leaving others alone to live their own lives. Even if her Christianity has made her accept, at least for a while, the inevitability of these relations of inequality and subordination, she is still very aware of the damage they cause people. She is aware of the ease with which relationships of subordination work to undermine a person's sense of individual identity. If she does not any longer want to question the basis of these unequal relationships, she insists upon people recognising 'that it is better not to command wherever one has power to do so' (*Waiting on God*, p. 105). She also assumes a need for self-denial so that people are ready to give others the 'creative attention' they need. This seems to be as necessary in relations between rich and poor, as it is within other relations of affliction.

In her Christian writings collected in *Waiting on God* Simone Weil is more accepting of the social order as a natural order, governed by God's will. But even here there is an abiding sense of how the structures of dependency and subordination can deprive people of what is vital to their existence as independent human beings. There is a sense of the ways people can be reduced to matter by the processes of social life. This will help us develop an understanding of what it means to treat others as means and of the ways people can be so easily hurt and damaged, not only in their relationships with others, but also through the very organization of social life. But there is also a continuing sense of the importance of how we relate to others, despite the structures of inequality and subordination that might divide us.[5]

CHARITY AND JUSTICE

Simone Weil seems to share the conviction that by refusing to acknowledge the power of social inequality in the ways we relate to others, we can help restore a person's belief in himself or herself. This is a gift which we can give to others. It involves holding ourselves from using a power which is ours, so it involves a form of self-denial. This might not be enough to support people through their everyday experience of subordination, but it can give people a sense of what is possible. Sometimes it seems as if this respite can only be temporary and that Simone Weil has come to believe people have to accept their affliction and suffering as God-given:

> He who, being reduced by affliction to the state of an inert and passive thing, returns, at least for a time, to the state of a human being, through the generosity of others, such a one, if he knows how to accept and feel the true essence of this generosity, receives at the very instant a soul begotten exclusively of charity. (*Waiting on God*, p. 103)

In contrast to the writings of Kant and Kierkegaard, our humanity can in no way be guaranteed, either in our rational capacities as moral beings or else in our individual relationships to God. If Kant comes near to recognizing the ways our ability to live a moral life is threatened through relations of subordination and dependency, Weil has a much more pervasive sense of the ease with which our very individualities can be undermined and our capacities damaged through the processes of social life. She understands the ease with which we can be reduced to mere matter. Our existence as independent human beings is not something that can be assumed in our relations with others. We are much more vulnerable in our relations of subordination and dependency to being undermined in our very individuality.[6]

There is a tension within Simone Weil's writings about charity and justice. At one level she wants people to be grateful for what they receive from others. She is teaching people about the correct attitude to take up to the help and generosity of others. At other moments she questions the distinction we make within liberal moral culture between charity and justice. It seems to open up the question of what we can expect from others as a matter of justice. It would seem to question the very basis of the unequal relationships she is taking for granted in these writings. Justice does not simply have to do with the distribution of goods, it has to do also with the ways people treat each other.

There seems to be a prior connection between treating someone justly and treating someone as a human being. This connection can be threatening to us if it challenges our sense of obligation to others:

> Christ does not call his benefactors loving or charitable. He calls them just. The Gospel makes no distinction between the love of our neighbour and justice. In the eyes of the Greeks also a respect for Zeus the suppliant was the first duty of justice. We have invented the distinction between justice and charity. It is easy to understand why. Our notion of justice dispenses with him who possesses from the obligation of giving. If he gives all the same, he thinks he has a right to be pleased with himself. He thinks that he has done a good work. As for him who receives, it depends on the way he interprets this notion whether he is dispensed from all gratitude, or whether it obliges him to offer servile thanks.
>
> Only the absolute identification of justice and love makes the co-existence possible of compassion and gratitude on the one hand, and on the other, of respect for the dignity of affliction in the afflicted – a respect felt by the sufferer himself and the others.   (*Waiting on God*, p. 97)

So Simone Weil would warn us about analytical procedures which limit themselves to exploring the distinction we find in everyday language between justice and charity. We also need to investigate this as a socially and historically specific distinction which works in a particular society to 'dispense him who possesses from the obligation of giving'. So this distinction will work in the interests of those who have wealth and power in society. It will work to legitimate the existing property relationships. A different conception of justice will challenge existing relationships and our sense of obligations towards others.

At the same time Simone Weil's critique remains very much within the framework of what it means for one person to act justly towards another. This can help her acknowledge that people have an obligation to give to others, even though the distinction that is drawn within the society between charity and justice might deny this.[7] If she helps us connect justice with the quality of our relationships with others, not simply the distribution of goods, she seems to stop short of questioning the basis of the inequalities reproduced within social life. This helps her reconcile herself to the implicit challenge to the prevailing relations of power when she challenges the distinction we make between charity and justice. In challenging a distinction within language we are also challenging the relations of power which sustain the distinction.

Simone Weil has raised a central issue of the relationship of language to power. She says that 'it is easy to understand why' we draw a distinction between charity and justice. She challenges the dispensation that this gives to 'him who possesses from the obligation of giving'. The powerful not only protect their position of power through sustaining this distinction, but they also guarantee themselves 'a right to be pleased' when they give to others. Kant was forced to worry in a similar way about the relations between rich and poor. Weil wants to restore the question of justice into our consideration of the relationships of people with each other. She knows that the person who receives a material advantage from an act of justice is receiving an 'object of contact and even a kind of nourishment' (*Waiting on God*, p. 97). She is working for 'the absolute identification of justice and love'.

In these Christian writings this does not involve the same challenge to the material basis of these unequal relationships, as it would have meant in her earlier socialist writings.[8] It meant learning to relate to others 'as though there were equality when one is the stronger in an unequal relationship'. In the later writing of *The Need for Roots* this meant a direct challenge to notions of justice in terms of equality before the law. This was to involve a notion of punishment and responsibility which would relate to the power and wellbeing different groups enjoyed in the organization of the larger society. But in these different periods it was important for her to develop a critique of the notion of rights. This involves an implicit critique of Kant's notion of respect for others as non-interference.

8 Respect, Rights and Injustice

OBLIGATIONS, RIGHTS AND INEQUALITY

Simone Weil helps us understand some of the difficulties in simply analysing the concept of respect, through analysing the ways we talk about 'respecting others' in our ordinary language. She makes us aware of the different traditions of thought that remain as latent tensions within our moral consciousness.[1] She also helps us become aware of the need for grasping the historical formation of our moral and political thinking, so we can understand *how* these different traditions enter our everyday understandings and language. This will help us ground some of the tensions and contradictions within the ways we think and feel about respecting others and treating them as equals.

Often we take these traditions of thought so much for granted that we are barely aware of their continuing influence upon our thinking and feeling. At the same time a recognition of the need for this kind of historical conscious- ness rests uneasily with the deeply rationalist strains in her writings. Weil tends to think of these different traditions as each attempting to articulate a single truth. This gives witness to the ongoing influence of Plato in her thinking.

She tends to assume that different formulations of our respect for others are to be understood as different attempts to articulate a single truth. Some of these inherited traditions express these original insights in a 'confused and imperfect form', so we have to become critically conscious of them. This is the way Simone Weil thinks about the tradition of positive rights.

In the early pages of *The Need for Roots* Simone Weil argues that the tradition of positive rights has had a distorting effect on the understanding of the nature of our obligations to others:

> The object of any obligation, in the realm of human affairs, is always the human being as such. There exists an obligation towards every human being for the sole reason that he or she a a human being, without any other condition requiring to be fulfilled . . .
>
> The recognition of this obligation is expressed in a confused and imperfect form, that is, more or less imperfect according to the particular case, by what are called positive rights. To the extent to which positive

rights are in contradiction with it, to that precise extent is their origin an illegitimate one.   (*The Need for Roots*, p. 4)

A moral and political theory which wants to express the nature of our obligations to others in terms of positive rights is bound to mislead and confuse us about the nature of our obligations. It is partly through a critique of the ways a tradition of positive rights works in our everyday consciousness and understanding, that she wants to make us more aware of the true nature of our obligations to others. Equally a language of rights is an inadequate basis for sustaining human dignity for as the experience of Jews in Nazi Germany showed, these can be withdrawn.

The tendency to see these different traditions of moral and political thought as attempts to articulate the same fundamental truths avoids the issue of relativism but only at the cost of minimising our understanding of the social and historical conditions of their emergence. It helps explain both the intensity of her thinking as well as the difficulties she sometimes has in coming to terms with historical realities that might otherwise bring into question some of her views. It becomes difficult to relate these different traditions of moral thought to the interests and power of different social classes, genders, or ethnic groups in society, though this is something Weil hinted at, say, in her discussion of the distinction we draw between justice and charity.

It is difficult to grasp the nature of our obligations to others if we are brought up to take for granted a tradition of positive rights. Whatever strength and clarity this tradition has given us, it confuses us about the nature of our obligations to others. This is particularly significant within a liberal moral culture, since we easily accept this tradition as guaranteeing our sense of individual freedom.

Weil sees a pervasive error in the ways we relate the notion of obligation to that of rights. She wants to argue for the priority of our obligation to others. She wants us to realise that these are not brought into existence within a particular form of society. This is how she begins her discussion in *The Need for Roots*:

The notion of obligations comes before that of rights, which is subordinate and relative to the former. A right is not effectual by itself, but only in relation to the obligation to which it corresponds, the effective exercise of a right springing not from the individual who possesses it, but from other men who consider themselves as being under a certain obligation towards him. Recognition of an obligation makes it effectual. An obligation which goes unrecognised by anybody loses none of the full force of its existence. A right which goes unrecognised by anybody is not worth very much. (*The Need for Roots*, p. 3)

Simone Weil wants us to remain clear about the centrality of the nature of our obligations to others as human beings. It is not subject to any conditions. These obligations are not conditional, nor do they depend in any way upon the kind of society we live in. There is no way for us to escape these obligations. It is not as owners of property that we have obligations, but we have obligations to others 'for the sole reason that he or she is a human being'. If we think in terms of rights it is easy to feel that if we have not infringed the rights of others then no harm can have been done. We slip into thinking that if people do not have rights for whatever reason, then we have no obligations towards them. Weil rejects the prevailing assumption. In a similar way to Kant's conviction that the source of our morality and so our obligations towards others lies in a realm of its own, Weil feels the need in these writings to discover the source of these obligations 'above this world':

Rights are always found to be related to certain conditions. Obligations alone remain independent of conditions. They belong to a realm situated above all conditions, because it is situated above this world.

The men of 1789 did not recognise the existence of such a realm. All they recognised was the one on the human plane. That is why they started off with the idea of rights. But at the same time they wanted to postulate absolute principles. This contradiction caused them to tumble into a confusion of language and ideas which is largely responsible for the present political and social confusion. The realm of what is eternal, universal, unconditional is other than the one conditioned by facts, and different ideas hold sway there, ones which are related to the most secret recesses of the human soul. (*The Need for Roots*, p. 4)[2]

Simone Weil saw the period of the French Revolution as crucial in establishing the language of rights. She recognised the fundamental ways in which this conception had influenced our moral and political consciousness. She thought that the way that rights had become a universal language in which our claims against others are made tended to mystify us about the nature of our obligations towards others. For one thing, it made it easier for us to assume that we were fulfilling our obligations to others in respecting them through not infringing their rights. This is the conception Kant was crucial in preparing. This made it easy for us to express our respect in a 'fictitious way'. We did not have to face the realisation that our respect can only be expressed 'through the medium of Man's earthly needs'.

This is where Simone Weil offers an implicit critique of Kant's conception of respect in terms of not interfering in the rights of others. There is the need for a deeper critique of the notion of rights which has an 'intrinsic inadequacy to fulfil the role assigned to it':

> To set up as a standard of public morality a notion which can neither be defined nor conceived is to open the door to every kind of tyranny.
>
> The notion of rights, which was launched into the world in 1789, has proved unable, because of its intrinsic inadequacy, to fulfil the role assigned to it.
>
> To combine two inadequate notions, by talking about the rights of human personality, will not bring us any further
>
> What is it, exactly, that prevents me from putting that man's eyes out if I am allowed to do so and if it takes my fancy?
>
> Although it is the whole of him that is sacred to me, he is not sacred in all respects and from every point of view. He is not sacred in as much as he happens to have long arms, blue eyes, or possibly commonplace thoughts. Nor as a duke, if he is one; nor as a dustman, if that is what he is. Nothing of all this would stay my hand.
>
> What would stay it is the knowledge that if someone were to put out his eyes, his soul would be lacerated by the thought that harm was being done to him.
>
> At the bottom of the heart of every human being, from earliest infancy until the tomb, there is something that goes on indomitably expecting, in the teeth of all experience of crimes committed, suffered, and witnessed, that good and not evil will be done to him. It is this above all that is sacred in every human being.   (*Selected Essays 1934–43*, p. 10)[3]

Simone Weil wants to make us aware that what stops us hurting others is not simply a respect for the rights they have. When we think of the respect we have for others we should not only think of respecting their rights. The notion of rights is inadequate to express the nature of our respect for others. If there are situations in which it is appropriate for us to think in terms of protecting or interfering in the rights of others, this does not mean that this notion can fully express the nature of our obligations to others.[4] If the notion of rights guaranteed to all has helped people believe that, in some sense, they counted as much as everyone else whatever the inequalities which divided them, it has also mystified people about the nature of human equality.

Even if the guarantee of certain legal and political rights has helped people believe they lived in a community in which they shared equal respect with others, Simone Weil is more aware of the different areas of people's lives, say at work or in the family, in which people have to bear subordination in their everyday experience. She warns us about taking to heart the self-conceptions of a liberal society. Sometimes she is so keen to establish her point that she will understate where a language of rights remains significant. She wants our respect for others to be 'effectively expressed in a real, not a fictitious way'. She was aware of the importance of the French Revolution in spreading the notion of rights as an integral aspect of the equality it wanted to bring into the world. She was suspicious of this notion of equality.

In *The Need for Roots* she seems to connect the increasing importance of money in mediating human relationships, which has been a consequence of the development of capitalism, with the kind of equality encouraged by the French Revolution:

> By making money the sole, or almost the sole, motive of all actions, the sole, or almost the sole, measure of all things, the poison of inequality has been introduced everywhere. It is true that this inequality is mobile; it is not attached to persons, for money is made and lost; it is none the less real.
> There are two sorts of inequality, each with its corresponding stimulant. A more or less stable inequality, like that of ancient France, produces the idolizing of superiors – not without a mixture of repressed hatred – and a submission to their commands. A mobile, fluid inequality produces a desire to better oneself. It is no nearer to equality than is stable inequality, and it is every bit as unwholesome. The Revolution of 1789, in putting forward equality, only succeeded in reality in sanctioning the substitution of one form of inequality for another. (*The Need for Roots*, p. 17)

Simone Weil wants to focus upon the lived experience of inequality in social life. She does not want us to take at face value the formal equality which is guaranteed by certain legal and political rights. She is suspicious of the effectiveness of these formal notions of equality, however important they might be in specific areas of people's lives, if the society is organised around competitive notions that everyone should prove themselves to be better than others.

As far as Weil is concerned, if the social world is organised as a vast ladder which people have to scramble up, this simply produces a 'mobile,

fluid inequality' which 'produces a desire to better oneself'. She wants to
bring us back from the formal definitions of 'equality' and 'justice' to the
lived reality of what people experience in their daily lives. This is part of
the meaning of her saying that our respect for others has to be expressed
'through the medium of Man's earthly needs'. In a way not too dissimiliar
to the ways Wittgenstein brings us back to the actual usage and context of
words, Weil brings us back to the everyday relationships people have with
each other.[5]

Simone Weil makes us sceptical about a conception of liberal society
which would argue that people are already guaranteed 'equality', 'justice'
and respect' in the institutions of society, so that all we need to do is make
sure that we do not infringe upon the rights of others. She is suspicious
of this conception of freedom, since it does not consider the everyday
reality of people's experience within the class relations of power and
subordination. This makes her critical of Kant's discussion of respect,
which would encourage us to think that people simply have to be left
alone to live their own lives. We should not be led away from thinking
seriously about the everyday realities of people's lives because of the
'rights' people are guaranteed. It becomes easy to think that individuals
just want to be left free to pursue whatever ends they have set themselves,
without having to deal with the realities of class, gender and racial power
and subordination.

We so easily think that as long as we respect the rights of others then
this fulfils our obligations to them. This makes it so much harder for us
to appreciate the ways in which people are hurt, damaged, undermined,
through the everyday processes of social life. We tend to think that as long
as people's rights are respected, then people cannot really be hurt by the
social relations of power and subordination. It is because of the ways our
conception of individuals each pursuing their own ends make it difficult
to appreciate the needs we share, that it is difficult to recognise the ways
people are hurt and damaged.

We fundamentally misconceive the nature of our obligation to others if
we conceive of this in terms of respecting the rights of others. This can
make us think that as long as we treat others with respect, then we are
absolved from any responsibility for the appalling housing conditions they
have, or the subordination they experience in the factories. As long as we
are concerned not to interfere in the rights of others, nothing more can be
expected of it.

This easily leaves us with a conception of the human community as a
place for mutual self-protection, rather than any involvement with others
for mutual fulfilment as human beings.[6] The language of rights so easily

limits our concern and involvement with others, without our really being
aware of how this happens. We think we cannot act more decently towards
others than by being careful to respect their rights. This can make us assume
that we cannot really be hurting others or causing them damage, if we have
been careful to respect their rights.

As long as rights are not being infringed then we do not have to feel
we have any responsibility for the suffering or misery of people. This is
something that does not have to be our concern. It grows out of a situation
that people have chosen for themselves. So, for example, it is easy within
a liberal moral culture to assume that people have freely chosen the factory
they are working in. As long as we can be assured that workers have the
right to sell their labour to whatever firm they want to work for, we can
assume they have voluntarily accepted the discipline and subordination of
the factory.[7]

It becomes difficult to understand the different ways in which workers
are made to suffer and the relations of power they have to subordinate
themselves to. Within a tradition of positive rights it becomes harder to
identify the sources of human suffering, where no rights seem to have
been infringed. People can be made to feel that they have no grounds for
protest. If people cannot themselves identify a clear infringement of rights,
their suffering has to be silenced.

It is easy to mystify our obligations to others if we think in terms of a
tradition of positive rights. Not only is Weil aware that injustice can be
done even if rights are scrupulously observed, but she knows that this
makes it difficult for people to identify and articulate their own suffering.
The language of rights might give people important protection, but this
will often be when they have property and position to protect. It will be
difficult to express some of the injuries and injustices that people suffer in
this language.

As Weil recognises, it will be an aspect of the relations of power and
subordination that those who are made to suffer most will often also be
dispossessed of their language.[8] With the language of rights so dominant
it will be hard for people to feel the legitimacy of their protest. This does
not mean that people are not made to suffer:

> And even in those who still have the power to cry out, the cry
> hardly ever expresses itself, either inwardly or outwardly, in coherent
> language. Usually, the words through which it seeks expression are quite
> irrelevant.
>
> That is all the more inevitable because those who most often have
> occasion to feel that evil is being done to them are those who are least

trained in the art of speech. Nothing, for example, is more frightful than to see some poor wretch in the police court stammering before a magistrate who keeps up an elegant flow of witticisms. (*Selected Essays 1934–43*, p. 11)

The available language of freedom which in a liberal moral culture speaks in terms of the infringement of rights, usually would be the words through which this suffering and oppression 'seeks expression'. But as Weil points out they 'are quite irrelevant'. People need to discover their own 'means of expression'. This will involve challenging the prevailing moral and political language, where this fails to identify and acknowledge the reality of human suffering, oppression and injustice. This is part of what Weil is preparing the ground for in her critique of the tradition of positive rights.[9]

RIGHTS, PRIVILEGES AND JUSTICE

Simone Weil shows in her essay 'Human Personality' the relationship of the language of rights to the question of power and property. She finds sources for this in a contrast between Rome and Greece:

It is singularly monstrous that ancient Rome should be praised for having bequeathed to us the notion of rights. If we examine Roman law in its cradle, to see what species it belongs to, we discover that property was defined by the *jus utendi et abutendi*. And in fact the things which the property owner had the right to use or abuse at will were for the most part human beings.

The Greeks had no conception of rights. They had no words to express it. They were content with the name of justice. (*Selected Essays 1934–43*, pp. 19–20)

Those who have power in society also have power over language. Simone Weil had learnt that our language was formed in the interests of those who have power and wealth in society. It does not exist as a neutral means of expression.[10] She was acutely aware of the ways in which the generalisation of the language of rights so easily becomes abused to protect the interests of those who have power. In the starkest examples: 'The Romans, like Hitler, understood that power is not fully efficacious unless clothed in a few ideas, and to this end they made use of the idea of rights, which is admirably suited to it' (*Selected Essays*, p. 19).

Simone Weil is critical of the connection we tend to assume between notions of equality and distributive conceptions of justice. This is related to the conception of rights. This becomes sharply institutionalised within liberal moral culture with the notion of 'an equal share of privilege for everybody':

> To the dimmed understanding of our age there seems nothing odd in claiming an equal share of privilege for everybody – an equal share in things whose essence is privilege. The claim is both absurd and base; absurd because privilege is, by definition, inequality; and base because it is not worth claiming.
>
> But the category of men who formulate claims, and everything else, the men who have the monopoly of language, is a category of privileged people. They are not the ones to say that privilege is unworthy to be desired. They do not think so and, in any case, it would be indecent for them to say so.
>
> Many indispensable truths, which could save men, go unspoken for reasons of this kind; those who could utter them cannot formulate them and those who could formulate them cannot utter them. If politics were taken seriously, finding a remedy for this would be one of its most urgent problems. (*Selected Essays 1934–43*, p. 22)

The language of rights easily serves to protect the interests of this 'category of privileged people'. They have the power to establish the terms of moral and political discussions. This establishes issues in particular ways. Its very generality tends to assimilate situations which should be thought about in very different terms. It makes us insensitive to the nature of the moral issues involved and to the ways people are hurt and damaged through the processes of social life.

Simone Weil thinks that the notion of rights is related to a particular conception of human relationships. It is hard to do justice to the Christian influence in this critique, especially to the contrast she develops between 'the personal and the impersonal'.[11] Sometimes she seems to argue that it is never appropriate to think in terms of rights since it always mystifies the nature of our obligations to others. At other moments it seems as if she thinks that it is mystifying to think in this way about some of the deeper sources of human misery and oppression. By the time she was writing this essay on 'Human Personality' she was very suspicious of what she called 'collectivity'.

She came to think that the very notion of the 'person' involved a subordination to 'the collective'. She also tended to think that the 'personal' involved making claims that we are better than others, or claiming our share is not as large as others. This made her intolerant of what she calls 'cries of personal protest':

> When the infliction of evil provokes a cry of sorrowful surprise from the depth of the soul, it is not a personal thing. Injury to the personality and its desires is not sufficient to evoke it, but only and always the sense of contact with injustice through pain. It is always, in the last of men, as in Christ himself, an impersonal protest.
>
> There are also many cries of personal protest, but they are unimportant; you may provoke as many of them as you wish without violating anything sacred.
>
> So far from being his person, what is sacred in a human being is the impersonal in him.   (*Selected Essays 1934–43*, p. 12)

I am left uneasy with the notion that these cries of 'personal protest' are 'unimportant' because they do not violate anything sacred. It is part of Weil's tendency to overstate the point she is making since otherwise she seems to fear that we will not take it seriously enough. She can make it difficult for us to think about the different kinds of hurt done to people, because of the ways she is focussed upon clarifying ways we fail to appreciate the depths of injury and suffering that is caused to people. This relates to her Platonism, that 'Truth and beauty dwell on this level of the impersonal and the anonymous'. It is this which makes her suspicious of any notion of respect for the person.

> The person, being subordinate to the collective both in fact and by the nature of things, enjoys no natural rights which can be appealed to on its behalf.
>
> It is said, quite correctly, that in antiquity there existed no notion of respect for the person. The ancients thought far too clearly to entertain such a confused idea.
>
> The human being can only escape from the collective by raising himself above the personal and entering into the impersonal. (*Selected Essays 1934–43*, p. 15)

These ideas can be difficult to follow. I can understand Simone Weil's critique of the cult of the personality, especially when she says 'it is precisely those artists and writers who are most inclined to think of their art as the manifestation of their personality who are in fact the most in bondage to public taste' (*Selected Essays*, p. 15). She knows how easy it is for us to identify ourselves with status or 'collective prestige', giving ourselves a sense of self-importance. Weil was also questioning 'the philosophy of personalism' which was popular among writers of her time who 'hope to acquire a name and a reputation'.[12]

She realised it was so much easier for those with power and status in society to 'feel something sacred in their own persons and believe they can generalise and attribute it to every person'. It is easy for them to overlook the workings of the class relations of power and subordination. They are easily supported in the sense they have of themselves through the status, wealth and prestige they enjoy. They remain unaware of the everyday realities of most people's lives:

> So they are mistaken in thinking they can generalise from their own case. Their motive is generous, but it cannot have enough force to make them really see the mass of people as anything but mere anonymous human matter. But it is hard for them to find this out, because they have no contact with the mass of people.
>
> The person in man is a thing in distress; it feels cold and is always looking for a warm shelter.
>
> But those in whom it is, in fact or in expectation, warmly wrapped in social consideration are unaware of this. (*Selected Essays 1934–43*, p. 16)

Weil is concerned to make us recognise different ways people can be hurt and damaged through the social relations of power and subordination. Often we do not want to face the sufferings of others. The language of rights can so easily protect us from this knowledge. People can be very seriously hurt and an injustice be done, even if it is not a matter of the infringement of rights. It is the deep and often unspoken expectation 'that good and not evil will be done' to us that is 'sacred in every human being'. As far as Simone Weil is concerned this is not involved when we agitate for our rights:

> This profound and childlike and unchanging expectation of good in the heart is not what is involved when we agitate for our rights. The motive which prompts a little boy to watch jealously to see if his brother has a slightly larger piece of cake arises from a much more superficial level of the soul. The word justice means two very different things according to whether it refers to one or the other level. It is only the former one that matters.
>
> Every time that there arises from the depths of a human heart the childish cry which Christ himself could not restrain, 'Why am I being hurt?', then there is certainly injustice. For if, as often happens, it

is only the result of a misunderstanding, then the injustice consists in the inadequacy of the explanation. (*Selected Essays 1934–43*, pp. 10–11)

This is intended to show us the limits of a conception of justice as fairness in a way that places it within a larger framework or discourse on justice. In watching to see I get as big a piece of cake as my brother I am jealously protecting my rights. I know it is unfair if we are not given the same size piece of cake. If I get a smaller piece on the first helping then I am going to make sure I make up for it on the next round. This could itself come to mean much more, if part of me feels my step-father never seems to give me an equal slice because I am not his real child. This would trigger much deeper feelings and hurt. What would matter would not simply be the same size of cake, but the feeling I was not loved as much as his other child. Weil wants to keep these levels clearly distinct, as she wants to distinguish the very different things justice can mean according to the level at which we are talking. Sometimes it seems as if she is protesting against the ways in which justice presented as the agitation for rights only makes one level available to us and attempts to assimilate different experience to this same level.

RIGHTS, INJURIES AND VIOLATION

The language of rights, for Weil, is implicitly connected with a 'bargaining spirit' which has 'a commercial flavour, essentially evocative of legal claims and arguments'. She tends to think that the notion of rights 'is linked with the notion of sharing out, of exchange, of measured quantity' (*Selected Essays*, p. 18). She does not say much to establish the emergence of this language, though sometimes she does suggest a connection with the dominance of monetary relations where money is made 'the sole, or almost the sole, motive for all actions, the sole, or almost the sole, measure of all things' (*The Need for Roots*, p. 17).

She sometimes seems to acknowledge the appropriateness of thinking in terms of rights in certain particular circumstances, while wanting to make us sharply aware of how mystifying this conception can be when it is generalised and made central to our moral and political understanding:

> Relying almost exclusively on this notion, it becomes impossible to keep one's eyes on the real problem. If one tries to browbeat a farmer to sell his eggs at a moderate price, the farmer can say: 'I have the right to keep my eggs if I don't get a good enough price for them'. But if a

young girl is being forced into a brothel she will not talk about her rights. In such a situation the word would sound ludicrously inadequate.

Thus it is that the social drama, which corresponds to the latter situation, is falsely assimilated, by the use of the word 'rights', to the former one.

Thanks to this word, what should have been a cry of protest from the depths of the heart has been turned into a shrill nagging of claims and counter-claims, which is both impure and unpractical. (*Selected Essays 1934–43*, p. 21)

Through using the notion of 'rights' to describe these very different situations we are 'falsely assimilating' them. We are being led astray by our language. This echoes something Wittgenstein was teaching in his later writings. We are implicitly suggesting an appropriate way of responding to the different situations. It becomes possible to think of both situations as an 'infringement of rights', so that it is difficult to grasp the very different kind of hurt and suffering caused in the two situations. It makes it difficult to understand the damage and pain caused to the young girl being dragged into a brothel. Making it an issue of whether her rights are being infringed allows us to avoid facing the nature of the suffering caused.

Yet within a liberal moral culture it can be difficult to discover the language which would help us grasp 'the real problem'. The very strength of utilitarian traditions makes us think in terms of causing people more or less pain. Too much of Kantian moral theory is tied to notions of respect in terms of not interfering with the rights of others. Weil helps us question the influence of both these traditions.

Simone Weil seems to take it as relatively unproblematic that the shop-keeper has a right to keep his eggs if he does not get a good price for them. They are his eggs so he can dispose of them as he wishes. Weil does not say enough about the market and contractual situation which are the basis for the 'appropriateness' of the language of rights.[13] The Bolivian film 'Blood of the Condor' has a moment which illustrates the historical and social specificity of these market assumptions of capitalism.

An Indian peasant woman is shown taking the eggs that she has collected to market. On the way she passes three American peace-corps people on the side of the road. They need some eggs for the medical centre where they are staying. They offer to buy all the eggs she has. She offers them one or two, but she refuses to sell them any more. This is incomprehensible to them. They have money and they want to buy her eggs. They would save her a long trip to the market. In the end they think that it is just her 'Indian stupidity' which explains her not wanting to sell the eggs to them.

They cannot understand that within the culture she lives in, these eggs are not simply her individual private property for her to dispose of in any way she wishes. Rather, she collects eggs within the context of a whole community and she knows people are dependent on her coming to the market for eggs for their families. She knows the whole community would be forced to go without eggs if she did not arrive. This is in conflict with the rationality of individual private property that we take very much for granted within a liberal moral culture. She does not have the 'right' to dispose of them at any price she wants. The situation is profoundly different. We are talking about a different kind of market situation in which individual rights do not have the same kind of meaning and significance.

It is crucial for Weil that 'if a young girl is being forced into a brothel she will not talk about her rights'. If we insist upon thinking of the situation in terms of the young girl's rights being infringed, it is hard for us to hear the 'cry of protest from the depths of the heart' but we will inevitably think in terms of 'claims and counter-claims'. The language of rights does not help us illuminate the moral realities of the situation or the nature of the injustice that is being done. It does not help keep our eyes 'on the real problem' of the nature of the hurt and damage being done to the girl. It could easily turn this into a psychological or medical question that has little bearing upon our moral appreciation of the situation.

We remain trapped by our moral traditions into thinking about what 'right' has been infringed and how. Our attention is shifted away from the experience and suffering of the girl herself. Nor is it that we can say we understand and appreciate the depths of the suffering, but that this is a personal matter that can have nothing to do with justice. This can easily be genuine and deeply felt, though it can also be a form of lip service because we do not really want to face the suffering ourselves. But we can still remain blind to the moral realities of the situation, if we do not have a moral language which can express and identify the nature of the suffering.

At the same time we have to appreciate that within a liberal moral tradition people might not feel it is 'ludicrously inappropriate' to extend the notion of rights to cover this situation. They might feel her rights have been infringed because she was forced into the brothel and had not been able to make the decision for herself. But suppose that the girl was older so that it could not be said that she was too young to make this kind of decision for herself. Would we then say she has every right to make this decision for herself? Would we say that it is her body and she has every right to use it as she wants to? Suppose she lives in a town with few alternative sources of income for a woman bringing up young children on her own? Surely we have to be aware of the kind of situation a woman is in when she makes this kind of choice. In many situations she has no effective choice, even though liberal moral theory would often want to insist there has to be.

Again this is different from the full horror of the situation Weil depicts of the young girl being forced into a brothel. She wants us to be able to hear 'a cry of protest from the depths of the heart'. She wants us to recognise the injustice being done. The heart hardens and the body can shrink away from the source of the pain.

> In those who have suffered too many blows, in slaves for example, that place in the heart from which the infliction of evil evokes a cry of surprise may seem to be dead. But it is never quite dead; it is simply unable to cry out any more. It has sunk into a state of dumb and ceaseless lamentation. (*Selected Essays 1934–43*, p. 11)

We cannot adequately express the ways a young girl is being violated if we continue to think and feel in terms of the infringement of rights. We need a moral language which can identify the *different levels* at which people can be hurt and the depths of the scars they will carry into the future. We need criteria for recognising the violation as a form of injustice. This involves questioning a utilitarian tradition which focuses upon the pain that is caused but does not have a way of illuminating the different kinds of hurt and damage we endure. It involves challenging the conception of a person which tends to limit itself to present pleasures and pains, as if our lives can be grasped as a series of discrete moments of either pleasurable or painful experiences.[14]

A utilitarian tradition encourages us to think we are living in a kind of constant present in which we are continually making decisions about how to maximise our satisfactions. We are discouraged from dwelling upon the pains, hurts and rejections of the past, since we do not want to lose the opportunities the present offers us. This is very much the conception of the rational person who is working to maximise satisfactions at each moment. This has a powerful influence upon all of us who have grown up within a capitalist society.

It is difficult not to think and feel this way about ourselves and the lives we live. This is a fundamentally ahistorical conception of ourselves. It encourages us to put the past aside, thinking we can always make a fresh start in the present. This carries little sense of the ways we carry our histories into the present so that the ways we relate to people and can be open and vulnerable to people very much depend upon the relationships we have internalised from the past. This involves a very different relationship with our histories and our past relationships, as we learn to acknowledge the injuries and violations to our integrity that we may have suffered, say, as children. It can involve us recognising that we cannot escape the influence of our pasts, unless we find a way of working through these experiences. This was an important challenge of Freud to the utilitarian conception of a person we still take very much for granted within liberal moral culture.[15]

Thinking solely in terms of the infringement of rights does not help us understand the injustices that we do to people in the way that we treat them. It tends to make us think that as long as rights are being respected, then little harm can be done to people themselves. It can mystify people as to the nature of the contract they are making, especially about the relations of power and subordination. This is something Weil learnt for herself in her factory experience. It remained crucial for her to understand this experience as a way of challenging traditions of moral thought that seemed to evade 'the real problem'. She was questioning Kantian notions of respect and dignity that continually failed to understand the ways human dignity is being continually undermined by the everyday relationships of subordination and dependency.

A rationalist tradition of moral thought is continually underestimating the moral relevance of social relations of power and subordination, thinking that dignity and self-respect need only be assured in people's rational faculties. Simone Weil recognises that we can have different relationships with social reality and that 'physical labour is a certain contact with the reality, the truth, and the beauty of this universe' (*Selected Essays*, p. 18). Our dignity and self-respect comes as much from what we do, as from what we think about ourselves. It has to be sustained in our everyday lives since it can so easily be undermined through the processes of social life:

> Physical labour may be painful, but it is not degrading as such. It is not art; it is not science; it is something else, possessing an equal value with art and science, for it provides an equal opportunity to reach the impersonal stage of attention.
>
> To take a youth who has a vocation for this kind of work and employ him at a conveyor-belt or as a piece-work machinist is no less a crime than to put out the eyes of the young Watteau and make him turn a grindstone. But the painter's vocation can be discerned and the other cannot. (*Selected Essays 1934–43*, p. 17)

Simone Weil's Christian writing was still reaching for a moral language which could show this to be the crime that it is. Since assembly-line production is such a central feature of twentieth-century capitalist production in both West and East, she was seeking a moral language which could come to terms with this reality.[16] It was through reflecting upon an experience of a young girl's violation that she discerned a non-distributive conception of justice. It also helped her to identify the weaknesses of an orthodox Marxist tradition that had lost a sense of moral outrage at the exploitation of human labour.

This involves a challenge to the available language of personal rights within which our thinking is so often trapped:

> If the workers felt this, if they felt that by being the victim they are in a certain sense the accomplice of sacrilege, their resistance would have a very different force from what is provided by the consideration of personal rights. It would not be an economic demand but an impulse from the depths of their being, fierce and desperate like that of a young girl who is being forced into a brothel; and at the same time it would be a cry of hope from the depth of their heart.
>
> This feeling, which surely enough exists in them, is so inarticulate as to be indiscernible even to themselves; and it is not the professionals of speech who can express it for them.
>
> Usually, when addressing them on their conditions, the selected topic is wages; and for men burdened with a fatigue that makes any effort of attention painful it is a relief to contemplate the unproblematic clarity of figures.
>
> In this way, they forget that the subject of the bargain, which they complain they are being forced to sell cheap and for less than the just price, is nothing other than their soul.
>
> Suppose the devil were bargaining for the soul of some poor wretch and someone, moved by pity, should step in and say to the devil: 'It is a shame for you to bid so low; the commodity is worth at least twice as much.'
>
> Such is the sinister farce which has been played by the working-class movement, its trade unions, its political parties, its leftist intellectuals. (*Selected Essays 1934–43*, p. 18)

Simone Weil is struggling for a moral understanding of the nature of wage labour in capitalist production. She was sharply aware of the conditions of factory production. She dwells upon the experience of work for she grasped it as a vital source of human dignity. At the same time what she was learning was also applicable to other areas of life in which a person's dignity or integrity could be compromised or violated. She wanted a language which would illuminate the moral reality of people's everyday experience.

A discussion of the 'rights' of the workers somehow being balanced by the 'rights' of capitalists to manage their firms, creates a sense of equality between two parties equally free to draw up a contract. This focuses the issue of 'freedom' on the moment at which a contract is drawn up, for which the parties are supposed to be equally responsible. In this situation it is easy to forget 'that the subject of the bargain . . . is nothing other than their soul'. For Weil our vision of freedom has to shift to include the relations of power and subordination within the everyday organisation of production. As far as she is concerned the modern factory 'reaches perhaps almost the limit of horror':

> Everybody in it is constantly harassed and kept on edge by the inter-ference of wills while the soul is left in cold and desolate misery. What man needs is silence and warmth; what he is given is an icy pandemonium.   (*Selected Essays 1934–43*, p. 17)

Marxist discussions of exploitation which simply focussed upon theories of surplus value often missed the crucial realities of exploitation which were written into people's everyday experience of subordination. In its own way Marxism had often seemed to foreclose the need for the development of our moral language and a critique of the prevailing traditions of moral and political thought. Simone Weil was tackling some of these issues, as I have tried to show with Lawrence Blum in *A Truer Liberty: Simone Weil and Marxism*.

She felt we were often trapped within our prevailing moral traditions, which would often distract our gaze from the real problems being repro-duced within the conditions of modern life. She was continually struggling to form a language which could help us recognise and express our outrage at the injustice continually done to people which we were continually refusing to identify for what it is, preferring to minimise its significance by learning to think of it as 'subjective', 'personal' or 'psychological'. We learn to do this for ourselves, especially as men who have learnt to take or withstand whatever mistreatment is offered as a sign of masculinity. Often it takes others to point our how hard things must have been for us. Weil also realises that: 'There are some people who get a positive pleasure from the cry; and many others simply do not hear it. For it is a silent cry, which sounds only in the secret heart' (*Selected Essays*, p. 11).

Kant has prepared the way to recognise the wrongness of treating people as means for our own ends. It is difficult to integrate this insight into our moral and political understanding. It is easiest to think this is not the way we should individually relate to others. Weil helps us understand not only the wrongness of behaving towards others in this way, but also what damage can be done to people if they are treated in this way. It was harder for her also to understand situations in which no individual seems clearly culpable.

So for instance, when we are faced with the situation of the young girl being forced into the brothel because this is the only way she can support her younger brothers and sisters, we also want this social reality to be grasped. It might be tempting to say, especially within the individualistic moral traditions we inherit, that this cannot be a question of morality since no individual is forcing her into this situation. This would be to create a false and mystifying distinction between moral discussion that has to do with the moral worth of individuals and what individuals should do in particular situations, and social and political discussion that has to do with the organisation of the larger society. This threatens to impoverish both our social and political understanding and also our moral language, which will be incapable of revealing the moral realities of a society in which class, sexual and racial relations of power and subordination have become so crucial.

Simone Weil looked to Christianity to develop a language which could illuminate depths of our moral experience that are so easily overlooked in our traditions of positive rights. She wanted a language which could reveal the ways in which individuals are violated through the processes of social life while not losing touch with issues of social justice.

9 Morality, Subordination and Oppression

EQUALITY, LIBERALISM AND MORALITY

As we have seen, for Simone Weil, respecting others as human beings cannot be thought about simply as a matter of respecting the rights of others. This is an inadequate conception when it is universalised, however important it has been historically for different people to struggle for their rights. Often these struggles have been fought very hard and long. Sometimes it seems as if Simone Weil is in danger of undervaluing these struggles and the contexts in which it might be quite appropriate to present claims in terms of rights. Or it could be said that she had an understanding of the ways that a language of rights was bound to limit our grasp of the injuries that people can suffer.

She recognises that the notion of respect as non-interference would be more meaningful if people were living in a society in which people were more or less equal, say, as small farmers having control of their means of livelihood. This was a situation Tocqueville saw being threatened with the rise of manufacturing industry in New England. He was watching the early developments of the class relations of power and dependency that were reorganising social relations with the development of capitalism.[1] This was going to transform the everyday conditions of people's lives profoundly. This was going increasingly to undermine some of the original impulses of liberalism we can find in Kant's moral writings.

Our moral and political theory either had to come to terms with the developing relations of class power and dominance, or else it had to abstract itself from these social and historical developments. The very rationalistic character of Kantian ethics made it easy for it to separate itself off from these developments, especially if it could also sidestep Kant's own worries about relations of inequality and dependency. It was easy to put these doubts aside, since they were potentially too threatening to the autonomy of morality Kant had so carefully prepared.[2] But if human dignity could not be assessed as an inner quality then morality and politics cannot be separated and we have to be careful about relying exclusively upon a language of rights as a source of human dignity.

144

Morality was very much established around the issue of what individuals ought to do, with the background assumption that individuals were living their lives to prove their moral worth and so prove themselves in the eyes of God. Morality was to help us understand how we should behave within relationships we found ourselves in. It was to educate us about how we should treat others. All the time it would very much assume we were free to treat others in a way we had decided upon, especially in our personal relations. Society was very much conceived of as a collection of individuals each pursuing his or her own lives and their individual relationships with others.

In its own way this made liberal moral and political theory invulnerable to social and historical transformations. This was confirmed in aspects of Kant's notion of respect for others which called upon us to abstract ourselves from the social relations of power and subordination. It made it seem as if we could show our respect for others and even treat others as equals, whatever relations of power and subordination separate us. If it is recognised that abstracting takes energy and effort, it simply proves our respect for others. This involves abstracting ourselves from the relations of everyday life, so that it means we can hardly affirm people, say, as miners or dockworkers. Rather we come to respect others, not through what they can do or how they live, but because of their shared humanity.

This sets up an opposition which can be investigated at its source in Kant's writings, and which meant for Weil that our respect for others threatened to become increasingly 'fictitious'. She directly challenges Kant's notion of respect when she says that our respect is only 'effectively expressed' if it is 'done through the medium of Man's earthly needs'. This is why our respect for others has to somehow be 'at once public, general, effective and genuinely expressed in institutions and customs'. A language of rights as the only acknowledged source of human dignity can offer a false sense of security as Jews were to discover to their cost in Nazi Germany for if the state is able to withdraw these rights then people are left powerless and disarmed as they are left without other ways of conceiving and protecting their dignity as human beings.

As relations of class, gender and racial power and subordination become central features of the development of capitalist society, liberalism becomes increasingly incapable of illuminating the moral relations that have developed. It becomes increasingly powerless to help people grasp the relations of power and subordination they meet in their everyday experience at work and in the community. It makes it increasingly difficult for people to locate their individual experience within the social relations of power of the larger society.

Liberalism encourages people to think of themselves as individuals with their own discrete talents and abilities, free to make whatever choices they want to make about their lives. This picture can help people feel better about themselves. It can encourage them to identify themselves with the legal and political rights they have in the public realm and the equality they are supposed to have with others, for instance as 'consumers', 'radio listeners', 'TV viewers', 'railway users' and 'travellers'.

Simone Weil is aware that it is much easier for people to identify themselves with these available identities, than to dwell upon areas of life in which people endure subordination and dependency. She thought that social and moral theory had to be able to reveal and reflect upon the relations of power and subordination since these have a power continually to bring individual identity into question. This is a crucial concern since it can involve undermining people's confidence in themselves. Sometimes this is to undermine their trust in their own abilities and capacities. The relations of power and subordination can undermine people's very sense of individuality and sense that they exist as individuals in their own right.[3]

This can be illuminated in the struggles women have fought for equality. When this was a struggle for equal rights, it was very much a struggle for the rights which men already possessed. It was a struggle for legal and political rights that women had been denied. It was often felt that the possession of these rights would make women equal to men.[4] It was only with experience that women had to learn that there were other equally important sources of women's oppression and subordination. These had largely been made invisible within the language of equal rights which had very much set the terms for sexual equality.

This is not to underestimate the historical importance of women's struggles for equal rights. It can make us aware of different traditions in which rights have been fought for. James Connolly makes us graphically aware of this in his discussion of women in *The Reconquest of Ireland*:

> The Irish peasant, in too many cases, treated his daughters in much the same manner as he regarded a plough or a spade – as tools with which to work the farm. The whole mental outlook, the entire moral atmosphere of the countryside, enforced this point of view. In every chapel, church or meeting-house the insistence was ever upon duties – duties to those in superior stations, duties to the Church, duties to the parents. Never were the ears of the young polluted by any reference to 'right', and, growing up in this atmosphere, the women of Ireland accepted their position of social inferiority. That, in spite of this, they have ever proven valuable assets in every progressive movement in Ireland, is evidence of

the great value their co-operation will be, when to their self-sacrificing acceptance of duty they begin to unite its necessary counterpoise, a high-minded assertion of rights.

We are not speaking here of rights, in the thin and attenuated meaning of the term to which we have been accustomed by the Liberal or other spokesmen of the capitalist class, that class to whom the assertion of rights has ever been the last word of human wisdom. We are rather using it in the sense in which it is used by, and is familiar to, the Labour movement.

We believe, with that movement, that the serene performance of duty, combined with and inseparable from the fearless assertion of rights, unite to make the highest expression of the human soul. That soul is the grandest which most unquestionably acquiesces in the performance of duty, and most unflinchingly claims its rights, even against a world in arms. (*James Connolly, Selected Writings*, ed. P. Berresford Ellis, pp. 191–2)[5]

The women's liberation movement has itself invoked the notion of rights, say in the importance given to 'A Woman's Right to Choose' in the National Abortion Campaign.[6] This is to recognise that men and women are in different situations in relation to childbirth. In this context the assertion of a right is a rejection of that very 'bargaining spirit' which Weil attached to the notion of rights. It is to say this is not something women are prepared to bargain over with men. It is something they want men to accept as a condition of working out the different responsibilities men and women can have for more equal child care.

But these rights are demanded within the context of a movement that has also had to challenge liberal notions of equality in the relations between men and women. The notion of equal respect had too easily concealed the relations of power and subordination that were discovered to be an integral aspect of relations between men and women. It had made it so much more difficult for women to identify the sources of their own oppression in domesticity, sexuality and work. It was harder for women to recognise the ways they were undermined in their very sense of themselves as independent individuals. These processes operated at very different levels. Sometimes they were expressed in a feeling that a woman was not being treated as a person in her own right, but only in relation to others as someone's wife or mother. We have already given examples to illustrate this.

The women's movement has understood how relations of dependency and subordination so easily work to undermine a woman's sense of her own individual identity. This identity is not something that can be guaranteed in her husband's attitude to her. Nor can it be thought about as a demand to have rights which men already enjoy, unless it is appreciated how this involves a transformation of the personal and social relationship that exists between men and women. To do this feminism has had to break with a language of rights to talk of oppression and liberation. It has been an integral part of feminism's challenge to a modernity whose moral and political theory, as Weil grants, is largely set in terms of rights. A woman might have to realise the ways in which her very sense of individual identity and her sense of what she wants and needs for herself, has been undermined as she has learnt to subordinate herself to the demands and needs of her husband and children.

She might discover she no longer has any confidence in her own abilities and skills. She might know her husband has always respected her wants and feelings, even if he has found it difficult to understand how the relationship has worked to undermine her sense of self. She knows they are going to have to find a way of sharing housework and childcare more equally, so she can have the time and space to recover a sense of what she wants for herself out of life. She wants her husband to respect her individual wants and needs, knowing this does not any longer simply mean leaving her alone with the house and the children, but involves transforming the relationship that exists between them.

At the same time it can be recognised that it is difficult for women to respect themselves as individuals able to decide what they want to do with their lives, if they live in a society in which they have to subordinate themselves. It can make issues of time and space crucial for often men will fail to appreciate that women have never had a chance to discover what they value assuming in a rationalistic way that if they cannot say immediately this can only mean that they are confused. A woman who is strong and forceful in her ideas can even be made to feel this is not a 'feminine' way to behave. She can be made to feel she should be grateful for her relationship with husband and children, as if making demands for more control over her life is a sign of ingratitude. There are limits to the transformations that can be made in a relationship, without the position of women within the larger society also changing fundamentally.

Feminism could turn out to be crucial in helping us to sort out when it might be useful and appropriate to talk in terms of a language of rights and when we might have to break with this tradition to reveal sources of oppression and misery. If the revolutions in Eastern Europe have reminded us of the potency of a language of rights as a challenge to authoritarian regimes it should not at the same time blind us into thinking that rights can serve as a universal language in which claims can be made or that it can serve as an adequate safeguard for human dignity. In this regard it is important to be reminded, as Weil does, of the historical Western liberal tradition of rights as well as the particular form of social relations it traditionally serves to sustain.

IDENTITY, POWER AND DEPENDENCY

Simone Weil understood how our very sense of self and the ways we exist as individuals is deeply vulnerable to the relations of power and subordination in social life. She could not assume that individuals come into social life with a clear sense of their individual wants and needs and a clear sense of the ends they want to follow. The structures of dependency within which we grow up in the family, school and, later, work, have a deep effect upon the formation of our individualities.

Since within a patriarchal culture boys and girls are treated very differently as they grow up, this makes a profound difference to the development of personal identity.[7] Simone Weil felt the need to understand the ways individuals can be hurt, damaged and undermined through these very processes. Feminist theory has expressed this as a matter of women being made to feel worthless and being rendered invisible within the public realm. This is not understandable within the categories of a utilitarian moral psychology. It is not simply a matter of causing people more or less pain. Nor is it simply a matter of people not being able to satisfy wants they have.

Individual senses of identity, their trust and confidence in themselves and their capacity to make meaningful relationships with others, are all vulnerable. This involves a very different personal, social and historical conception of the growth and development of people in their individualities. It also involves recognising the ways we can undermine and hurt people to the core if we attack their expectation 'that good and not evil will be done' to them since 'this is sacred in every human being'. This damage is not easy to repair. People will have to learn to trust themselves with others again. People will not want to make themselves vulnerable if they expect to be hurt again.[8]

We can think for a moment about the example of Diana who has become aware of the scars she still carries because of the ways she was called 'fatty' at school. She could not have let the other children know how hurt she felt since she knew this would have made matters worse. Thinking back she knows she learnt to defend herself against the pain she felt by learning to laugh at herself before the other girls had a chance of poking fun at her. This became her personal style. She was seen by others as a jovial girl who did not mind laughing at herself. At one level we might say she learnt to live with it, and that after a while it did not hurt her much. Within a utilitarian moral psychology it can become difficult to identify the hurt, let alone the scars it left.

Simone Weil can help us to understand the ways Diana learnt to hold the hurt inside herself. Even if she seems to have reached a stage at which she does not seem to feel her own hurt, she can come to realise this is partly because it is too painful for her to get in touch with all the suffering and misery this created for her. The fact that Diana did her best not to acknowledge these feelings did not mean they did not continue to influence her. Looking back she knows that it had something to do with why she has had very few real friendships. She finds it hard really to believe that others would want to be friends with her. She knows she learnt when she was very young not to let other people get close to her.

Weil helps us question ways we might think Diana is happy enough, because she has always been able to laugh and joke at herself. She encourages us to question the notions of 'character' and 'personality', as if they are simply a set of discrete qualities people have been born with. She helps us become more conscious of ways our very identities have been formed and sustained within the human relationships we have experienced. Our very understanding of how we have become the people we are, has to be reformulated within this broader personal, social and historical context of relationships.

Diana has had to learn this for herself. She has become conscious of the ways she has become funny in order to defend herself against possible ridicule. She did not want to show others she was vulnerable. She did not even want to let herself know how hurt she felt. She knows this had a deep impact upon the ways she relates to herself, let alone the ways others would relate to her. She has found it difficult to take her own wants and needs seriously. She found it difficult to acknowledge her loneliness and isolation as she felt forced to put on a show for others. She knows that few people at school treated her with respect. This made it difficult for her to learn how to treat herself with respect too. She constantly felt she had to prove herself to others. She never felt good enough. She was so used to hiding herself from others, that she knew she did not really have much respect for herself.

 We do not only cause people momentary hurt and pain, we can also undermine them. We violate people. We also learn different ways of defending ourselves and of not making ourselves vulnerable to others. We learn to protect ourselves against the sources of possible hurt, ridicule, humiliation. Sometimes people withdraw from contact with others, or learn not to make themselves vulnerable to others. People can find ways of hiding themselves, even as they seem to be acting in an open and extrovert way. This is not a process we have easy control over. If it has been an intensely damaging experience such as a concentration camp it can mean that something has died inside. Sometimes we would want to be much more open with people than we can be. Often this means we cannot get the kind of contact and nourishment from others that we need.

Of course this has to be learnt at different levels of our experience. Certainly Weil appreciated that we could be hurt in different ways. She knew that sometimes it was much easier for us to recover from the hurt. It was also important to recognise that sometimes people never recovered but were scarred for life. She knew this was connected with the details of people's everyday experience and the social relations of power and subordination within which we live our lives. It is not simply a question of the ways individuals learn to treat each other. Nor it is something that can be redeemed through a liberal assurance that people at least have equal legal and political rights. We also need a language which helps us identify the ways people are used and abused through the institutions and practices of social life.

Simone Weil gives a graphic example of the power of social institutions over the lives of individuals when she talks about the law and its penal machinery:

No state is beneath that of a human being enveloped in a cloud of guilt, be it true or false, and entirely in the power of a few men who are to decide his fate with a word. These men do not pay any attention to him. Moreover, from the moment when anyone falls into the hands of the law with all its penal machinery until the moment he is free again – and those known as hardened criminals are like prostitutes, in that they hardly ever to get free until the day of their death – such a one is never an object of attention. Everything combines, down to the smallest details, down even to the inflections of people's voices, to make him seem vile and outcast in all men's eyes including his own. The brutality and flippancy, the terms of scorn and the jokes, the way of speaking. the way of listening and of not listening, all these things are equally effective.

There is no intentional unkindness in it all. It is the automatic effect of a professional life which has as its object crime seen in the form of afflic-tion, that is to say in the form where horror and defilement are exposed in their nakedness. Such a contact, being uninterrupted, necessarily contaminates, and the form this contamination takes is contempt. It is this contempt which is reflected on every prisoner at the bar. (*Waiting on God*, p. 110)

When Simone Weil says that 'There is no intentional unkindness in it all', she wants us to be aware that it does not depend upon the kindness and consideration of individuals. She wants us to be aware of how this contempt is produced as 'the automatic effect of a professional life which has as its object crime seen in the form of affliction'. The mere contact with this penal apparatus can leave deep scars. In her Christian writing she came to believe that 'However the code may be reformed, punishment cannot be humane unless it passes through Christ' (*Waiting on God*, p. 111).

The very details of social institutions can seriously affect the ways people feel about themselves. She acknowledges the power of social institutions to affect the ways people think and feel about themselves. She knew how important it was in her own experience working in factories, to receive a moment of kindness and consideration from others. She knew how much more it cost people even to make this gesture. Often she draws upon this experience of work but it has a broader significance for her because it illuminates the moral workings of institutional relations of power. She grasped the need for a moral language which is not simply focussed upon saying how individuals should treat each other, without also illuminating the social relations of power within which this relationship is working.

This relates to her understanding of how the institutions of modern life have such a powerful effect over the lives of individuals. They have the power to damage our very individuality and sense of self. Our prevailing moral traditions do not help us identify damage being done to people's lives, let alone help us think creatively about the kinds of social relations which would help people flourish through satisfying different needs.

Simone Weil articulates the *priority* of a conception of justice which relates more directly to the ways people can be invalidated and undermined in their very sense of self. This is why she thinks it misleading to think of justice solely in terms of just distribution. She drew from her sense of Greek conceptions of injustice as mistreatment and violation to challenge a modernity that seemed unable to think of justice in anything other than distributive terms. I may feel it is unfair if I do not get as large a piece of cake as my brother, but I will not usually feel my very identity has been damaged, threatened or undermined. She thinks the injustice of 'modern forms of social oppression' works to undermine and attack individuals in precisely these ways. It is inadequate to think we can only approach these issues once we have sorted out what is a just distribution, since within our prevailing moral traditions we can feel reasonably confiden. we are talking about in this kind of situation. This is not simply t. there are other conceptions of justice besides that of distributive ju..

DIGNITY, SUBORDINATION AND OPPRESSION

Simone Weil recognised the difficulty of respecting others equally as human beings, when the very circumstances of people's everyday lives denied this. It is not simply a matter of learning to take up the correct moral attitude towards others. She was working to develop a moral language which could grasp the difficulties of relating to others as equals while not ignoring the modern forms of social oppression. Weil maintained her recognition that capitalist society fundamentally divided people into 'people who count for something and people who count for nothing'. She recognises how the conditions of modern factory life reproduce these conditions in the everyday reality of people's lives, despite the political and legal rights a democratic society guarantees to people.

She remains suspicious of these rights since they made it so much harder to understand the ways people are systematically undermined through the everyday conditions of subordination at work. This is a lesson she learnt working in factories. It was to motivate so much of her writing right up till her death. It helped set the fundamental issues for her:

> . . . the second lesson is that humanity is divided into two categories – the people who count for something and the people who count for nothing. When one is in the second category one comes to find it quite natural to count for nothing – which is by no means to say that it isn't painful. I myself found it natural; in the same way that now, in spite of myself, I am beginning to find it almost natural to count for something . . . The question at present is whether, in the existing conditions, one can bring it about, within a factory, that the workers count, and have the feeling that they count, for something . . . (*Seventy Letters*, p. 35)

Weil recognises that 'the sense of inferiority . . . is necessarily induced by the daily assault of poverty, subordination and dependence' (*Seventy Letters*, p. 22). She wanted to do everything that would help workers retain a sense of their dignity, which was being continually undermined through their conditions of work. She knew that this would also be a pressing need in a socialist society. She knew that it was not simply a question of the

ownership of the means of production, but also of the social organisation
of production in its smallest details.

A Kantian moral tradition tends to assume that people's dignity can be
guaranteed to them regardless of the social life they live. Weil came to
understand how much more vulnerable we are to the processes of social
life. Weil knew how relations of subordination and dependency would
continually work to undermine people's sense of themselves. Our dignity
cannot be guaranteed as an 'inner quality', unless we also understand how
it can be undermined through the everyday conditions of our lives. Morality
should not be conceived of as an individual search for moral worth, but
must be connected with issues of social justice.

This is something Simone Weil had to learn from her own experience,
since she had been brought up to think her dignity and self-respect solely
depended upon her inner qualities:

> What working in a factory meant for me personally was as follows.
> It meant that all the external reasons (which I had previously thought
> internal) upon which my sense of personal dignity, my self-respect, was
> based were radically destroyed within two or three weeks by the daily
> experience of brutal constraint. And don't imagine that this provoked in
> me any rebellious reaction. (*Seventy Letters*, p. 21)

We have to come to terms with basic changes in the labour process of
capitalist production[10], if we are to be able to think about the nature
of freedom and subordination in modern society. This was not simply
a question of the abstract choices available to people, say about what
kind of factory they work in, if they were to meet similar conditions of
subordination and oppression. This involved her in a critique of negative
conceptions of freedom found within liberalism, but also of the political
theory which had taken hold within a Marxist tradition.[11] She wanted to
bring people back to an investigation of the 'real conditions which make
servitude or freedom for the workers':

> Only when I think that the great Bolshevik leaders proposed to create
> a *free* working class and that doubtless none of them – certainly not
> Trotsky, and I don't think Lenin either – had ever set foot inside a
> factory, so that they hadn't the faintest idea of the real conditions which
> make servitude or freedom for the workers – well, politics appears to
> me a sinister farce. (*Seventy Letters*, p. 15)

In a letter that Simone Weil wrote to a factory manager in an attempt to persuade him to adopt certain reforms in his factory, she contrasts the conditions of modern workers in pre-World War II France with those of Stoic slaves. She shows how hard it is to maintain a sense of self-respect within the conditions of factory production:

> It is true that a man of strong soul, if he is poor and dependent, has always the resource of courage and indifference to suffering and privation. It was the resource of Stoic slaves. But that resource is not available to the slaves of modern industry. The work they live by calls for such a mechanical sequence of gestures at such a rapid speed that there can be no incentive for it except fear and the lure of the pay packet. The Stoic who made himself proof against these incentives would make it impossible for himself to work at the required speed. The simplest way, therefore, to suffer as little as possible is to reduce one's soul to the level of these two incentives; but that is to degrade oneself. So if one wishes to retain human dignity in one's own eyes it means a daily struggle with oneself, a perpetual self-mutilation and sense of humiliation, and prolonged and exhausting moral suffering; for all the time one must be abasing oneself to satisfy the demands of industrial production and then reacting, so as not to lose one's self-respect, and so on indefinitely. That is the horror of the modern form of social oppression; and the kindness or brutality of one's superiors makes little difference. You will perceive clearly, I think, that what I have just described is applicable to every human being, whoever he is, when placed in such a situation. (*Seventy Letters*, p. 38–9)

So it becomes impossible to think about the meaning of freedom within industrialised society, be it capitalist or socialist, without fully understanding the kind of subordination people have to endure in their work. In many ways the features that Simone Weil was talking about in the 1930s have become more general with the rationalisation of labour processes in factories, offices, hospitals and schools. People have much less control over their work processes, even within areas of professional work. The jobs have been broken down into small activities that can more easily be regulated. This is something Harry Braverman has drawn attention to as the degradation of work in the twentieth century.[12] He has demonstrated the importance of investigating in detail changes in the labour process so that our discussions of freedom and exploitation are firmly grounded in the everyday conditions of work, rather than simply in issues of ownership.

Our moral and political theory has hardly reflected upon the significance of some of these basic changes in social organisation. Issues of respect and dignity at work are marginalised and treated as if they have little bearing upon questions of freedom and justice. We have easily assumed individuals have control over their lives and that somehow the work people do expresses ends individuals have chosen for themselves. The political and moral theory of liberalism has barely touched the social relations of power and dominance that have starkly emerged with the reorganisation of capitalist production in the twentieth century. The lack of freedom is built into the very technology and organisation of work. This is something people have to submit to. It is not a matter of the ways individuals treat each other.

It becomes so much harder to identify the sources of oppression and misery. Often at work the machine is the only focus for one's frustration and rage. The speed of the machines demands their own subordination:

> There are two factors in this slavery: the necessity for speed, and passive obedience to orders. Speed: in order to 'make the grade' one has to repeat movement after movement faster than one can think, so that not only reflection but even day-dreaming is impossible. In front of his machine, the worker has to annihilate his soul, his thought, his feelings, and everything, for eight hours a day. If he is irritated, or sad, or disgusted, he must swallow and completely suppress his irritation, sadness, or disgust; they would slow down his output. And the same with joy. Then orders: from the time he clocks in to the time he clocks out he may at any moment receive any order; and he must always obey without a word. The order may be an unpleasant or a dangerous or even an impracticable one; or two superiors may give contradictory orders; no matter, one submits in silence. To speak to a superior – even for something indispensable – is always to risk a snub, even though he may be a kindly man (the kindest men have spells of bad temper); and one must take the snub in silence. As for one's own fits of irritation or bad humour, one must swallow them; they can have no outlet either in word or gesture. All one's movements are determined all the time by the work. In this situation, thought shrivels up and withdraws, as the flesh flinches from a lancet. One *cannot* be 'conscious'.   (*Seventy Letters*, p. 22)

It is because Simone Weil understood how the reorganisation of work involved the systematic subordination of people to the demands of technology, that she felt crucial questions of human freedom, dignity and equality had to be raised in different terms. The control skilled workers had been partially able to win over their work had been threatened as management learnt to break down tasks and subordinate workers to the speeds set by

the machines themselves. It was harder for people to realise the
their freedom and respect were being denied by other people, as this all
became part of the conditions of the job. Often people were set to prove
themselves against the machines. People had become subordinated to an
assembly line in which 'All one's movements are determined all the time
by the work'.

This was not simply a feature of capitalist production, since these changes
in the organisation were also introduced into the Soviet Union in the early
1920s, where conditions were further exacerbated as workers had no right
to strike. Working to 'make the grade' makes it difficult for people to have
their own feelings, thoughts and desires. As Simone Weil says, 'in front of
his machine, the worker has to annihilate his soul, his thoughts, his feelings,
and everything for eight hours a day'. People must learn to suppress their
irritation, sadness or disgust because this would threaten the output they
could reach.[13] In a very real sense they cannot afford to be their own person
in this kind of situation but have to learn to adapt themselves to the demands
of the machines.

In this situation 'the kindness or brutality of one's superiors makes little
difference'. Our moral understanding cannot limit itself to a consideration
of how people treat each other in this situation. Certainly Weil appreciated
that 'in the midst of it all a smile, a word of kindness, a moment of human
contact' helps you know 'what human brotherhood is'. But she also realised
that 'there is little of it, very little. Most often, relations between comrades
reflect the harshness which dominates everything else' (*Seventy Letters*,
p. 22–3).

The 'modern forms of social oppression' make it impossible to continue
thinking of human dignity and self-respect as 'inner qualities'. The resource
of 'courage and indifference to suffering and privation' available to the
Stoic slaves is 'not available to the slaves of modern industry' because 'the
work they live by calls for such a mechanical sequence of gestures at such
a rapid speed that there can be no incentive for it except fear and the lure of
the pay packet'. People no longer have control over their bodily movements
but have continually to keep up with the rhythms set by the machines. This
involves a very real subordination and lack of freedom.

So Simone Weil wants our thinking about respect and dignity to consider
the everyday realities of people's experience at work. She does not want
to assume that people have certain resources available to them to resist
the subordination and dependency, unless we have carefully specified the
particular forms of subordination and dependency they have to endure. She
was aware that 'the modern forms of social oppression' challenged some of
the fundamental assumptions of liberal moral and political theory.

People are more vulnerable than we take them to be. Often the damage cannot be repaired as something dies inside. The violation of the young girl through sexual abuse becomes the primary example for Weil for the injury cannot be adequately described as an infringement of rights. At this level the personal cannot be separated from the political so that the abuse cannot be adequately thought about in personal and psychological terms. It is this insight which is to become crucial to later feminist theory that for Weil necessites a language of violation. It is an insight that a Marxist theory locked into distributive conceptions of exploitation and justice was constantly losing so that Weil had to use a potentially feminist insight into a young girl's violation to recover what is at issue in the situation of wage labour.

Simone Weil carried on her investigations on the assumption 'that any suffering, no matter what, is less overwhelming and less likely to degrade a man if he understands the complex of necessities which cause it' *Seventy Letters*, p. 36). This involves developing a moral and political language which can illuminate 'the horror of the modern forms of social oppression'. This can mean questioning the prevailing liberal notions of freedom, respect, dignity and equality where these are defined very much in contractual terms. So it could be said workers have 'freely chosen' the jobs they have got. They have to realise that while they are at work this is the 'boss's time', so they have to be ready to do whatever is demanded of them.

It is further assumed that workers and employers are very much 'equal parties' to the contract they agree. This very much denies any relationship of power that exists between a capitalist class that owns and controls the means of production and a working class that needs to find work through the sale of their labour. Within liberal theory it becomes possible to think of labour as a commodity workers are prepared to sell. As Simone Weil puts it 'they forget that the subject of the bargain . . . is nothing other than their soul' (*Selected Essays*, p. 18).

A language of the soul is crucial if we are to grasp how people are vulnerable to violation; if we regard exploitation as a matter of surplus value we do not grasp that the injustice has fundamentally to do with how people are treated. This echoes a recognition that Marx makes in the Paris Manuscripts of 1844 to question the nature of the equality involved:

In general it has to be observed that in these cases where the worker and capitalist equally suffer, the worker suffers in his very existence, the capitalist in the profit of his dead mammon.

The worker has to struggle not only for his physical means of sub-sistence: he has to struggle to get work. (*Economic and Philosophical Manuscripts*, p. 24)[14]

Weil challenges any separation between the moral lives people live and the everyday relations of subordination and dependency. She questioned the assumption that individuals are in more or less an equal situation to work out their relationships with the moral law. Even if she acknowledged that you find people living very different kinds of moral lives in the different social classes, this only confirmed her sense of the need to grasp the everyday realities of people's lives. She needed to understand the 'sense of inferiority which is necessarily induced by the daily assault of poverty, subordination, and dependence' (*Seventy Letters*, p. 24). It is only if we can grasp the everyday conditions of subordination of people's everyday lives, that we can know the difficulties people face in maintaining a sense of dignity and self-respect. This is something that neither Kant nor Kierkegaard makes clear for us. They make it seem as if dignity and self-respect can be guaranteed to people regardless of the social relations they are in.

If Kant comes to the edge of recognising this challenge, he does not formulate the need for a fundamental transformation of social relations. Rather he helps foster a language which is mystifying in its universality, since it does not help us acknowledge the significance of the class, sexual and racial relations of power and subordination over people's everyday experience. This is a disjunction which Simone Weil experienced for her-self in her move from the university to the factory:

In the university I have rights and dignity and a responsibility to defend. What have I to defend as a factory worker, when I have to renounce all rights every morning at the moment I clock in? All I have left to defend is my life. It would be too much to be expected to endure the subordination of a slave and at the same time to face dangers like a free man. To compel a man in that situation to choose between incurring a danger and fading away, as you put it, is to inflict a humiliation which it would be more humane to spare him. (*Seventy Letters*, p. 34, Bourges, 3 March 1936)

Human dignity was something that was being continually undermined through the everyday subordination of factory life. It was not anything that was guaranteed to people. This was something Simone Weil made clear in her letter to Monsieur B., who was the manager of a factory ᴩᵣᵒ.uucing stoves near Bourges. We have already quoted her saying that 'if one wishes to retain human dignity in one's own eyes it means a daily struggle with oneself, a perpetual self-mutilation and sense of humiliation, and prolonged and exhausting moral suffering'. This is because 'all the time one must be abasing oneself to satisfy the demands of industrial production and then reacting, so as not to lose one's self-respect' (*Seventy Letters*, p. 38). This is a contradiction many working-class people face. It leaves people fundamentally divided against themselves. This shows the difficulties people face, if they want to retain a sense of their dignity and self-respect.

Both the necessity for speed and the passive obedience to orders create a situation of subordination and dependency which challenges liberal moral and political theory. It can no longer simply be a matter of whether people are treating each other with equal respect that they are owed. We have to grasp the ways people are being mistreated, even damaged, within these conditions of production. This is not because work provides the only place where people can be violated. It remains central for Weil because it provides people with an important contact with reality. People can experience themselves being used and dispensable within the conditions of modern factory and office production. It is not simply a question of the organisation of personal relationships, however significant these might be in people's experience of their work. It can be difficult to square the recognition that one has a 'sublime moral disposition' and 'has duties laid upon him by his own reason' with the everyday experience of subordination. It becomes difficult to find the vocabulary which can help working class men and women make sense of this experience of disjunction.

DIGNITY, LANGUAGE AND OPPRESSION

People often have to struggle against conditions of subordination and dependency to experience a sense of dignity and self-respect. Weil questioned the notion that dignity was an inner quality that people could secure for themselves. She knew that a transformation of social relations would be necessary, if people were to retain a sense of human dignity. This would also involve challenging the prevailing traditions of moral and political theory which failed to help people identify and articulate the nature of the oppression they endured.

A sense of dignity was related to the ways people were brought up to think and feel about themselves within a liberal moral culture. It encouraged people to deny the subordination, boredom and humiliations of their experience at work, so they could identify themselves more equally with others through the political and legal rights they shared. People are mystified about the working of the class, gender and racial relations of power and subordination.

Simone Weil never lost touch with her experience of work in a factory. She knew what power the foreman had over her. She was forced to feel grateful for the chance to prove herself. She tells of an experience that left a deep mark on her, in a letter to Boris Souvarine:

Yesterday I was on the same job the whole day (stamping press). I worked until four o'clock at the rate of 400 pieces an hour and I felt I was working hard. At four o'clock the foreman came and said that if I didn't do 800 he would get rid of me: 'If you do 800 tomorrow, *perhaps I'll consent* to keep you'. They make a favour, you see, of allowing us to kill ourselves, and we have to say thank you. (*Seventy Letters*, p. 18)

Weil thought it was wrong for someone to have this kind of power over others. Along with the example of the young girl being dragged against her will into a brothel it was a touchstone for her thinking about the nature of power and violation. She constantly returns to those situations as if they provide moments of truth that we are continually led to avoid. The inequality of power is written into the individual relationship. Of course the foreman could talk to her with more or less respect and consideration. He can be more or less polite. She might even feel grateful that he is giving her the chance to prove herself. He might say he does not have any choice in the matter himself, since 800 is just the required speed of production. She knew she had to endure the frustration and humiliation in silence, if she was to keep her job. The foreman could behave more or less brutally, but this hardly touched the brutality which already existed in the subordination to the requirements of production, even if this was done in the name of greater efficiency and productivity.

The conditions of life in a factory as Weil experiences them never cease to undermine people's sense of human dignity and self-respect. Weil knew the class relations of power left people in such fundamentally different situations, that we could no longer assume individuals are in an equal position to live moral lives. If she came to question the possibilities for a revolutionary transformation of social relations, she firmly believed that the power capitalists had over the lives of others should go along with much higher responsibilities. She had to come to terms with the relations of subordination and dependency created through the class relations of power. She was concerned with the everyday organisation of work, knowing that the necessities for work would not disappear with a transformation of ownership.

She could not think, as Kant was often able to, that forms of dependency are somehow always created within otherwise equal relationships. They are much more deeply embedded in the very organisation of social life. Within an individualistic moral culture we hardly have to connect the wealth of some with the poverty of others. This is simply taken to reflect within market liberalism the qualities and abilities of individuals. Often we do not thank people who encourage us to make connections we do not want to form. So Simone Weil could recognise the sincerity of a factory owner who might be sorry for the lot of his workers:

> The owner of a factory: 'I enjoy this and that expensive luxury and my workmen are miserably poor'. He may be very sincerely sorry for his workmen and yet not form the connection.
>
> For no connection is formed if thought does not bring it about . . . We hate people who try to make us form connections we do not want to form.   (*Gravity and Grace*, p. 125)

Often what Simone Weil calls 'the modern forms of social oppression' work to undermine people's sense of human dignity. This is a crucial insight for it refuses to separate an empirical sociology of work from moral theory, as has so often happened to the impoverishment of both. Weil wants to help people to a sense of the ways they are violated in these conditions of work, though sometimes she is so taken with this central insight that she fails to envisage how it might work out in different circumstances of work. She wants their resistance to these conditions to 'have a very different force from what is provided by the consideration of personal rights'. We have to recall the moment in her essay on "Human Personality" where she says 'It would not be an economic demand but an impulse from the depth of their being, fierce and desperate like that of a young girl who is being forced into a brothel' (*Selected Essays*, p. 18). The comparison here is clearly intended. There is a fundamental sense in which people's humanity is being violated and abused within these conditions of work. This involves a sacrifice of people's minds and bodies.

As long as people's experience of work involves the necessity for speed in order to 'make the grade' and has to involve the passive obedience to orders, this is bound to violate. But again it is crucial to be specific about the particular conditions of work and the ways they might be said to violate. Rather than work in any sense being an expression of self, a genuine contact with reality, or a way people discover their dignity, it has increasingly become, with the conditions of twentieth-century assembly-line production, a form of human degradation. It does not even allow people to have their own feelings of disgust and irritation, since they would threaten the output set. Weil realised that changing conditions of work raise fundamental if unacknowledged questions for our moral and political theory. It becomes important to understand the ways people can be hurt, and literally be made ill, through working in conditions in which one has to swallow one's irritation and bad humour. This can be true in different ways of factory work as it can be of money brokers and merchant bankers getting ulcers being all night glued to their Reuters' screens.

We need to understand the ways people's abilities and capacities are thwarted when they are forced to work in these kinds of conditions. Weil realises how easy it is for people to focus upon the wages people receive for work since 'it is a relief to contemplate the unproblematic clarity of figures', especially if people are made to feel grateful they have a job in a period of high unemployment. It is much harder for people to recognise the ways labour has been degraded and the ways people are being violated and damaged through the particular forms of subordination and dependency. This sense of violation 'surely enough exists in them' but 'it is so inarticulate as to be indiscernible even to themselves'. Weil also warns us in the same passage that 'it is not the professionals of speech who can express it for them' (*Selected Essays*, p. 18).

This is to recognise the power of the prevailing moral and political traditions over the ways in which people can experience themselves. Within her more depressed moments Weil tends to forget that within a class society there are bound to be challenging traditions of thought and feeling. It is as if Weil was caught by a single insight that she felt others had failed to see as when she recognised that the power of those over language goes hand in hand with the power they have over the lives of others. Often the powerless and the oppressed in society are dispossessed of the very language which could help them identify and express their own experience. The very universalism of a Kantian moral tradition with its assumption that equal respect and dignity is available to all has made it more difficult for people to recognise the very different conditions of life they have within a society divided by class, race and gender. If this has helped to strengthen people's conviction that they deserve equal respect and consideration with others more fortunate than themselves, it has also made it more difficult for people to recognise the sources of their suffering and oppression.

Simone Weil is very attentive to the power and influence of words. She knows the depths at which ideology works within people's experience and the difficulties people face in finding ways of expressing themselves

truthfully. This involves challenging prevailing moral and political traditions where they distract people from what they need to express about
themselves. We grow up into a society which has already prepared certain
means of expression and which has powerfully institutionalised certain
ways of thinking and feeling about ourselves. But as the revolutions in
Eastern Europe have shown, the power of moral example can spread and
bring new terms into moral and political resistance. To some extent established traditions carry a certain level of conviction partly because they help
illuminate certain aspects of our experience.

But as her critique of the notion of personal rights shows, it is often at
the cost of mystifying us about how to express other truths. She is searching
for a language which can help people express the nature of their experience
within the 'modern forms of social oppression'. This involves recognising
the ways our very individuality and sense of self can be undermined and
violated through the processes of social life. She identified herself with the
oppressed and wanted to help give their experience a voice. This would
help confirm people's own experience of suffering and oppression but this
could not happen without challenging 'the men who have the monopoly
of language' which is 'a category of privileged people' (*Selected Essays*,
p. 22).[15]

To express the experience of the poor and afflicted meant using words
'which express nothing but good, in its pure state'. Weil thought words
that can be 'associated with something signifying an evil are alien to pure
good':

> . . . To possess a right implies the possibility of making good or bad
> use of it; therefore rights are alien to the good. On the other hand, it
> is always and everywhere good to fulfil an obligation. Truth, beauty,
> justice, compassion are always and everywhere good.
>
> For the aspirations of the afflicted, if we wish to be sure of using the
> right words, all that is necessary is to confine ourselves to those words
> and phrases which always, everywhere, in all circumstances express
> only the good.
>
> This is one of the only two services which can be rendered to the
> afflicted with words. The other is to find the words which express the
> truth of their affliction, the words which can give resonance, through
> the crust of external circumstances, to the cry which is always inaudible:
> 'Why am I being hurt?'   (*Selected Essays 1934–43*, p. 24)

Weil was working to discover a language fitting to this task. It involved a
recognition that with the modern forms of social oppression people could

not live lives in which they could fulfil themselves. The prevailing organisation of work involved systematic oppression and denial of the self.

The spread of scientific management had involved the subordination of people to the routines of production. People could experience themselves being used as means for the goal of production organised around profits, though it could also be argued that people have grown accustomed to this because of the very real satisfaction they are offered as consumers. But this does not deny that the dependency Kant had found so threatening to the autonomy of morality, had become institutionalised into the very organisation of production in the twentieth century. People are obliged to work in conditions in which 'all the time one must be abasing oneself to satisfy the demands of industrial production and then reacting, so as not to lose one's self-respect' (*Seventy Letters*, p. 38). This produces a very different form of 'abstracting ourselves' than we learnt from Kierkegaard, so the routines of one's everyday work do not completely undermine one's self-respect. Weil is under no illusions about the 'perpetual self-mutilation and sense of humiliation' that this daily struggle with oneself involves.

This brings us to the recognition that the modern forms of industrial production continually treat people as dispensable commodities. Marx had long realised this to be the truth of capitalist production. Possibly it has become easier to recognise this with the fundamental de-skilling of work with assembly-line production in the twentieth century, though it also has to be set against the ability to provide a range of consumer goods that state socialist societies manifestly failed to provide. This has set different terms for the character of the struggles against capitalist production as the revolutions in Eastern Europe have so powerfully demonstrated.

Often this has meant people do not have the compensations of a tradition of skill with which to identify themselves, though within Western liberal capitalist societies those who are employed are offered a range of consumer goods. Especially for those who are unemployed or underemployed, this produces particular tensions for the inherited conceptions of masculinity, conceptions which have been so closely tied to the ideologies of work.

Unskilled workers are often left with much less control over their work lives, as they have had to subordinate themselves to the pace set by the assembly lines. Work for many people has become more fundamentally dehumanising, though some would argue that it is also much less significant in people's lives. Sometimes this dehumanisation has shown itself in the violence which has been a feature of modern forms of industrial opposition. This has not simply involved a demand for higher remuneration, but has involved a much broader refusal of the conditions of work themselves.[16]

People cannot respect themselves if they do work which so totally sub-ordinates them. Weil recognises this when she says that 'the work they live by calls for such a mechanical sequence of gestures at such a rapid speed that there can be no incentive for it except fear and the lure of the pay packet'. She also understood that 'the simplest way . . . to suffer as little as possible is to reduce one's soul to the level of these two incentives; but that is to degrade oneself' (Selected Essays, p. 38). These conditions of work cannot treat people with respect. We could also say these conditions are inhuman and are bound to remain so as production is organised around profits and so inevitably involves the subordination of people's needs to the requirements of production. If Weil recognised this, she also wanted to do everything in her power to reform these conditions to help people recover their sense of dignity.[17] Though work always remained a central source of human dignity and self-respect, it was also a metaphor for other areas of people's lives. It was the humiliation at work that also helped her reflect upon other relationships of power and domination. If work provided a crucial contact with reality, so could love, friendship and beauty.

Simone Weil felt the inadequacy of a moral tradition which simply focussed upon the ways individuals treat each other, but could not understand how people were forced to degrade themselves because of the 'humiliating conditions' of their lives. If Kant recognised the ways in which relations of dependency undermine the respect people can have for each other and how relations of subordination threaten the autonomy of morality, he did not grasp fully enough that social and personal relations have to be transformed to create a more genuine basis for respect and equality. Kant was too focussed upon how people should learn to treat each other with respect, even if they are in an unequal relationship. He helps us understand the ways a degree of respect between people can be maintained without having to question the basis of the relationship. This becomes too threatening to the notion that individuals are in an equal position to obey the moral law. This was why it was so important for him to assume individuals could live lives which are fundamentally independent of each other. The question of dependency was crucial to him because it threatened the very basis of the autonomy of morality.[18]

This was not an issue which Kierkegaard had to face. He could always assume that it was possible for people to abstract themselves from the prevailing relationships of power and dependency. This was systematically to deny the significance of social life for people. The meaning of life comes from another realm, so the social world is simply a place in which we can prove ourselves to be worthy for salvation. This is also an important feature in Kant's writings. It is part of the history of the denial of the significance of social life and social relations of power and dependency over people's everyday experience, within individualistic moral and political traditions.

This is something Simone Weil was forced to challenge, even if she understood the strengths of these traditions. She helps us come to terms with the ways class, gender and racial relations of power and subordination have become an integral aspect of the organisation of life within twentieth century capitalist societies. She had to find a way of recognising the moral significance of these relations, even if it meant challenging some of the basic assumptions about the autonomy of morality and the separation of morality from politics. The social and historical transformations of capitalist society have undermined the assumption that individuals are living more or less independent lives. It becomes pressing to grasp the moral significance of the class relations of power and dependency.

Simone Weil was trying to come to terms with the modern forms of social oppression. She recognised the inadequacy of our inherited moral traditions for this task. She recognised the ways people's misery and suffering were being hidden and avoided. Often they were marginalised through being treated as 'personal' or 'psychological'. If they were acknowledged at all, it would often be said that we could not expect politics as a public discourse to deal with these intensely personal concerns. In her later writings Weil was drawing upon Christian notions to help her with this task. They were helping her identify some of the pain and suffering people lived. Sometimes this is suffering that people have not wanted to acknowledge themselves, anxious to maintain an acceptable image in the social world. She felt the inadequacy of calling upon people to treat each other in a different way to show the equal respect and consideration due to them. This was too easy for it failed to acknowledge how people had been damaged through their treatment and the human cost of healing their wounds, if they could be healed at all. She knew she had to find a way of voicing the humiliating conditions of so many people's lives.

She wanted to help people acknowledge the ways they were made to suffer and hurt within the prevailing organisation of social life. She recognised the forms of class relationships of dependency and subordination that had become a central feature of social life. She might have appreciated insights of modern feminism which show how the sexual relationships of power between the sexes can work to undermine a woman's sense of existing as a person, and how women were made to feel invisible. In these different, but inevitably related situations, it is not enough for people to take up a different attitude of respect towards others. It involves changing the very basis of relationships so that people can have more control over their lives.

We cannot adequately show our respect for others through abstracting ourselves from the relationships of power and subordination and relating to others simply as individuals. If this tradition helped people feel they deserved equal respect and consideration, it did not help them grasp how their very individualities could be weakened and undermined within relationships of dependency and subordination. This had become crucially important in a social world in which the class, ethnic and sexual relationships of power and dependency had become so central to the organisation of society. This was why it was so crucial for Simone Weil to recognise that the obligation to respect others 'is only performed if the respect is effectively expressed in a real, not a fictitious, way; and this can only be done through the medium of Man's earthly needs'.

10 Love, Dignity and Oppression

IDENTITY, DIGNITY AND OPPRESSION

Within a liberal moral culture we learn to think of inequality and injustice in terms of the distribution of goods and services. We think about injustice as the unfairness of some people having more while others have less. Much of the social theory we inherit is concerned with the legitimation of these social inequalities. Within a liberal theory we tend to think of them as the outcome of individual differences. It is because individuals are blessed with different abilities and talents that they can make different lives for themselves. So it is that issues of social inequality tend to be individualised or psychologised as if individuals only have themselves to blame for the position they have within the larger society. Within a liberal democratic state these inequalities of wealth, status and power supposedly do not affect our equality as citizens, which is guaranteed through legal and political rights. As we are equal before God, so we are equal before the law.

Simone Weil challenges the adequacy of a language of rights to sustain a sense of human dignity. Somehow the inadequacy of rights has to do with their incapacity to articulate and give expression to the deeper violations and injuries that people suffer within social life. Our individuality, identity and integrity is much more vulnerable to social relations of power and subordination than a liberal moral theory that can assume the integrity and inviolability of the person and is assuaged by the notion that human dignity can be sustained by the legal and political rights of citizenship can allow. It was possible for Kant to assume that dignity is an inner quality that can be preserved regardless of the social relations of power and subordination. Simone Weil came to question this through her own experience of factory work and so forces us to rethink the weaknesses of a liberal moral theory that can assume the integrity of individuals, as I have argued in *Kant, Respect and Injustice*.

The sense of individuality which is taken to be a strength of Kantian ethics when compared with a utilitarian theory that would more readily subsume individual wants and interests in the quest for general welfare, is still too weak and attenuated. Often Marxist theory has been too quick to contrast the individualism of liberal theory with the collectivism of socialism. This polarity proves itself to be too quickly drawn and with it the conventional political distinctions between Right and Left, capitalism and socialism. It is the inadequacy of our inherited moral and political languages that Simone Weil was beginning to question.[1] In the new realities that we face the inadequacy of the Enlightenment vision of the rational self that underpins our inherited sense of modernity and the notions of freedom and equality has to be reworked.[2]

Feminist theory has understood how much of the pain and suffering of women's oppression has been rendered invisible within a liberal moral theory. It has helped in its own way to question an inherited tradition of rights which has tended to take for granted the structures of patriarchal power. It has assumed that the inequalities that women suffer can be put right by extending to them rights that are already shared by men and by giving them access to institutions, such as the law and medicine, from which they were traditionally excluded.

Feminism questioned the terms on which access was being granted and the tendency to normalise existing practices and relationships as rational and universally appropriate.[3] Similarly in the context of the family women questioned the supposed equality that they were being offered where respect for women's responsibilities for housework and childcare was supposedly equal to the respect owed to men for their task of providing income for the family.

The private sphere was not simply a realm of free choice and responsibility as liberal theory had it, but a space in which relationships of power and subordination were being worked out. Love could not be separated from inequality. This was not to diminish the importance of the private realm but to rethink the ways that the personal is political. Again this would challenge our inherited sense of 'politics' as being exclusively concerned with issues of power in the public realm.[4] In large part this was a point of agreement between liberal and Marxist theory.

They both operated with a distinction between the public and the private and both tended to accept that justice has to do with distribution of power and resources within the public realm. This is especially true in the orthodox tradition of Marxism that tends to accept Marxism as a theory of economic determinism. It has less space for Marx's sense of how people are estranged from themselves in capitalist conditions of work and how our identities are fragmented in having to make ourselves through these relationships.

Feminist theory appreciates the ways that women were undermined within social relations of power. Women did not exist in their own right but only in relation to men and children. It showed that a sense of worth and dignity would not be sustained as inner qualities for they were vulnerable in a way that liberal theory could not grasp. Even though women enjoyed a different position in relation to the market, they would often be left feeling that they did not exist as persons able to make their own choices, in their relationships. This had to do with the way that the relationship was structured and worked out, not as Kant put it, with the attitudes of respect that people take up towards each other. It showed that we are not equal as rational beings, nor can we assume along with Kant and the Enlightenment that our identities as individuals are secured through the equal relationship we have to the moral law.

Feminism showed that women cannot take their identity, independence and autonomy for granted. Identity cannot be presumed to exist prior to a person's involvement with relationships. A recognition of the precarious and fragmented character of identities, of the rational self that Descartes forged, is part of the crisis of modernity.[5] But this is not new for it was in part anticipated in different terms by Nietzsche, Freud and the Frankfurt School.[6]

But what Christianity offered to Simone Weil was a language of the soul that allowed her to bring into focus the weight of both material and spiritual needs. It was her experience of life that taught her how people could be made to suffer. She learnt about the efforts that needed to be made to sustain a sense of human dignity in a position of subordination and oppression. She appreciated Kant's formulation that people should not be treated only as means to the ends of others as one of the clearest starting points for our thinking about oppression, though I have showed in *Kant, Respect and Injustice* that Kant's rationalism, which defined reason in opposition to nature, could not provide an understanding of how people can be emotionally undermined to the extent of losing a sense of self.

It is a strength of feminism to question a pervasive Enlightenment distinction between reason and nature, so showing that autonomy and independence cannot be substantiated through reason alone. In part this awareness is there in Spinoza's challenge to Descartes. Spinoza has been too readily assimilated into a rationalist tradition, thus blinding us to the Jewish sources in his ethical writing that suggest a more embodied self which is vulnerable both emotionally and spiritually. Little wonder that Spinoza remains a crucial influence on Weil. He helps her towards a more substantial conception of the person.[7]

Simone Weil also anticipates a feminist insight into the violation that is done to a woman through rape. This remains a crucial example for her to show that it is inadequate to say that her rights have been infringed. This is to assimilate the injury and harm that is being done to other situations where the hurt is far more superficial. Only gradually is a liberal moral culture learning to respond to the injustice of rape. Often it insists on an invidious separation of the 'moral' from the 'psychological' as if we can think of the violation of abuse and rape purely as 'psychological damage'. This is to place boundaries around the pain that prevent it from bringing into question more central institutions such as marriage, family, masculinity and male violence.[8]

It also raises issues about how we conceive of justice and whether we have lost touch, as Weil crucially recognises, with a sense of injustice as violation that was known to the Greeks. We too readily assume that if no law has been broken, no right been infringed, then no injustice has been done. This renders invisible many sources of misery and injustice which have no language in which they can be expressed.

So it was that women developed feminism to give voice to their own sense of outrage at the suffering that they had so long been forced to suffer in silence. Women found that they could *validate* their experience by sharing their experience with other women. This broke the spell of a liberal theory that says that our experience is private, individual and unique. If it could be shared at all it could only be in the intimacy of a sexual relationship or on the psychoanalyst's couch, where women often found themselves when they dared to speak of their condition. It was proof that 'something was wrong with them' if they were miserable and unhappy in a situation in which there were 'no rational grounds' for their husbands were providing them with 'everything they could want' and other women would be only too ready to accept the conditions of their life.

But women discovered that they could gain confidence and strength through *sharing* their experience and being *listened to* by other women. There was a dignity in speaking out their misery and suffering, a sense of the worth of what they had for so long suffered in shame. Sharing emotional life in this way was a matter of forming connections that could otherwise stay invisible. It showed how what was taken to be private was in fact an experience shared by others and was the experience of a particular form of power and relationship. This helped to substantiate the self as its emotional life found form and place within the context of ongoing institutions and relationships. Rather than being a drag on individuality, this helped women define their identities in connection with others. It showed how the self exists in relationship with others and so brought into question the isolated self of liberal moral theory.

The challenge which feminism makes to the Enlightenment conception of the rational self is part of a break with a modernity that has been defined so exclusively in rationalistic terms. Because of this it would be a mistake to assimilate feminism to modernity but it is important to recognise how a feminist exploration of women's oppression has set the terms for many of the insights associated with post-modernism. It is the difficulties that philosophy and social theory have had in coming to terms with the identification of masculinity with reason that have blinded us to these insights.[9]

For it was feminism that showed that there was not a single path to be discerned by reason that could be followed by men and women alike. Women had to define their own terms for involvement in institutional life if male norms could not be universalised. Women had their own experience and had to explore their own meanings and values. This was an exploration that called upon emotion as well as reason, upon intuition as much as analysis, upon feeling as much as insight. It involved a recognition that there are different ways of knowing and each has to find its own place. What is more, they were each a source of dignity and worth and should not be derided or placed within a hierarchy that assumed the sovereignty of reason.

Feminism challenged traditional notions of sovereignty that had for so long gone unquestioned and which were impatient of differences. If the great chain of being had been replaced, its resonance lived on in the hierarchy of reason over nature, men over women, white over black. Progress was identified with the control and domination of nature. Culture was to be in control of nature just as reason was to be in control of emotions and feelings. But feminism brought into question these dualities which had structured our experience of modernity since the Enlightenment. It had implicitly set up a white, masculine, Protestant experience as rational and universal, against which the experience and traditions of others were to be marginalised and found wanting.

The dominant Enlightenment culture was to establish a secularised Protestantism as setting the terms of citizenship through which all others were to judge themselves. It was to set the terms in which others had to prove themselves. So it was that women had to prove themselves to be rational, while men could take it for granted, blacks had to prove themselves to be 'civilised' and Jews had to reaffirm that they were 'citizens'. It meant that within a modernity defined by the Enlightenment people had to be prepared to treat differences – whether of religion, ethnicity, class or gender, as if they were contingent and incidental. As free and equal individuals we can separate ourselves from our histories and culture, proving that we are no longer determined by external forces of culture, history or nature but that we are self-determining rational selves able to make our own lives.

The point is that it is only as rational selves that we can be self-determining beings. Both Marxism and feminism have challenged the conditions of self-determination, which turned out be be far more complex than an issue of mind over matter. It is too easy to assume that the sources of misery and disappointment will disappear if we have sufficient will and determination. So it is that within a secularised Protestant tradition we learn of emotions and feelings as forms of self-indulgence that need to be resisted.

Similarly as we learn to separate and distance ourselves from our emotional lives, learning to identify freedom with rational control, so we learn that to be 'modern' involves establishing a distance between ourselves – as rational agents – and our sense of class, race or ethnicity. To allow these traditions, histories and cultures to have *weight* in our experience is to compromise our freedom and self-determination as rational agents. It is to allow ourselves to fall back into ways of thinking and feeling that would determine our behaviour and so make us less free than we could be.

Within modernity we can only expect to be respected, let alone accepted and loved, if we show ourselves prepared to make these 'sacrifices'. They are the liberal conditions for equality and citizenship. It is to deny the significance of *difference* as we learn to identify with a universality that is supposedly more fundamental because it defines the conditions of a rational humanity. So it is that there is no sacrifice to be made for it is a movement out of the darkness of tradition, habit and faith into the light of freedom, self-determination and reason. As Simone Weil recognised, modernity has an important source in the Enlightenment dismissal of religion as superstition and the underpinning distinctions between science and the humanities.[10]

The 'modern' period in philosophy is defined through Descartes' and Kant's distinction that identified our humanity with our rationality. In Kant's ethics this separated the dignity that was due to us in our moral relations within the intelligible realm from the determination of our behaviour by social forces within the empirical realm. This undercuts the sources of human dignity for it treats both cultural and natural emotions and feelings as bereft of any human dignity. It is only as rational selves that we have dignity. Our histories and traditions, for example as blacks or Asians, or as Jews, Hindus or Moslems can have no dignity as they can be no part of our identities as rational selves. Rather they become part of private concerns to do with individual self-perfection, to be concealed almost as something shameful within the public realm of freedom, citizenship and politics. It is these terms of modernity and citizenship that are irredeemable after Auschwitz.

When we think about inequality we think about the public realm of wealth and power while, when we think of love, we think of the private realm of freely chosen relationships. As a citizen I can expect to be respected, not loved. Notions of liberal citizenship that are built upon rights automatically abstract people from their histories and cultures and treat individuals as instances of these universal rights, as Sartre recognised. Rather than existing as individual men and women who have individual wants, needs and desires, we exist as the abstract bearers of these rights.

Our individuality is defined very much in these terms. It is as if we are almost encouraged to abstract from the personal qualities that people have, in the respect we owe them as human beings. It is almost as if we do not want to know too much about them, since this respect is due to them regardless of the particularities of their history, experience and background. It is as if knowing more will serve as a temptation to discriminate, and can easily be interpreted as a form of interference. It is as if saying that it is the 'individual' who is owed respect is to abstract someone from their personal, sexual and class histories. This is something that Sartre notices:

> He has no eyes for the concrete syntheses with which history confronts him. He recognises neither Jew, nor Arab, nor Negro, nor bourgeois, nor worker, but only man – man always the same in all times and in all places. He resolves all collectivities into individual elements . . . And by individual he means the incarnation in a single example of the individual traits which make up human nature. (*Anti-Semite and Jew*, p. 55)

Within the liberal democratic state our legal and political rights stand as evidence of our humanity, for with Kant and the Enlightenment tradition it is only as rational beings that we have dignity and humanity. But when the state suspends these rights, as the Nazi state did to the Jews, they are bereft of both citizenship and humanity. Jews were not 'neighbours' who could be appreciated, even loved, as Jews. Since they were no longer citizens they were no longer human – they were represented as vermin in the kitchen. A clean Germany had to rid itself of the Jews. What seems crucial is the ways that Enlightenment and modernity had turned out to be a mixed blessing for they worked to disempower the Jews at the very moment that they offered freedom and emancipation.

But the costs of this emancipation were never made clear, for Jews were to be acceptable as 'citizens' to the extent that they were prepared to forsake themselves, or at least privatise their experience as Jews. As

Sartre has it, the liberal democratic state could not tolerate the emergence of a 'Jewish consciousness' and it could not tolerate 'class consciousness'. Liberal individualism worked to dissolve these identities. It is part of the discussion around post-modernity to recognise that if identity remains a critical issue, the terms in which these fragmented identities now work have radically shifted, although the ways in which these issues of difference have been treated within post-modernism have precluded the assertion of a crucial relationship between difference and integrity.

The Enlightenment worked to identify modernity with progress. Emancipation was being offered to Jews as long as they recognised that their continuing loyalty to their religion was backward-looking. The movement towards citizenship was a movement away from Judaism as more than a set of individual beliefs. As Franklin Littell has put it, recognising that Hegel and Voltaire were vehemently anti-Semitic, for the Enlightenment 'the solution to "the Jewish question" was the disappearance of the Jews through assimilation. The Jewish faith, redundant through its mysteries and particularisms, should evaporate in an enlightened modern age' (*The Crucifixion of the Jews: The Failure of Christians to Understand the Jewish Experience*, p. 32).[11]

The Enlightenment vision of progress allowed for a secular form of a common Christian displacement theory that Judaism is a thing of the past and that, even in the context of religion, the Old Testament had been replaced by the New. The integrity and self-identity of the Hebrew Bible was attacked. Jews can only find emancipation as individuals. There was a pervasive resentment against any sense of a Jewish people with its own history, culture and integrity. Within a liberal moral culture there is a predisposition towards universalism and abstraction that I have traced in the writings of Kant and Kierkegaard. Everything that recognised and emphasised differences between individuals and groups is threatening. Modernism has opposed a dream world of a universal humanity to all particularities.

It is crucial to grasp, as Littell reminds us in his *The Crucifixion of the Jews*, that, 'in Nazi Germany, the very centre of Protestant anti-Semitism was this type of "liberal" Christianity' (p. 35) which rejected particularity and repudiated the peculiar history of any religious community. There was a powerful drive towards homogenisation in the Nazi party platform from 1920 in which the party identified itself with a 'positive Christianity' without binding itself in the matter of creed to any particular confession. Littell quotes Professor Cajus Fabricius of the University of Berlin, personally a Pietist and professionally a liberal, who gave the specifics of such a universalised Christianity of accommodation:

Every singling out of individuals, every separation of interests, confusion of opinions, every irregular appearance of selfish interests, everything that calls forth and emphasizes differences between individuals and between various groups is repellent to the spirit of National Socialism, since it disturbs the unity of the Volk, breaks up the team spirit and menaces the powerful solidarity of the nation.   (*Positive Christianity in the Third Reich*, p. 13)

Tragically most Christians accommodated, leaving the Jews exposed as the signs of a discordant particularity.

Emancipated thought, whether liberal or Marxist, has always had difficulty with the Old Testament and the Jews.[12] It was concerned to identify modernity with universality and progress. It could identify with Jews as individuals but not as part of a particular history and culture. Modernity inherited a disembodied and unemotional vision of individuals as rational agents. Moral theory had to be universal if it was to be rational. Within this context it is uncomfortable to say the least to place the Holocaust within the context of Western culture and to argue that Christian anti-Semitism helps prepare the ground that made it possible.

Too often the Holocaust is treated as an aberration – a moment of irrationality, even madness, that means that it does not have to be grasped and understood within the context of Western history, culture and philosophy. There has been a guilty silence within the disciplines that have denied its significance by too often passing over it in silence.[13] It is yet to challenge and reformulate our moral and political theory that is still fundamentally cast within an Enlightenment tradition. Coming to terms both personally and intellectually with the Holocaust remains a crucial part of the crisis of modernity.

As Franklin Littell has expressed it, 'the slide into the abyss began with the enlightened affirmation of 'spirituality', 'humanity', 'universalism': the language of speculation replaced the language of events.' He quotes André Lacocque's writing about those Christians of the post-Enlightenment period who have sought timeless truths and high spirituality and wished to divorce themselves from the paradoxes and concreteness ('materialism') of the Old Testament:

Within such a perspective, it was not without frowning that pious and moral Christians read the records of men too 'human' for their taste. Jacob the liar, Moses the murderer, David the adulterer . . . the concept of God's intervention in human history is desperately materialistic, and the people's feelings on being elected and chosen so particularistic, that it is really hard to 'spiritualise' this Jewish book in order to match it with a truly Christian religiosity.[14]

So it is that spirituality is identified with an abstract universality that is more attuned to a Kantian ethics. It defines spirituality as Kant does, our rationality in fundamental opposition to our natures. It seeks to redefine our 'humanity' so that it can be identified with our reason alone. So it is that love becomes universalised for it cannot concern our emotional and sexual relationships with particular persons. To particularise is to diminish and compromise. If Jews insist on their particularity then they are forsaking the possibility of a higher universal morality and spirituality. Charging the source of anti-Semitism to Jewish particularism, and so blaming the victim, has for centuries been a major anti-Semitic ploy.

An Enlightenment rationalism is intolerant of difference. It asserts that at a fundamental level we are alike, so that what separates us in our histories and cultures is superficial and arbitrary. It is as rational beings that we sustain a primary vision of equality. This is clearly formulated in Kant. This helps illuminate a dilemma that J. S. Mill voices in *On Liberty* where he says that our claims for individuality are denied by a fear of difference.[15] Within a liberal moral culture we can still be struck by a pervasive conformity.

Similarly there is a sense, stronger possibly in men than in women, that we do not really need others, that as Kant often suggests, it is better that we do things ourselves rather than share the moral worth of our actions with others. An aspect of a pervasive individualism and a dominant masculinity that prides itself in its independence and self-sufficiency is that we lose a sense of the value of friendship. As Iris Murdoch recognises, this goes along with a loss of the moral place of love in our moral culture and lives.[16]

Within a competitive culture we are often forming our sense of identity through comparing ourselves with others. It is as if we are left with such a weak and attenuated sense of self, within a Kantian tradition, that we can only feel that we exist in relation to others. So often people admit to a sense of having no secure centre, but as existing in quite different ways with different people. This is a fragmentation that post-modernist theory identifies and even welcomes, for it shows the falsity of the Cartesian vision of the rational self that has guided so much of a Western philosophical tradition. Yet if this helps us question the notion that our identities remain untouched by our histories and experience it loses touch with the dangers of a fragmentation that signals a lack of self-definition and integrity – a willingness to accommodate to whatever is expected of us.

In *Kant, Respect and Injustice* I argue that this is integral to the weakness of a Kantian tradition that otherwise sustained a sense that individuals should stand up for what they knew to be right, regardless of external authority. Again the weakness of German resistance to Nazi rule shows that this tradition produces its own forms of submissiveness and accommodation. I argue that our emotional lives – our desires and feelings – have to be understood as part of our 'humanity' – so that our individuality is not a matter of reason alone but involves the clarification and self-definition of our needs and desires. It is this which *strengthens* our sense of individuality, bringing into focus what we share with others and how we are different.

Both Kierkegaard and Simone Weil are struggling in their different ways to recognise the separateness and autonomy of others. So it is that love involves recognising the separateness and reality of others, rather than simply seeing others in relation to ourselves. This is to love others in their concrete individuality, not as we would like others to be. Kant's rationalism wants to see others as ends in themselves, but it is doubtful, as I argue, whether he can do this adequately. It is Kierkegaard who usefully challenges the universalism of love as a rational feeling, recognising that it is only if I can love another individual, that I can learn to love others. But his vision is too tied to the possibilities of abstraction to illuminate seriously the difficulties of loving other individuals.

Simone Weil comes to terms with the difficulties of loving those who are poor and afflicted. She also appreciates the sacredness of friendship for she knows how hard it is to allow others their individuality. Her sense that it is everything about another that is sacred could have opened up her vision to what it means to be created in the image of God. But this Hebraic vision is constantly undercut by her Platonic rationalism, which finds it hard to provide space for our somatic and emotional lives. The feminist challenge to the distinctions between reason and feeling is the best possibility we have for opening up the terms of this investigation. With therapy it opens up the terms of what we share with others as well as how we grow in our autonomy and individuality.

LOVE, IDENTITY AND DIFFERENCE

Who is my neighbour? A rationalist tradition echoes a universal Christian response and says that everyone is my neighbour. It is wrong to make distinctions, for as we are all equal in the eyes of God, so we are all equal before the moral law. In *Kant, Respect and Injustice* I argued that if we are capable of morality, we do not have the same relationships with the moral law. People have different experiences of life and are involved in relationships of power and subordination that mean that we do not stand as independent and autonomous individuals before the moral law. Nor is it, as Kant and Kierkegaard have it, that we can abstract from these relationships to exist as rational selves before the law.

For Kant morality is an affair of reason, not of feelings of the heart. It is a matter of doing our duty as the moral law dictates. Gradually as we make this law our own we transcend our selfish interests, to take on a more loving and disinterested attitude towards others, but this involves a rejection of our natures that we can often learn to be ashamed of. It is only as rational beings that we are supposedly made in the image of God, not as emotional and sexual beings.

Feminist theory and practice has understood that as we share our feelings and emotions with others, we can learn not to be ashamed of them. Of course there is also a strong rationalistic strand in feminism that would argue moralistically that certain feelings, say of jealousy or possessiveness, are unacceptable and so have to be rejected. We can hear echoes of Kant's earlier moralistic voice. This makes our emotions and feelings threatening to us because we can never be sure of what we will discover about ourselves.

We learn to close off from these parts of our experience, only allowing ourselves to have those feelings, say of anger or sadness, that we know we can rationally defend in advance. It is as if we work to hold our anger or sadness in check until we know that we can rationally justify it. As we are left fearful and ashamed of our natural feelings, it is difficult to acknowledge that these are equally part of our humanity – equally made in God's image. Elie Wiesel puts some of these issues together when he reminds us of an old Chasidic saying that:

> Any man who loves God while hating or despising his creation will in the end hate God. A Jew who rejects his origins, his brothers, to make a so-called contribution to mankind, will in the end betray mankind. This is true of all people. (*Souls on Fire*, p. 32)[17]

The terms of the Enlightenment project enforced a rejection both of our inner natures – that were denigrated as 'animal' and therefore to be considered as less than human – as well as any sense of difference that drew attention to a particular history and culture. As people learnt to identify themselves as 'rational selves' in the moral sphere and as 'free and equal citizens' within the political realm, so they learnt to hide and feel shame for those parts of themselves that no longer fitted with this movement towards modernity. This is the classical vision of the 'essential self' that exists outside of history. It was to separate people from a sense of their class, race and ethnicity. People were to remake themselves in this new vision of freedom and self-determination. Again the experience of Jews stands as a powerful example of the progress involved. The injuries to integrity and self-respect were rendered invisible as people were often only too willing to take refuge in this new found universality.

In an important discussion of Polish-Jewish relations inaugurated in the Polish Catholic journal *Tygodnik Powczechny*,[18] Jan Blonski in his article 'A Poor Pole Looks at the Ghetto', reflecting on the experience of the Polish-Jewish past that ended so tragically, says:

> We must stop blaming political, social, or economic conditions, but must first say; yes, we are guilty. We accepted Jews into our house, but we told them to live in the basement. When they wanted to enter the rooms, we promised them admission if they ceased to be Jews, if they became 'civilized', as they used to say in the nineteenth century, and not only in Poland . . . There were some Jews who were ready to accept this condition. Then talk began about the invasion of Jews, the dangers posed by their entrance into Polish society! We began . . . to posit conditions, such as stipulating that only Jews who would co-operate in limiting Jewish influences would be accepted as Poles. That is – to put it plainly – only those who would turn against their own kind, or against their parents! Eventually we lost our house and the new occupants began to kill Jews. Did we show solidarity by offering help? How many of us asserted that it wasn't our business?

Another contribution to the symposium, 'In some sense I am an anti-Semite' by Janina Walewska, helps us take this a little further. She recalls how as a young girl during the war, she and her friends, all brought up in pious homes, had been completely indifferent to 'those people who were perishing in the ghettos. This was "they" and not "we". I saw the smoke rising from the burning ghetto, I heard what was happening there, but it was "they"!' (quoted by Abraham Brumberg, 'Poland and the Jews', *Tikkun*, vol. 2, no. 3, pp. 15–20).

What makes it difficult to recognise others as 'neighbours'? Do people have to be 'like us' to be recognised as neighbours? To what extent does a liberal moral culture, established in the image of the Enlightenment, make us fearful of difference? It tends to foster the idea that people can be accepted as long as they are prepared to assimilate into the dominant culture, as long as they are prepared to conceal those aspects of themselves which signal some kind of difference. A challenge to modernity is beginning to make a liberal moral culture more pluralistic as different groups such as blacks, women, gays and lesbians insist on defining their own terms of acceptance and identity. Issues of visibility have recently become crucial as notions of respect and equality are redefined.

Women have learnt to accept their own experience, rather than constantly judge themselves in terms not of their own making. Emotion and intuition are being reasserted as forms of knowledge as feminists rework their experience of subordination and oppression within a patriarchal culture that, when it talked of them as equals, refused to respect their autonomy and independence. Issues of identity have been connected with questions of inequality as the struggle to rework identities within new historical situations is recognised as a moral and political issue of integrity and dignity. Similarly there is a black movement that is forced to come to terms with the historical experience of slavery and colonialism in the remaking of its identity – in learning to value different, often conflicting aspects of an historical experience of oppression.

Identity is inseparable from history and a process of historical and cultural self-acceptance. We cannot wish our histories to be different, but we have to work through them for what they are. This does not mean that there is a single unified identity, but that people will seek different ways of coming to terms with their experience and history. History is not simply an intellectual or conceptual construction, as post-structuralist theory often has it, nor is it given as some kind of birthright.[19] It can be a painful and difficult process which takes attention and patience for often it cannot be rushed, since it has a time and a movement of its own. So it is that some blacks look to Africa for a sense of a positive identification with a history and a culture that goes beyond a blanket rejection of the identities available within a white culture.[20]

This is part of a process of individual and collective transformation for it involves a process of self-acceptance. This does not make identities provisional, in the sense of new clothes that we can put on and discard. It is too easy for post-modernists to think that all fixed and stable identities have been rendered redundant so that we are all left with the endless play of appearances that are presented to us in the media. This is to suspend issues of value and individuality and to surrender to the market as the sole legislator not only of prices, but also dignities, values and identities.

Within an Enlightenment culture people can unconsciously feel ashamed and despise those aspects of themselves that make them different. We learn to emphasise what it is we share with others which makes us acceptable to them. It is only recently that we have learnt to value marginality and the insights and understandings that this can yield into the prevailing relationships of power and subordination.[21] Blacks, women, Jews and gays were all marginalised within an Enlightenment rationalism and made to feel inadequate unless they could *prove themselves* within the terms of the dominant culture. The *costs* and *injuries* of invisibility have gradually been brought to the surface as people recognise that what they are being asked to leave behind is what gives vitality and definition to their experience.

So it is that a liberal vision of freedom is flawed if it has to assume that along with our inclinations, our history, class and ethnicity can play no real part in our identities, but are simply contingent and accidental aspects which are externally constraining upon an 'inner reason' that is alone the source of our freedom and autonomy. For Kant the 'true self' is the 'inner self' untouched by history and culture. Its integrity remains intact whatever its external conditions of inequality and oppression.

For Simone Weil the 'inner' cannot be separated from the 'outer' and it is part of the struggle for integrity, dignity and autonomy to give expression to the 'inner' in the ways that we live our everyday lives. So it is that respect is not simply an attitude we take up in our personal relations with others but has to be expressed in the institutions and practices of society. She also recognises that our integrity can be violated as our lives can be damaged beyond repair. Sometimes suffering becomes a form of affliction that cannot be healed. But it is crucial for Weil that loving others does not involve *a denial* or a seeing through our differences. It is not a matter of being ready to overlook the poverty or misery of a person's condition, as if this were a sign of our respect or love for him or her. Rather it is through *affirming* the situation that someone is in that we help them to a sense of the *reality* of their situation.

We do not help people to validate their experience through ignoring these differences in the firm conviction that 'underneath it all' we are all rational selves or people in our own right. This is a strategy that is nurtured by Kant and the Enlightenment traditions that might, for instance, encourage school teachers to insist that they do not consider a person's religion, class, race or ethnicity, since they pride themselves on being indifferent to those contingencies. They are just concerned with treating everyone the same in the class and they are clear that their task is to recognise only the abstract and impersonal abilities which children show.[22] Kierkegaard might foster a similar practice though he might make us more sensitive to the quality of the individual relationship that the teacher has with each child. He could be more aware of the pitfalls in treating all the children impersonally, thinking that in this impartiality we demonstrate our respect.

Weil would be more aware of the institutional relationships of power within teaching and from her earliest writings was concerned to validate the different class and cultural experiences that children bring into education. She would help us be more aware of the injuries that we can do through overlooking these particularities. For her we show our love by being able to affirm the particularities of a child's experience, rather than through making him or her ashamed for who they are because most people in the school live in different circumstances. Issues of class, sex and race have to be faced rather than overlooked. And for Weil philosophy is centrally concerned with giving voice to an experience of those who are injured or oppressed.

Reason itself does not make people's reality visible to themselves, for it might encourage them to see themselves through different eyes. From her early student days she was wary of Western claims to civilisation which in the name of science, progress and modernity, left colonial peoples cheated of a sense of their own rich histories and culture.[23] While deeply identified with French culture herself, to the extent of being estranged, even hostile, to the Judaism of her background, Weil was often sensitive to the mechanisms of class and cultural humiliation that were suffered by others.

Weil was less aware in her writings of the ways that women could be emotionally invalidated, which is a theme that has been raised by feminism and psychotherapy. Within a Kantian framework that has done so much to shape dominant modes of masculinity, emotions and feelings have to be rationally accounted for. In this context it carries little weight to say that anger or sadness or rage or fear are quite natural feelings so that we have to separate issues about the emotions and feelings that we have from questions about their 'appropriateness' or 'rightness'.

In some fundamental sense that Kant fails to grasp, it is part of our respect – even love – for people that we recognise that they have a right to their own emotions and feelings. This is as much part of their individuality – or their integrity as individuals – as is their reasoning. The fact that our emotions change should not count against their validity. Kant uses an inadmissible standard whereby the certainties of geometry or algebra are somehow to stand as some kind of ideal or model of certainty. This is integral to the Cartesian vision, but as Wittgenstein shows in *On Certainty*, it is not a standard that can usefully be general ised to other spheres of life without creating considerable confusion.[24]

A simple example might illuminate possible areas of investigation. Often it is men who are more identified with a Kantian framework through being brought up to treat feelings as a sign of weakness.[25] So, for instance, if Tom's partner is feeling upset or angry because the weather on their holiday has turned out so badly, he might think that it is his task somehow to make things better. It is a sign of love. Tom might even say to her that there is no point feeling angry because that will not change the weather, or upset, since it would be 'more rational' just to get on and make the best of things. Since these comments might be made with the best of intentions it can be hard to accept that they make the situation worse. Kant can unwittingly help to foster such an approach. Sheila might feel completely unrecognised in the situation, as if she is not being understood. These are her feelings and she wants to be listened to. She wants her partner to *affirm* and *validate* her experience – her reality. She does not feel that she is asking very much but somehow it seems difficult to appreciate what she needs. This is not new to her since, as feminism has attempted to explain, it is quite common for men to want to make the situation better. She does not want her feelings taken away from her. She just wants them validated as part of her reality. It is when this happens that, in her experience, things begin to change.

Our emotions and feelings are part of our relationships and they are an important part of our lived reality, even if our intellectual traditions rarely give them credibility. A Kantian tradition only recognises our reasoning as establishing our dignity and individuality. It tends to see morality in terms of principles and, as Jean Baker Miller and Carol Gilligan have stressed, it tends to minimise moral relations of care and concern.[26] Living up to principles for Kant involves avoiding being led astray by our inclinations. Our values are supposedly established through reason alone. This leaves no space in which we can recognise the place of feelings in establishing our beliefs and values. Often our beliefs are established by attending to what it is that we have feelings for.

This is to suggest a possible distinction between emotions and feelings so that we can acknowledge the importance of the *feeling* that we have for what we do. Am I working with a sense of love of what I do? Do I have a feeling for the students that I work with? Is love, as Iris Murdoch learns from Weil, connected with bringing us in touch with the reality of what it is that we are doing? Kant's sense of acting out of a sense of duty sometimes carries this awareness, but the framework out of which it emerges – a framework that fundamentally sets reason against nature – is powerless to develop some of these insights. In this deeper sense love is connected to a recognition of particularity and as Kierkegaard sometimes recognises, this has to be the basis on which we learn to love others. As

Murdoch recognises in *The Sovereignty of Good* this is no easy task. It is the struggle of a lifetime.

Kierkegaard recognises in his challenge to Hegel how easy it is for the individual to be subsumed in an Enlightenment vision which would identify reason, history and progress.[27] To this extent he also forces us to rethink an Enlightenment inheritance within Marxism and the difficulties that Marxism has had as a future-oriented theory deeply involved with conceptions of progress in taking seriously individual expressions of needs and desires. It is too easy to discount these expressions as trapped within a 'bourgeois consciousness' that is soon to be superceded. It can leave people feeling confused and uncertain about what they empirically experience as their aspirations, needs and desires, thinking that these are exclusively the product of being brought up within a capitalist society. It is the ease with which it discounts *present* experience that is part of an Enlightenment inheritance. So it is that progress is separated from human wellbeing and, within an orthodox reading of Marx, placed within the historical development of the forces of production.

As I have argued with Lawrence Blum in *A Truer Liberty – Simone Weil and Marxism*, Weil recognised the falsity of equating moral development with the development of the forces of production. This is a deep flaw in the orthodox position which readily assumes that people should endure the miseries of the present in order to deliver a regime of freedom and equality in the future. Weil, like Benjamin, felt that the sufferings and miseries in the present could never be so justified. They both broke with the identification of history and progress and were both ready to acknowledge that values and relationships in the past need to be retrieved to remind us of possibilities for a more human and decent life in the present.[28]

An Enlightenment rationalism tends to see the meaning and value of life as existing separate from our experience as embodied human beings. Paradoxically though, it was deeply suspicious of religion. Its universalism and its readiness to abstract involved a spiritualisation of politics. It was as if only as rational beings could people be permitted to enter the discourses of morality and politics. It was assumed that people would separate themselves from their natures – their emotions, feelings and desires, as they would also separate themselves from their history, class, gender and ethnicity.

All these aspects of life and value were effectively marginalised for they were discounted in advance as sources of human dignity, integrity or self-respect. It was in being ready to separate ourselves from these different realms of determination which would each seek to compromise our freedom and autonomy through influencing our behaviour externally, that we could prove ourselves as free and equal rational agents.

This is to leave us with a thin and attenuated vision of individuality as the 'rational self'. This was part of Hegel's argument against Kant, but it could not be reconciled with his identification of reason with history. The recognition that our rational consciousness is a particular form of historical consciousness was too readily fixed into a series of discrete stages, each superseding and somehow retaining what is 'historically significant' in what went before. It was this that gave secular form to the idea that Christianity had somehow superseded Judaism, as love superseded law. Judaism was declared to be historically redundant, a form of historical irrationality that had outlived its moment. It is this vision of discrete stages of development moving towards a period of freedom and reason that was to fix and mesmerise orthodox Marxism.

If individuals only have dignity and integrity as rational selves, our personal relationships become formal and impersonalised. This creates distance in the relationships between people so that we learn to live separate lives, even while being in a relationship. Within a liberal moral culture the very notion and experience of relationship becomes problematic. For a long time this is hidden since marriage as a sanctioned relationship of power was normalised so that people learnt to accept what was expected of them. Feminism has questioned these patriarchal assumptions and raised critical issues of how we can be ourselves as individuals and be committed to the concerns and responsibilities of relationship. Kierkegaard was also acutely aware of some of these issues, though in the end he chose to stay distant from an ongoing relationship involving marriage. He is aware of a tension between reason and intimacy and the way that love can be instrumentalised if it is turned into a rational affair.

Possibly it should come as no surprise – though it is still shocking – to read Kant's writings on marriage and sexuality.[29] It has to do with an exchange of use so that marriage provides partners with an exclusive right over the use of each other's body. If it strikes an unsentimental note about particular forms of relationships, it is blind to the issues of intimacy, concern, responsibility and love within relationships. If there is a vision of personal transformation in Kant, in rational selves gradually transcending their empirical lives as they more easily identify with their duties, it is bereft of any grasp of how a transformation in our feelings and emotional lives might be integral to retaining a sense of integrity and love in relationships. Kant has no sense of how we might work on ourselves emotionally without suppressing our 'inclinations'.

A continuing strength in Kant's ethical writings is in the way that they are constantly reminding us of issues of responsibility. To what extent are we responsible for the lives that we live, for the misery and strife around us, for the destruction of human life and planetary life? Kant reminds us that we are far more responsible than we tend to think and that it is wrong to discount these issues by saying that morality depends on the prevailing moral rules in a particular society. Kant cuts through a moral and cultural relativism that has since reasserted itself as the common sense in the human sciences.

So it is that people are excused from their treatment of blacks, women, Jews, gays and lesbians since this behaviour accords with the prevailing standards in society. We inherit a fear of making moral judgements as if this has to mean judging other societies by the standards of our own. This is an understandable fear since the West has for so long appropriated to itself the wisdom of science, civilisation and progress and it has been part of the modernist project – in the different guises of imperialism – to set the terms in which other, supposedly 'less developed' societies and cultures are to judge themselves.

But we have learnt that to accept the integrity and dignity of different cultures is to accept the terms in which they do things, and it is certainly important to put our own house in order before we can pass judgement on others. And we can be sure that there is more than enough to consider in our own society. But the problems do not go away. The world is affected by what happens to the Amazon forest and it is right to care about it. It is our responsibility and we are part of a world that has made such destructions seem legitimate. It might be wrong to put the blame at the feet of the Brazilians, for this is to fail to grasp the power that multinational companies have over the Brazilian economy. Kant's universalism can help us feel responsible and can focus our care and concern, but its rationalistic framework too readily assumes that the planet is there to be used and exploited.

It carries with it a false vision of progress and civilisation that blocks the possibility of our love for nature and the conditions of the planet. Kant was not insensitive to the ways we treated animals, but the focus was on the consequences for human relations. If we learn to mistreat animals we are less likely to be sensitive in our relations with people. For Kant moral relations have to do with the relationships between people.

Animals and nature are part of an empirical world that is bereft of any dignity of its own. It is only in relation to values and meanings that humans assign that it acquires any dignity at all. It is only as rational beings that we can live moral lives. An ecological vision that cherishes the planet and wants to restore our relationship with nature has to challenge an Enlightenment vision of progress. It also has to come to terms with its Christian antecedents if this investigation is to move further.

Kant reminds us that we are responsible not only for what we think but also for what we do. Words come cheap. It is important to judge people not just on what they say but on what they are doing for others. He knew that the intentions with which we act are also important, so that it matters if someone acts out of a pure motive. The focus for Kant is on not acting in a selfish or self-interested way and the surest guarantee of this seems to be provided by acting out of a sense of duty. This shows that our will is pure.

This is to give secular form to a deeply embodied Christian notion that somehow we prove our love for others by denying or sacrificing ourselves. Sometimes the example of Jesus himself gives rise to a tendency, as John Raynor has put it in his 1982 St. Paul's lecture 'The Greatest Commandment': 'To look upon self-sacrifice as the supreme manifestation of love, and therefore to understand the ideal as being, not merely to love your neighbour yourself, but to love him more than yourself: "Greater love has no man than this, that a man lay down his life for his friends" (John 15:13). A certain noble extremism enters into the Christian preachment of love . . . ' (p. 7).

Rational love is not to be tainted by emotions and feelings for Kant. It is to be shown in our impartiality and disinterested universality. This connects his rationalism with an 'other-worldliness' for we do not act out of our feelings for concrete others, but from our reason. The heart has been transposed into a rational faculty. Love has become an affair of reason. For Kant our natures can only lead us astray. As long as we follow our desires and inclinations we are as strangers wandering in an unredeemed world. It is through the faculty of reason alone that we can escape from this fallen human state. Was it not the temptation of desire that was responsible for the exclusion from Eden? We carry this predicament in our beings for it is only if we turn away from our natures and towards our rational faculty that we will overcome our estrangement from our true self.

Our natures have no intrinsic value and they cannot be a source of dignity and moral worth. So it is that our finitude is akin to our natures that have to be transcended. This is a source of the other-worldliness of Kant's rationalism that gives secular expression to a particular form of Christian theology. It sees the consciousness of our finitude as an estrangement from our true being. It is only if we anchor our existence not in our transitory bodily natures but in the eternal voice of reason that we can discover freedom and redemption. Reason is our link with an eternal realm, though it presents itself in other guises.

In the Biblical story of creation, God confirms and legitimates our natures: "And God saw all that he had made, and it was very good." (Genesis 1:31). We stand as dignified finite creatures before our creator.[30] Finitude and human limitation are often identified with corporeality, while the intellect alone in medieval discussions might be immortal. But in Genesis, however, the whole human being – intellect as well as body, reason as well as nature – is anchored to finitude and terminality. As David Hartman has reminded us:

> As a biological creature, the human being does not inhabit the world of eternity. Our biology is a constant reminder of our finitude and limitations. Yet the intellect, when not heedful of the body's message of finite human existence, may be tempted to believe that it can totally transcend temporality and context, be freed from finitude, and think the thoughts of God. That illusion has produced dogmatisms and can set off wars in the name of truth. An intellect conscious of its connection to the body, on the other hand, is always anchored to particular temporal moments in history. Rooted in our bodies, we are always reminded of the limited, fragile, but dignified quality of human finitude. (*A Living Covenant*, p. 260)

Our natural feelings and sexuality do not need to be accompanied by a sense of guilt. They do not need to lead us astray unless we delude ourselves about their place in our lives. They have a dignity and integrity that needs to be listened to and learnt from. They should not be suppressed in the name of a reason that can alone set up a moral path. As Hartman says, 'They are willed by God, provided that we never forget our finitude and delude ourselves we are the absolute masters of nature. "And God saw all that he had made, and it was very good" (Gen. 1:31). The finitude of God's creatures does not require sanctification, and nature as a creation of God is not in need of redemption. Human existence has intrinsic justification' (p. 260). So it is that dignity is conferred upon human existence by creation, not simply upon parts of us that form our rational selves.

Morality does not have to seek to redeem us from our 'creaturely finitude' as Hartman says, as if human freedom can be separated from the contradictory character of our emotions and desires. There is no resolution that can be reached by turning away from our natures, as if freedom can be guaranteed in a realm of reason alone. We have to learn to take responsibility for our emotions, feelings and desires and this can only be done by developing an ongoing relationship with them, rather than turning our backs on them in the hope that they will disappear, or at least that their hold over our expressions will weaken. This is a form of emotional death that can injure deeply. As Freud comes to express a once familiar insight for a secularised western culture, the repressed will return in many guises to haunt our dreams and waking lives. Out of sight does not mean out of mind.

Freedom involves making mistakes, getting things wrong so that we can learn. This is one of the ways that we can grow in our responsibility as human beings. Love involves accepting others in all their imperfections and limitations as responsible beings able to make decisions for themselves. The covenantal moment of Sinai demonstrates God's love and willingness to build his vision of history with vulnerable human beings. This is very different from Kant's Protestant vision in which it is only as rational beings that we can be loved, as long as we suppress our natures. We inherit an abiding sense in the Protestant ethic that we are not lovable or acceptable as we are but only if we change ourselves into something different.

So it is that we turn against ourselves – against our unacceptable feelings and emotions, thinking that we are inadequate and worthless because we cannot live up to standards that we have set for ourselves by reason. This sense of inadequacy haunts us, Christian, Jew or Moslem, atheist or agnostic alike, for we all grow up shaping ourselves within these taken-for-granted moral assumptions. So it is hard to feel that we are *deserving* of love and partly because of this we learn not to need others but to do things for ourselves. Especially as men we learn not to need, for needs can make us vulnerable to the rejections and put-downs of others. So it is difficult to learn to nourish ourselves. This is paradoxical within a liberal moral culture that is informed by a utilitarian stress on the satisfaction of wants, interests and desires.

This abiding sense of inadequacy is often hidden, remaining as it does as a sign of our unworthiness. We learn to show only those aspects of ourselves that will find favour in the eyes of others. We learn to present ourselves as we think that others would want us to be. If this seems natural, it can also block intimacy within a relationship. If love is connected with self-acceptance, then Kant's fragmented vision does not help us love ourselves. It insists on *rejecting* our natures. We can only be loved to the extent that we aspire to a rational perfection.

For Kant it is always possible for us to choose to do the right thing, so that it is our own responsibility if we fail to make ourselves admirable in this way. This Protestant vision of responsibility supposedly echoes the Jewish Bible where we are admonished: 'Behold, I have set before you this day life and good, and death and evil; . . . therefore choose life'

(Deuteronomy, 30: 15, 19). This is the burden of responsibility which goes along with freedom.

But for Kant moral righteousness is given a particular Protestant form for it is within our grasp for as long as we do not suffer from a weakness of the will. It is only our 'inclinations' that stand in the way of our acting out of a sense of duty. There is a hard edge to this vision that does not tolerate failure. There is also a sense that we are flawed beings and that we have to prove ourselves worthy, otherwise others will know us as the worthless beings that our natures would have us be if left to themselves.

LOVE, INTEGRITY AND REDEMPTION

As it is described in Exodus and Deuteronomy, the Covenant with Israel does not suggest any promise of resolution for the tensions and contradictions of the human condition. It does not suggest that we can abstract ourselves from social relationships of power and subordination to meet on another level in which our humanity remains pure, equal and untainted. The Covenant offers no security against the misuse of human freedom. The community has to learn to be responsible for its social and political existence within the uncertain conditions of history.

It cannot transcend these conditions but must learn to live with dignity and integrity in the conditions in which it finds itself. Moral relations cannot be transcendent relationships lived out in a realm of reason or spirituality. Both reason and spirituality have to be discovered and worked for in the realm of human and social relationships as we find them. As Hartman has it, 'Failure, uncertainty, and unpredictability are permanent features of life under the Covenant, since human freedom is constitutive of the covernental relationship' (p. 261).[31]

A Covenant does not free us from the limitations of the human condition. This is underlined in the story of the golden calf following directly after the moment of election. It does not prove that people are unworthy in their natures, but that they are likely to fail. It is human to make mistakes and to fail and it is reassuring to know that we can be forgiven. It can help us to forgive ourselves and recognise how unforgiving we are within a culture that is so organised around a fear of failure. Whenever they felt threatened, thirsty or hungry, the Children of Israel longed to return to Egypt. They fled from freedom and responsibility when they met difficulties, crying out to Moses: 'Was it for want of graves in Egypt that you brought us to die in the wilderness?' (Exodus 14:11)

This reminds us how vulnerable human beings are and also how willing they are to succumb to slavery, but the Covenant is still reconfirmed as if to remind us that the relationship with God can be reinstated despite weakness and vulnerability to sin. This does not mean that people are loved the less, for love does not have to be earned or proved in this way. We do not have to prove that we are deserving of love, as if our good deeds can somehow secure love for us. Taking responsibility for ourselves can mean acknowledging our difficult and unwelcome feelings, knowing that only if we learn to accept ourselves can we expect others to love us.

In a relationship it is easy to feel that love will somehow compensate for everything lacking in one's own individual life. There is a sense that love can fill the holes that we carry inside us, as if it can make us whole and redeem us. In time a relationship can become a wall between two people and the rest of the world, as early expectations give way to unexpected realities. People can cling to each other in their insecurity, hiding a pervasive sense of inadequacy from others. It is a painful realisation to discover that love does not heal all and that it cannot compensate for whatever we feel we lack in our lives. It is not possible for each partner in the relationship to redeem the other. As Hartman says helpfully:

> They come to the hard-won realization that neither of them can single-handedly give dignity and a sense of wholeness and worth to the other. The feeling of personal integration and self-confidence that makes for dignity never comes exclusively as a gift from the other, but is always the fruit of enormous personal effort. (*A Living Covenant*, p. 273)

Love expresses itself in the ability to accept the separate reality of the other. It is a struggle to see the other in his or her reality, rather than in the images and fantasies that we have prepared for them. This is something that both Simone Weil and Iris Murdoch talk about, though probably with different senses of what such a struggle involves. In part it involves a recognition that in the end individuals have to create themselves and take responsibility for themselves in relationships. We can support our partners and our friends in what they have to go through themselves, but we cannot do it for them. We have to go through the process of healing ourselves so that we can begin to undo the effects of a culture that has left us feeling inadequate, unable to face our own history and experience.

We can help others to feel confident in our support for them, but we have to face these feelings of loss and worthlessness ourselves. We can hide from these feelings and we can be hard on ourselves as we constantly blame ourselves for our failings but often this is a form of avoidance. If our partners stay with us through the hard times as we acknowledge our fears, hurts and insecurities to them, rather than hiding them away in the fear that we will be rejected, if we show more of ourselves, then our relationships will strengthen.

As we trust more of our feelings so we will grow in our authority and sense of adequacy. We will be less fearful in revealing ourselves and we will learn to treasure the contact and intimacy that this brings with it. So it is that we do not lose our autonomy and integrity within a relationship of equals. We can learn to appreciate the struggles of our partners and friends, while knowing that they have to discern their path for themselves. It has been argued that the idea that people must create themselves is the idea that Judaism introduced into the world.

The adequacy and integrity of human beings which means that they can act with dignity and self-awareness before God is integral to the Biblical account of creation where it is said that men and women are created in the image of God. The creation of beings who are capable of saying no to divine commands and who are to be in an important sense partners in the creation of the world is taken as an expression of divine love. God makes room for humans as independent free creatures. As Hartman describes it:

> Though covenantal relatedness does not imply the equality of the parties to the covenant in all respects, it does presuppose mutual recognition of the separate existence and rights of the parties involved.   (*A Living Covenant*, p. 25)

There is an uncompromising commitment to safeguard human freedom and integrity. It ultimately depends on human beings ourselves, what we make of the world. The human community has its own responsibility for its own spiritual growth and development. The difference of emphasis is that within Kant's writing it is only as rational beings who have separated ourselves from our natures that we can be said to be created in the image of God. It is only as rational beings that we can discern what duties we have. A Judaic tradition sustains the notion that our natures, even our negative feelings and desires, are part of our integrity. These are equally ordained by creation and they are nothing that we have to regret or apologise for. They are integral to our humanity, which cannot be defined by our autonomous faculty of reason alone.

A Kantian tradition sustains within a liberal moral culture the idealisation of morality and politics. It sustains a Platonic notion that reality does not exist in our experience in our everyday lives but it exists as a realm of its own that is only dimly reflected in what we can know through our own experience.[32] For Kant it is reason that gives us access to this separate intelligible world that is separated once and for all from the empirical realm. There is an ideal realm that exists beyond our experience – a transcendent realm that alone is able to give meaning and value to our lives. So it is that we have to aspire to a life of reason that involves the rejection of our natures.

This is a dualistic vision that discovers the meaning of life in salvation. It is by doing our duty that we transcend the desires and shadows that would otherwise lead us astray. It is through accumulating moral worth that we can dedicate our lives to salvation. As Max Weber recognised, this vision has been secularised in part. It is an ethic that is integral to capitalist society. We learn to sacrifice ourselves for the work that we do as work and money become ends in themselves. As Weber agrees with Marx, we live in order to work, so that we take for granted an ethic that is basically irrational for it involves a form of self-denial that is rendered invisible as it is taken for granted.[33]

Liberalism learns from its Protestant antecedents that we can abstract ourselves from the all-too-human contradictions of everyday material and emotional life. We can wish ourselves into a different realm in which we are supposedly free and equal rational beings. Since the moral worth of our actions can only be guaranteed in this realm, nothing is lost. We do not want to be reminded of the contradictory nature of a Jacob or Joseph in the Hebrew Bible for we learn within a liberal culture to deny those parts of ourselves – our emotions and desires – that do not accord with the image that we have of ourselves. As long as we can discern through reason alone what is expected of us, then we do not have to accept responsibility for these other aspects of our lives. We learn that they are only signs of an inadequacy that we had to learn to transcend in the only process of self-transcendence that Kant acknowledges.

As we move beyond our selfish, egoistic selves we will more easily identify with the demands of our reason. There is little awareness of an earlier idea, rediscovered in some psychotherapy and feminist writings, that transcendence or growth in human beings involves a coming to terms and working through of our emotional lives. It involves a process of *self-acceptance* of those very parts of ourselves that a liberal moral culture so often teaches us to denigrate and disown. Our dignity and integrity lies as much in our feelings and desires as it does in our reason. The moral demarcation should not be drawn along the line of reason and nature for we have good and bad impulses. This is to evade the reality of our moral lives.

Iris Murdoch sustains an idea of perfection that helps explain her appreciation of Kant. It helps us avoid a simplistic reading of his ethics to be reminded that:

> Reason itself is for him an ideal limit: indeed his term 'Idea of Reason' expresses precisely that end less aspiration to perfection which is characteristic of moral activity. His is not the 'achieved' or 'given' reason which belongs with 'ordinary language' and convention, nor is his man on the other hand totally unguided and alone. There exists a moral reality, a real though infinitely distant standard: the difficulties of understanding and imitating remain.   (*The Sovereignty of Good*, p. 31)

Yet there is something unsettling about the notion of perfection since it can so easily lead people to blame themselves and feel inadequate for not reaching standards or ideals that they have set themselves. Murdoch might be right to remind us that love is knowledge of the individual and that this involves an endless task of attention, care and concern, but I am less clear that the notion of perfection helps. It is the very fact, as she acknowledges, that it can reflect on our 'fallen' human condition that leaves me unsettled. It is striking to be reminded that: 'Words are often stable while concepts alter; we have a different image of courage at forty from that which we had at twenty. A deepening process, at any rate an altering and complicating process, takes place' (p. 29). Murdoch draws from Weil to talk of 'efforts of attention directed upon individuals and of obedience to reality as an exercise of love' (p. 42).

If we assume that it is an endless moral task to see people as they are in their reality we must also recognise what it means to come to terms with ourselves, for similarly it can be an endless task to learn to be ourselves. Why has it become so hard for so many of us to be ourselves with others and why do we so easily feel false and unreal? Is it because we are so used to a morality and politics that has been idealised, so that the way that ideals come to inhabit our lives is part of the problem. It is part of a turning away from our own experience because it does not live up to the ideals we have set.

D. H. Lawrence recognised a connection between the place of ideals and the fear of our bodily and emotional experience. In *Introduction to These Paintings*, a polemic of his last years, he gives a history of that battle against the old Adam, 'the physical, instinctive-intuitive "man"', which he suggests was provoked in its modern form in the sixteenth century by the panic fear of syphilis. Fear, at any rate, he declares, 'is the great clue to bourgeois psychology', and since it was 'fear and hate of one's own instinctive, intuitive body, and fear and hatred of every other man's and every other woman's that caused 'the collapse of the feeling of physical flesh and blood kinship, and the substitution of our ideal, social or political oneness' (*Phoenix*, p. 771 (Introduction to Pictures)).

After Blake, Lawrence was, indeed, the first writer to see the Puritan onslaught on sex for what it was. As F. A. Lea has written, 'his own onslaught on Puritanism . . . would always be part and parcel of a campaign against that abstract love of an abstract neighbour which had blasted Shakespeare's England' (p. 12),[34] Lawrence differed from many other objectors to the First World War in his absolute repudiation of the duty to 'love one's neighbour'. He found objectionable the idea of 'sacrifice to one's neighbour':

> Our leaders have not loved men; they have loved ideas, and have been willing to sacrifice passionate men on the altar of their blood-drinking, ever ash-thirsty ideal. (*Fantasies of the Unconscious*, Ch. 9)

From 1915 Lawrence never abandons his war on that 'love and benevolence ideal' which, unlike Blake, he identified with the Christian. He knew how deeply this ideal of goodness as self-sacrifice had damaged his own youth and how it had been the dominant ideal that ended up in the useless slaughter of 1914–18. As he said more than once, the war changed him for ever. He stood out bravely against the war: 'to fight for possessions, goods, is what my soul *will not* do. Therefore it will not fight for the neighbour who fights for his own goods' (Letter 9 July 1916).

He could never forget the English conscripts at Bodmin, waiting to go to war, as he recalls in the same letter:

> They all seemed so *decent*. And yet they all seemed as if they had *chosen* wrong. It was the underlying sense of disaster that overwhelmed me. They are all so brave, to suffer, but none of them brave enough, to reject suffering. They are all so noble, to accept sorry and hurt, but they can none of them demand happiness. Their manliness all lies in accepting calmly this death, this loss of their integrity. They must stand by their fellow man: that is the motto. That is what Christ's weeping over Jerusalem has brought us to, a whole Jerusalem offering itself to the cross. To me, that is infinitely more terrifying than Pharisees and publicans and sinners, taking *their* way to death. This is what love of our neighbour has brought us to, that, because one man dies, we all die. (Letter 9 July 1916)

Lawrence was deeply hostile to the secularisation of Christian virtue that he saw embodied in a utilitarian moral and political culture. He thought it wrong for people to accord priority to their own self-sacrifice, before they understood what was important to them – the way they needed *to live* themselves. What enchanted the utilitarians was precisely the opportunity their ideology afforded them to sacrifice, in the name of equality, the subsistence that they pronounced indispensable to 'the good'. It was a way of practising the Christian virtue of altruism. As Lea has put it:

> Such men would never have mistaken a mathematical abstraction for a unique, flesh-and-blood human being, if they had not believed it their duty to pursue the general happiness here; they would never have believed this their duty, if they had not been made to pursue it hereafter; and they would never have done either, if they had not been commanded to 'love their neighbour', whether they loved him or not.   (*Voices in the Wilderness*, p. 8)

We often learn to identify a struggle against selfishness and egoism with a morality of selflessness and self-denial. It is this ethic that can make it difficult to attend to others in their reality for we can only recognise others and ourselves as idealised or spiritualised beings. We fail to recognise our emotional lives and desires as part of our reality for within Kant's secularisation of a Protestant tradition it is only as rational beings that we can recognise ourselves as human. We learn to deny or forget other aspects of our emotional being that are part of the contradictory reality presented to us in the stories of the Hebrew Bible. Similarly we prefer to believe in a formal and spiritualised vision of human equality before God or as embodied in legal and political rights rather than turn our attention to the concrete conditions of hardship and oppression.

So it is that we blame others if our rationalistic image of ourselves seems to be threatened, for a Kantian tradition teaches us to suppress our emotional lives, rather than to take responsibility for them. So if we find ourselves with unwanted feelings and desires that bring into question our image of ourselves, then it must be others to blame. It becomes so much easier for us to blame others than for us to take responsibility for ourselves. If we are so used to denying aspects of our reality in this way, it is difficult to appreciate the reality of others.

Simone Weil's experience of the civil war in Spain taught her to be very wary about the place of ideals in human life.[35] She recognised the ease with which people would live and die for abstractions, constantly losing touch with the lived experience of people's lives. Her developing focus upon the ways that institutions sustained human dignity was a move towards a sense of morality and politics that took seriously this issue. Lawrence moved in quite a different direction but he shared some sense of the false place which ideals had assumed. Unlike a Kantian tradition that opposed reason to nature, Lawrence wanted 'each individual to be helped, lonely, reverently, towards his own natural fulfilment' *(Phoenix,* p. 594, 'Education of the People'). If his vision is in many ways misogynist, there are insights that we still need to learn from.

Similarly if we reject many of the elitist conclusions he reaches, we should still value the light that he sheds along the way. He was crucially aware that any genuine emotion can be nourishing whereas the dissemblance of anger is as poisonous as the semblance of love. We have to be wary of ideals that are externally imposed rather than generated out of a person's consciousness and experience. We can hear echoes of Kierkegaard in Lawrence's rejection of idealism, even if we are uncomfortable with the direction of his thinking. It is a tendency that Wittgenstein was also concerned with in his later writing. Again Lawrence is thinking of utilitarianism when he explains what he means by 'idealism':

> For instance, if I teach a man the idea that all men are equal, now this idea has no foundation in experience, but is logically deduced from certain ethical or philosophical principles. But there is a disease of idealism in the world, and we are all born with it. Particularly teachers are born with it. So they seize on the idea of equality, and they proceed to instill it. With what result? Your man is no longer a man, living his own life from his own spontaneous centres. He is a theoretical imbecile trying to frustrate and dislocate all life. *(Fantasies of the Unconscious,* Ch. 7)

For Lawrence it was important to recognise life as a process that needed to be learnt from and respected. We had to learn 'how not to *interfere'.* That is how to live dynamically, from the great source, and not statically, like machines driven by ideas and principles from the head, or automatically, from one fixed desire. At last, knowledge must be put into its true place in the living activity of man. And we must know deeply, in order even to do that' *(Fantasies,* Ch. 6). So it is up to each person to discover for himself or herself what obstacles, internal or external, interfere with his or her growth.

This involves patient experiment for we have to discern not general rules that can be applied impartially to all, but what particular sunshine and soil this particular person requires. Ideal, impulse and tradition each have to be listened to in their own hour while recognising in the same words as Nietzsche that reason 'is the finest instrument we have'. He knew it is a faculty that could not be refined if it was simply set against our inclinations for it would then dislocate our instincts and emotional lives, for there is no soul apart from the body.

The denigration of the body as part of the suppression of nature is embedded within western culture so that individuals have become virtually incapable of an immediate, instinctive and hence individual perception or response.[36] It is often our preconceived, stereotyped notions of what should be seen or felt – our 'images' of ourselves – that dictate our feelings. Our intuitive faculties have atrophied as they have been dismissed as 'irrational'. Lawrence's sketch of the Anglo-Saxon visitors to the Uffizi, in his 'Introduction to these Paintings', still strikes a powerful chord:

> They can see the living body of imagery as little as a blind man can see colour. The imaginative vision, which includes physical, intuitional perception *they have not got*. Poor things it is dead in them. And they stand in front of a Botticelli Venus, which they know as conventionally 'beautiful', much as a blind man might stand in front of a bunch of roses . . . They stare so hard, they do so *want* to see . . .   (*Phoenix*, p. 557)

There is also a grasp of how the inner self cannot be separated from the situations and relationships we find ourselves in. It is not simply a matter of staring at what is inside as we might stare at the picture. The Delphic notion of 'know thyself' can too easily encourage introspection and self-analysis. We live in interaction and relationship with those around us and this is the only way that we can know ourselves. But this is to connect the 'inner' and the 'outer' which a Protestant tradition has too often torn apart. It is to discover a task that we are often blind to, as Frieda Lawrence says:

> It isn't at all easy to know what you really feel and most of us are too beastly lazy to find out how we respond genuinely to this or that. It's hard work to be a genuine human being such as we were meant to be . . . (F. Lawrence, *The Memoirs and Correspondence*, pp. 150–1)

It is hard to know what we feel if we are constantly denying our emotions and feelings when they do not accord with the ideals that we have set for ourselves. We often deny our strength, sadness or resentment when we think that these emotions will reflect badly on ourselves. So it is that we learn to deny reality at the same moment as we might declare that we are concerned to be impartial and objective. Even when it comes to ourselves the point is that we inherit a modernist Enlightenment tradition that learns to think of 'reality' as something impartial and objective and so which blinds us to a recognition that if we deny our emotions and feelings we are denying part of our reality. We are making our lives less truthful than they would be. We do not recognise the injuries that we do to ourselves during the process. We learn to look away. Similarly we learn to look away from the injuries and mistreatments of others. So it was that the Jews in Nazi Germany became invisible. They were not neighbours – individuals that had been significant – but 'others' who could not be neighbours because they were no longer visible.

It is so much easier to blame others than to take responsibility for ourselves. The Treaty of Versailles and the Jews were blamed by Hitler for the condition of Germany – people should learn to ignore the mistreatment of the Jews, knowing that this was a small price to pay for the renewal of Germany. Within a Protestant tradition goodness is in our reach as long as we are prepared to turn away from our inclinations. There always has to be someone to blame for our misery or misfortune for it cannot be of our own making. We learn to apportion blame, rather than work out how responsibility is shared, for we are set to prove ourselves blameless. For it is as individuals that we have to give an account of ourselves. We are concerned with the moral worth of individual action, for it is as individuals that we secure salvation.

Our moral theory, founded as it is on individualistic assumptions which see freedom as a matter of individual will and choice, fails to illuminate these issues as the self-denial is taken for granted. As Murdoch has recognised:

> A working philosophical psychology is needed which can at least attempt to connect modern psychological terminology with a terminology concerned with virtue. We need a moral philosophy which can speak significantly of Freud and Marx, and out of which authentic and political views can be generated. We need a moral philosophy in which the concept of love, so rarely mentioned now by philosophers, can once again be made central. (*The Sovereignty of Good*, p. 46)

In its absence we have to make difficult connections for ourselves. It can also be important to learn from the experience of others.

Until 18 March 1958 Thomas Merton, the American trappist monk and author, had seen his life in isolation from others. He had been attracted to a Trappist monastery as a place of radical apartness from others. But on his trip to Louisville, Kentucky, standing still on a street corner, he 'suddenly realized that I loved all the people and none of these were, or could be, totally alien to me. As if waking from a dream – the dream of my separateness, of my "special" vocation to be different'. As he described it in his journal, 'the sense of liberation from an illusory difference was such a joy that I almost laughed out loud . . . It is a glorious destiny to be a member of the human race'. This was to strengthen his conviction that love and justice had to be connected.

For some time he had valued the active stance that Dorothy Day and the 'Catholic Worker' took against war, but now it came to have a more pressing significance for him. He identified their nonviolent action with Gandhi's Satyagraha, which literally means the power that comes from living in truth. But the more Merton engaged with groups involved in protest the more aware he became of the difficulties of growing in patience and compassion. He learnt that people can easily become centred in anger and self-righteousness. Assuming that truth is all on their side they can become an obstacle to changing the attitudes of others. In a letter to Jim Forest of the *Catholic Worker* he notes that '[people] do not feel threatened by the bomb . . . but they feel terribly threatened by some . . . students carrying a placard . . . We have to have a deep patient compassion for the fears of men, for the fears and irrational mania of those who hate or condemn us . . . ' (Letter to Jim Forest, 5 January 1962).[37]

Simone Weil came to recognise the failings of an orthodox Marxist theory that assumed that the proletariat has an exclusive identification with truth and morality. Since they were the victims of injustice they could do no wrong because history was on their side. In a different context Professor Ezra Mendelsohn has wisely observed that 'victims are extremely reluctant to admit that they have victimised others'.[38] Poles certainly have the right to see themselves as victims of a cruel history but this does not absolve them from the obligation to pursue the truth about their relations with the Jews. Negative stereotypes die hard especially if they imbue those who believe them with a sense of self-righteousness.

This is part of an idealisation of politics that has been so endemic in liberal and Marxist politics. We lose a sense of the dignity and human worth of individuals as we become lost in abstractions. Both Simone Weil and Merton became aware of the difficulties and limits of politics, even if it remains inescapable. Politics should communicate liberating possibilities to people, but this is often foreclosed. As Merton has it:

One of the important things to do is to keep cutting deliberately through political lines and barriers and emphasising the fact that these are largely fabricated and that there is another dimension, a genuine reality, totally opposed to the fictions of politics: the human dimension which politics pretends to arrogate entirely (to itself) . . . This is the necessary first step along the long way . . . of purifying, humanising and somehow illuminating politics . . . Is this possible? . . . At least we must try . . . (Letter to Jim Forest, 8 December 1962[39])

Love has to do with concrete relationships with others. Love is inseparable from politics if we are concerned with the wellbeing of others, rather than with myths and abstractions. As we become less concerned with the consequences and results of our actions and more 'in the value, the rightness, the truth of the work itself', as Merton has it, 'gradually you struggle less for an idea and more and more for specific people. The range tends to narrow down, but it gets much more real. In the end it is the reality of personal relationships that saves everything . . . ' In the same letter to Jim Forest he recognises that 'the great thing, after all, is to live, not to pour out your life in the service of a myth: and we turn the best things into myths' (Letter to Jim Forest, 22 February 1966).

Merton had awoken from his own myth of separateness. With Simone Weil, he knew not to underestimate the power of myths and the need to come to terms with them in our own lives. We had to learn of the limits of politics for it had been a powerful myth that politics alone could bring human emancipation. Orthodox Marxism had in its Leninist incarnations come to believe in the sovereignty of politics and the need to subordinate the institutions and practices of civil society to the state. In contrast liberalism talks of the sovereignty of the individual but inherits a vision of the separateness of individuals that is often blind to the injuries of social injustice.

Some black and feminist writing allows us to rework our inherited political and moral traditions by connecting issues of morality with oppression, love with inequality. It sustains a notion of dignity and self-respect which is not simply an inner quality of Kantian liberalism nor something that can be delivered to people through the socialisation of the means of production. If Simone Weil helps us to rethink the relationship of morality to politics, feminism helps to restore the connection with our emotional lives.

With the black and gay movement it provides a language of empowerment which is more than an issue of will and determination. It recognises, as Kierkegaard does, the importance of transforming the quality of our relationship with ourselves if we are to learn to love and respect others as they are, rather than as we would want them to be in our idealisations. The black movement carries within itself the importance of spiritual resistance, of not losing faith with oneself or one's soul. It has persisted with a language of the soul, when it has long lost its grip with a culture of modernity. It recognised implicitly that we also, as Weil has it, have needs of the soul.[40]

These social movements have come together with a sense of the importance of being able to speak as a victim to see and hear other people's victimisation. People are victims of the evils of violence, poverty and racism that they cannot control and in no way deserve. Within a liberal moral culture this is very hard to hear and for many people very hard to say. As Sara Ruddick has recognised, 'It is so much easier to believe that if only they – or we – had been a little stronger, more resourceful, more active, terrible suffering would have been avoided. One element of the transformative vision, coming from feminists, is just this ability to see and hear and remember the suffering of victims, and to cast their lot, to stand with the victim against the oppression' (*Tikkun*, vol. 2, no. 3, p. 42).[41]

It is a matter of somehow holding this in balance with the need to take responsibility for your life, so that we do not assume that victimisation carries with it a kind of purity, as if being a victim somehow gives one moral privilege. As Catherine Stimpson says in the *Tikkun Roundtable* on 'Feminist Consciousness Today' (*Tikkun*, vol. 2, no. 3), some women are 'very loath to give up the notion of women's victimization, clinging to a notion of universal victimization. They didn't want to see that women are sometimes mean to other women and that women can do vile and horrible things' (p. 42). This involves a recognition of complexity and difference that is so often denied. It involves taking seriously differences as a source of strength and learning a true sense of entitlement that gives vision to life.

This involves remaking the connections between morality and politics in a way that comes to terms with the moral limits of modernity. It involves a recognition of complexity and a sense that differences need to be understood as a source of dignity and integrity for there is no single path that can be sanctioned by reason alone. There are different traditions of thought, feeling and action. We need to transcend traditions of modernity which prevent us from learning a new reverence for nature as well as a sense of the dignity of our emotional lives. We need to explore the resources within our inherited moral, political and spiritual traditions both to reflect upon the contradictions of our lived experience as well as to provide new visions of love, freedom, equality and justice.

Notes

1 Introduction: Love, Inequality and Oppression

1. In *Kant, Respect and Injustice*, I explore notions of respect in Kant's writing but also in the way that they underpin liberal moral and political theory as it has recently been discussed by Rawls, Hart, Dworkin and others. This depends upon an idea of the autonomy of morality that Kant himself came to have serious doubts about when he considered the moral relations between rich and poor.

2. Simone Weil places a discussion of both bodily and spiritual needs in the opening section of *The Need for Roots*. Recently David Wiggins has written in *Morality and Objectivity*, ed. Ted Honderich. Michael Ignatieff in *The Needs of Strangers* provides an interesting and incisive account in the history of ideas.

3. The traditional vision of the social order conceived as part of a larger order of nature is discussed by A. O. Lovejoy in *The Great Chain of Being*. Keith Thomas' *Religion and the Decline of Magic* also provides interesting historical background.

4. See the discussions in Part 3 of *The Prison Notebooks* entitled 'The Philosophy of Praxis'. A useful introduction to Gramsci's writings is provided by Carl Boggs' *Gramsci's Marxism* and the collection *Gramsci and Marxist Theory*, ed. Chantal Mouffe. For a useful intellectual biography see Alastair Davidson's *Antonio Gramsci: Towards an Intellectual Biography*.

5. Interesting selections on Marx's conception of human needs are to be found in Agnes Heller's *The Theory of Need in Marx*. From a different structuralist tradition of Marxist work it has also been usefully discussed by Kate Soper, *On Human Needs*, and Norman Geras, *The Concept of Human Nature in Marx*. I have discussed the issue of human needs in 'Trusting Ourselves: Marxism, Human Needs and Sexual Politics' in *One Dimensional Marxism* by S. Clarke, T. Lovell, K. Robins and V. Seidler.

6. John Rawls' *A Theory of Justice* has provided an enormous discussion of the continuing relevance of theories of social contract. Some of these papers have been collected in *Reading Rawls*, ed. Norman Daniels. See also the critical discussion in Michael Sandel's *Liberalism and the Limits of Justice*. I have discussed some of the strengths and weaknesses of Sandel's account in the concluding chapter of *Kant, Respect and Injustice: The Limits of Liberal Moral Theory*, entitled 'Liberalism and the Autonomy of Morality'.

7. An appreciation of the Enlightenment which carries with it a sense of the importance of its critics is provided by Isaiah Berlin's *Against the Current*. See in particular the essays 'The Divorce between the Sciences and the

Humanities', 'The Counter-Enlightenment' and 'Vico and the Ideal of Enlightenment'.

8. These contradictions have been further discussed in the concluding chapter to *Kant, Respect and Injustice: The Limits of Liberal Moral Theory*, entitled 'Liberalism and the Autonomy of Morality'. See also Victor Seidler's 'Kant: Respect, Individuality and Dependence' in *Kant's Practical Philosophy Reconsidered*, ed. Y. Yovel, pp. 235–54.

9. Sartre's 'Anti-Semite and Jew' is crucial in illuminating the contradictory inheritance of emancipation. It connects with the difficulties of affirming a positive cultural or ethnic identity within an Enlightenment culture. Samuel Trigano recently asserted 'that revolutionary France of 1789 did not truly emancipate the Jew but rather prohibited the emergence of the "positive Jew", that is the Jew who is utterly faithful to the heritage and traditions of the Jewish people while remaining an active and creative member of the surrounding society'. Simon Sibelman, 'Liberty, Equality and Identity' (Jewish Chronicle Literary Supplement, 18 August 1984, p. 2).

10. The relationship between masculinity and reason as a central feature of an Enlightenment inheritance is discussed by Genevieve Lloyd in *The Man of Reason* and by Victor Seidler in *Rediscovering Masculinity: Reason, Language & Sexuality*.

11. The need to find a place for the importance of love within our moral theory is stressed by Iris Murdoch in *The Sovereignty of Good* and in the opening part of 'On God' and 'Good'. She says: 'We need a moral philosophy in which the concept of love, so rarely mentioned by the philosophers, can once again be made central' (p. 46).

12. Carolyn Merchant's *The Death of Nature* illuminates the important historical transformation whereby with the scientific revolution our relationship with nature became a relationship with dead matter. It is also a continuing theme in Susan Griffin's writings. See, for instance, *Women and Nature* and *Pornography and Silence*.

13. A useful introduction to Max Weber is provided in the Collection *From Max Weber*, ed. H. Gerth and C. Wright Mills. See also Wolfgang J. Mommsen, *The Age of Bureaucracy*. The relationship of Weber to modernity is a continuing theme in Alastair MacIntyre's *After Virtue*.

14. Herder's challenge to Kant is discussed by Isaiah Berlin in his paper 'Herder and the Enlightenment' in *Vico and Herder*, pp. 143–216.

15. See Wittgenstein's Introduction to the *Philosophical Investigations*, trans. G. E. M. Anscombe, and remarks collected in *Culture and Value*. Some sense of how Wittgenstein saw his work is provided in *Ludwig Wittgenstein; Personal Reflections*, edited by Rush Rees, in particular M. O. C. Drury's 'Conversations with Wittgenstein', pp. 112–89.

16. Some of these connections are illuminated by James Hillman's *Revisioning Psychology*. He explains that the idea of soul-making can be found in William Blake's *Vala* but that it was John Keats who clarified the phrase in a letter to his brother: 'Call the world if you please "the vale of

soul-making". Then you will find out the use of the world . . . ' Keats goes on to say: ' . . . I say *"soul-making"* – soul as distinguished from intelligence. There may be intelligence or sparks of the divinity in millions – but they are not souls till they acquire identities, till each one is personally itself . . . How then are souls to be made? . . . How but by the medium of a world like this? This point I sincerely wish you to consider because I think it is a grander system of salvation than the Christian religion.' *The Letters of John Keats*, letter dating from April 1819, p. 326 (London, Reeves and Turner, 1895).

17. Max Scheler dwelt on the themes of self-denial and resentment in his *Ressentiment*. It is also a theme in his *Man's Place in Nature*. For a useful background to the intellectual life of Max Scheler see *Max Scheler* by John Raphael Staude. In many ways Scheler is yet to assume a proper position in philosophy and sociology.

18. The place of Weber as a voice of modernity is a theme in Alastair MacIntyre's *After Virtue*. It is also a theme taken up in Gerry Doppelt's critical discussion of *After Virtue* in 'Modernity and Conflict' *Analyse und Kritik* 7 (1985) pp. 206–33.

19. Walter Benjamin's ideas on the relationship of history to progress are partly developed in his 'Theses on the Philosophy of History' in *Illuminations*. See also his 'Critique of Violence' and the 'Theologico-Political Fragment' which are in *One-Way Street*, pp. 132–54 & pp. 155–6. The essay by Hannah Arendt, 'Walter Benjamin: 1892 –1940' which is published as an introduction to *Illuminations* provides a useful historical and intellectual background.

20. The notion of rootedness is discussed by Simone Weil in *The Need for Roots*. This tension in her writing is one of the themes discussed by Robert Coles in *Simone Weil: A Modern Pilgrimage*. It is also a theme in the concluding chapter of *A Truer Liberty: Simone Weil and Marxism* by Lawrence Blum and Victor Seidler.

21. This quotation is taken from Raya Dunayevskaya's *Marxism and Freedom*. In interpretations of Marx this grasp of individuality is often lost as we confine ourselves to a false polarity which identifies socialism with collectivism. Attempts, such as Gerry Cohen's *Marx's Theory of History: A Defense*, to defend Marxism as a form of economic determinism, lose touch with this tension in his writings.

2   Respect and Love

1. In this chapter I draw heavily upon Kant's discussion in Part 2 of *Doctrine of Virtue* entitled 'On Duties of Virtue to Others', pp. 115–39, trans. Mary Gregor. It is possible to sense a shift in moral sensibility between these writings and Kant's more formalistic writings. This is an issue often avoided by diminishing these writings as 'less systematic'. As I argue in *Kant, Respect and Injustice*, they recognise moral issues that

were formally denied or side-stepped. It is part of the greatness of Kant's thought that he recognised some of these tensions and contradictions.

2. I am saying little about the processes of secularisation though I would want to argue that a religious morality in which we have to prove ourselves worthy in the eyes of God prepares the ground for the social relations of individual achievement and competitiveness which are so central to the nature of morality in capitalist society. It is the strength of Max Weber's *The Protestant Ethic and the Spirit of Capitalism* that he illuminates some of these connections.

3. It can be difficult to think about estrangement within a rationalistic moral tradition. It is a strength of Marx's writings that he refused to separate the 'psychological' from everyday material relations. This has been difficult to sustain within an orthodox Marxist tradition that insists on interpreting Marxism as a form of economic determinism. In Marxist writings touched by Hegel and phenomenology we find more recognition of 'estrangement', though often its moral significance is lost. See, for instance, Georg Lukacs' *History and Class Consciousness*. More recently there is John O'Neil's 'The Concept of Estrangement in Marx' in *Sociology as a Skin Trade*, pp. 113–36.

4. Weber's appreciation of the dominance of capitalist relations is often lost on those who focus too narrowly on a contrast between Weber and Marx on the place of values in history. We find a similar recognition of the power of capital in Alexis de Tocqueville's *Democracy in America*. When the impact of the growth of capital on the organisation of manufacturing can still be seen clearly on the Eastern seaboard of the United States, moral theory has been slow to recognise the challenge this makes to its prevailing individualistic assumptions.

5. These themes are discussed further in the concluding chapter, 'Liberalism and the Autonomy of Morality', of Victor Seidler's *Kant, Respect & Injustice: The Limits of Liberal Moral Theory*.

6. The link that an Enlightenment culture has drawn between masculinity and reason gives this a particular emphasis in the lives of men. It suggests a link between masculinity and a morality that values independence and self-sufficiency. This is a theme explored in Victor Seidler's *Rediscovering Masculinity: Reason, Language & Sexuality*. The ways that it has worked to render women's moral experience invisible within the dominant moral traditions is a theme in Carol Gilligan's *In a Different Voice*. A stimulating discussion of some of Gilligan's ideas that connects them with broader issues of social theory is provided by Seyla Benhabib 'The Generalized and the Concrete Other: The Kohlberg-Gilligan Controversy and Feminist Theory' in *Feminism as Critique*, edited by Seyla Benhabib and Drucilla Cornell.

7. Themes of isolation and loneliness within an individualistic culture are reflected upon by Erich Fromm in his *Fear of Freedom*. C. B. Macpherson's *The Political Theory of Possessive Individualism* also helps to illuminate the market relationships which helped sustain a

political culture of possessive individualism. We tend to take it for granted within a Protestant culture that because our emotions and feelings are 'personal' they are thereby different from the feelings of others. It can come as a revelation to recognise that we can share our feelings with others, especially if they have suffered a similar experience. Such a recognition has been central to the role of 'consciousness raising' as part of the tactics of the women's liberation movement in recent times.

8. The issue of the moral law within Kant's conception of morality is discussed in Chapter 4, 'Respect, Impartiality and the Moral Law', of *Respect & Injustice; The Limits of Liberal Moral Theory*.

9. Max Scheler's discussion of Kantian ethics can help illuminate some of the weaknesses of a moral tradition that is defined in rationalistic terms. He senses the difficulties of such a tradition to come to terms with the complexities of our moral experience. This can still be appreciated even if we do not follow the solutions that he provides. Scheler's most extensive discussion of Kant is to be found in his *Formalism in Ethics and Non-Formal Ethics of Values*.

10. The relationship between a Protestant distrust of our natures and the formal or rationalistic character of our prevailing moral traditions is difficult to explore because we take the universalistic claims of Kantian rationalism so much for granted. We have swallowed the idea that because it is rational it must be universal and so available to all. This has blinded us to the particularity of the Protestant assumptions that underpin so much of our moral theory. Bernard Williams' *Ethics and the Limits of Philosophy* can help us to identify the rationalistic character of our inherited moral traditions.

11. The place of altruistic emotions within Kant's ethics is discussed by Lawrence Blum in *Friendship, Altruism and Morality*. See also Bernard Williams' paper 'Morality and the Emotions' In *Problems of the Self*, pp. 207–29, and the papers collected in *Explaining Emotions*, edited by Amelie Okensberg Rorty.

12. The challenges which Freud and different forms of psychoanalytic theory and practice make to our established moral traditions remains to be explored. Interesting issues are raised by Richard Wollheim's 'On Persons and Their Lives' in *Explaining Emotions* ed. Amelie Okensberg Rorty. See also Richard Wollheim's William James lectures at Harvard, published as *The Thread of Life*.

13. The ways that we unwittingly adopt an instrumental attitude towards others even whilst being explicitly warned against it by Kant is a theme in Part 2, 'Means and Ends', of the concluding chapter, 'Liberalism and the Autonomy of Morality', of my *Kant, Respect and Injustice: The Limits of Liberal Moral Theory*.

14. The links between a particular form of masculinity and rediscovering a sense of emotion as a sign of weakness are further explored in Victor Seidler, *Rediscovering Masculinity: Reason, Language and Sexuality*.

The connection between masculinity and self-denial is firmly grounded within a Protestant moral culture. This is explored further in Victor Seidler, *Recreating Sexual Politics: Men, Feminism and Politics*

3 Love and Equality

1. A sense of the significance of Kierkegaard for Wittgenstein's later philosophy is provided by M. O'C. Drury. See his 'Conversations with Wittgenstein' in R. Rhees' *Ludwig Wittgenstein: Personal Recollections*, pp. 112–84 See also M. O'C. Drury's *The Danger of Words*.
2. This makes it possible to understand at least one of the reasons that Kierkegaard could have been such an influence on Wittgenstein, especially for some of the themes of the *Philosophical Investigations*. See also Norman Malcolm's *Nothing is Hidden*.
3. This conception of 'free and equal rational persons, is crucial to John Rawls' *A Theory of Justice*. It is challenged in the name of a form of communitarian theory by Michael Sandel's *Liberalism and the Limits of Justice*. These claims are explored in the concluding chapter of Victor Seidler's *Kant, Respect and Injustice: The Limits of Liberal floral Theory*, entitled 'Liberalism and the Autonomy of Morality'.
4. Relatively little attention seems to have been given to the conceptions of personal change which are implicit in particular moral theories. If this exists at all it seems to be separated off into a more distinctly psychological discussion of moral development.
5. The relationship of altruism to extensivity which suggests that altruism could be measured by the degree of extensivity is a theme explored in Samuel and Pearl Oliner's study of Christian rescuers of Jews in the war, entitled 'The Altruistic Personality'. It is a strength of this work that it senses the limits of a Kantian framework when it comes to exploring the nature of care and concern for others. It is more difficult to recognise the ways Kantian universalistic notions are implicit in such psychological frameworks.
6. Sometimes this recognition, which can exist in Kant's writings, gets lost as he separates the 'duties to oneself' from the 'duties or virtues to other men' as the two parts of *The Doctrine of Virtue*. Kierkegaard has a fuller appreciation of the dialectical quality of our relationships. Sometimes it is only as we change our relationship to ourselves that our relationships to others can genuinely be transformed.
7. The ways in which moral theory since the Enlightenment has been trapped within a framework that separates 'egoism' from 'altruism' is illuminated in Bernard Williams' paper 'Egoism and Altruism' in *Problems of the Self*, pp. 250–65. See also discussion in Bernard Williams' *Morality*.
8. Within an analytic tradition Richard Wollheim seems to be illustrating some appreciation of lived experience. It is no accident that he opens up his *The Thread of Life* with an entry from Kierkegaard's journal for the

year 1843 saying 'It is perfectly true, as philosophers say, that life must be understood backwards. But they forget the other proposition, that it must be lived forwards'.

9. In this kind of reflection we can discern the continuing influence within a liberal moral culture of what C. B. Macpherson has identified historically as possessive individualism, in his *The Political Theory of Possessive Individualism*. See also Charles Taylor's essay 'Atomism' in his *Philosophy and the Human Sciences*, Philosophical Papers 2, pp. 187–210.

10. Some of these themes are further explored in Victor Seidler's 'Fathering, Authority and Masculinity' in *Male Order*, ed. Rowena Chapman and Jonathan Rutherford, pp. 272–302.

11. This is illustrated historically in Philip Aries *Centuries of Childhood*. For some contemporary reflections see *Sex and Love: New Thoughts on Old Contradictions*, ed. Sue Cartledge and Joanna Ryan.

12. Kierkegaard has been a direct influence upon the work of Frank Lake in *Clinical Theology* as well as more generally in the school of existential psychology. See, for instance, the collection *Psychoanalysis and Existential Philosophy*, ed. Henrik M. Ruitenbeck.

13. The relationship of masculinity to power and emotional life is explored further in Victor Seidler's *Rediscovering Masculinity: Reason, Language and Sexuality*. An interesting investigation of the relationship of emotionality to power is provided by Jean Baker Miller in *Towards a New Psychology of Women*. This work seems to have been generally formative in relating issues of identity, power and sexuality in non-structuralist ways.

14. Forms of individualism are discussed further in Victor Seidler's 'Kant: Respect, Individuality and Dependence' in *Kant's Practical Philosophy Rediscovered*, ed. Y. Yovel, pp. 235–54.

4 Morality and Inequality

1. Functionalist theories of social inequality have had a powerful influence on sociological theory. Some idea of the discussion is given in *Class, Status and Power* edited by K. Bendix and M. Lipset. An early questioning of this tradition was in Ralf Dahrendorf's *Class and Class Conflict in Industrial Society*. See also Frank Parkin's *Class, Inequality and Political Order*. The guiding notion is that social inequalities can be legitimated if they can be shown to work in the interests of society in general.

2. C. S. Lewis, *The Screwtape Letters*.

3. The relationship between inequality and a sense of worthlessness is usefully reflected on by Gregory Vlastos in 'Human Worth, Merit and Equality' in *Moral Concepts*, ed. Joel Feinberg.

4. See Herbert Marcuse's historical discussion of this as 'The Foundations of Positivism and the Rise of Sociology' which is in Part 2 of *Reason and Revolution*. For more recent discussion, see *Positivism and Sociology*, ed. Anthony Giddens, and the translation by Glyn Adey and David Frisby

of the important German discussion, *The Positivist Dispute in German Sociology.*

5. It has been a strength of feminist theory to introduce issues of power and subordination into realms of personal life where we are not used to identifying them. It challenges a prevailing conception which would recognise power exclusively as an issue within the public realm of politics. We are encouraged to rework our inherited senses of power, identity and politics. See, for instance, Steven Lukes' *Power* and Sheila Rowbotham's *Woman's Consciousness, Man's World*, and 'Woman, Power and Consciousness' in *Dreams and Dilemmas*, pp. 5–32 and 136–60.

6. Questions about the place of law are illuminated by H. L. A. Hart in *The Concept of Law* and Ronald Dworkin's *Taking Rights Seriously*. Some sense of the discussion this work has provoked is given in *The Philosophy of Law*, ed. R. Dworkin. To set some of the challenges that Marxist theory makes in context, see, for instance, *Law and Marxism* by Eugene Pashukanis.

7. The notion that if people are poor it is because they lack will and determination has been central to conservative libertarian thought. For a discussion of equality which emerges from this tradition that has reasserted itself in the political culture of the 1980s, see *Equality* by Keith Joseph and Jonathan Jumption.

8. Conceptualising the differences between people in terms of an idea of moral grading is a feature of J. O. Urmson's 'Saints and Heroes' which is reprinted in *Essays in Moral Philosophy*, ed. A. I. Melden. See also the discussion in David Heyd's *Supererogation* and J. Feinberg's 'Supererogation and Rules' in *Ethics*, ed. J. J. Thompson and G. Dworkin.

9. This vision of respect as involving a willingness to abstract from structures of inequality is developed in Bernard Williams' influential article, 'Equality'. It shows how liberal moral and political theory has given a secular form to a fundamentally Protestant conception. Its universalistic claims mean that it is rarely recognised as such.

10. The notion of privacy is reflected upon historically in Barrington Moore's *Privacy*. It is also an issue in Mary Midgley and Judith Hughes' *Women's Choices*.

11. The difficulties of abstracting personal relations from the context of relationships of class, race and gender and so the difficulties of regarding moral issues as if they are exclusively matters of individual choice and decision, is a theme in Victor Seidler's *Kant, Respect and Injustice: The Limits of Liberal Moral Theory.*

5 Inequality and Subordination

1. This begs questions about the relationship of social theory to the character of the social relations we live out. Different 'images' are available to help us make sense of the distinctions of social life. The pervasiveness

of role theory is a theme in Erving Goffman's work. See, for instance, *The Presentation of Self in Everyday Life*. For some critical comments on Goffman's work see Alvin Gouldner's *The Coming Crisis of Western Sociology*, pp. 378–90 The connection between philosophy and the everyday images that are structured into our 'common sense' is a theme in Antonio Gramsci's *The Prison Notebooks*; see in particular 'The Study of Philosophy', pp. 323–77. It is crucial that 'common sense, rather than being something that can be taken for granted, is something that is contested within relationships of Power. As Alice Walker reminds us, it is difficult after centuries of horror to talk about shared assumptions. She thinks that black people cannot rely on anything so nice and cosy as shared assumptions. As she says, 'It makes a difference to have lived among people who have challenged oppression and won' (Observer, 17 September 1984, p. 35).

2. The vision of the world as a stage continues to have considerable influence both as a guiding metaphor within a liberal moral culture and also in the social theories we inherit. Its currency reveals something about the precarious character of identities where we are left assuming that if identity is not something fixed it has simply to be a reflection of the different roles we play. This theme is further explored in Victor Seidler's *Rediscovering Masculinity: Reason, Language and Sexuality*. The difficulties of a post-structuralist tradition to deal adequately with issues of identity is symptomatic of a crucial blindness.

3. Some sense of the inadequacy of the way that Wittgenstein has been interpreted, especially in regard to the distinctions between 'inner' and 'outer' – the private and the public – is shown in Iris Murdoch's essay, 'The Idea of Perfection' in *The Sovereignty of Good*, pp. 11–45.

4. A discussion of class inequality that is able to connect it to issues of dignity and human worth is provided by Richard Sennett and Jonathan Cobb's *The Hidden Injuries of Class*. See also the study by Lillian Rubin, *Worlds of Pain: Life in the Working-Class Family*.

5. This is a theme explored in E. P. Thompson's critique of Althusserian Marxism in *The Poverty of Theory*. It is also a theme in Victor Seidler's 'Trusting Ourselves: Marxism, Human Needs and Sexual Politics' in *Dimensional Marxism* by Simon Clarke et al. A more general discussion of the relationship of Marxism to morality is provided by Steven Lukes' *Marxism and Morality*.

6. An appreciation of the ways that both Wittgenstein and Austin in quite different ways are struggling to heal the disconnection that takes place when language is used in an empty and false way, is a guiding theme in Stanley Cavell's *The Claims of Reason*. Some sense of his reading of Wittgenstein and Austin is given in his papers 'The Availability of Wittgenstein's Later Philosophy' and 'Austin as Criticism' in *Must We Mean What We Say?*, pp. 44–72 and 97–114.

7. A sense of the historical sources of our experience is a possible link that could be explored between the Gramsci of *The Prison Notebooks* and the

investigations of the later Wittgenstein that we find in *Philosophical Investigations*. The resonances are there even if they echo from very different traditions of theory and practice.

8. The difficulties of abstracting personal relations from the larger gender relations of power is a theme in Sheila Rowbotham's *Woman's Consciousness, Man's World*. This is not to eradicate the significance of personal relationships, as you might think from the critical remarks in Jean Bethke Elshtain's *Public Man, Private Woman: Women in Social and Political Thought*.

9. The ease with which the poor, powerless and oppressed can be blamed for their condition is a theme in *Blaming the Victim* by William Ryan. See also the interesting discussion in *Regulating the Poor* and *Poor People's Movements: Why they Succeed, How they Fail*, both by Francis Fox Piven and Richard A. Cloward.

10. An exploration of Simone Weil's relationship with Marxism at different moments in her life is given in Lawrence Blum and Victor Seidler's *A Truer Liberty: Simone Weil and Marxism*.

6 Respect, Human Needs and Equality

1. It is significant that Weil prefers to talk in terms of obligations rather than rights. She develops a connection between obligations and needs that is vital if people are to thrive. See the early sections of *The Need for Roots*.

2. The connection between being able to respect others and the social relations of power and subordination is a theme in Victor Seidler's *Respect and Injustice: The Limits of Liberal Moral Theory*.

3. For a discussion of Simone Weil's conception of oppression see Lawrence Blum and Victor Seidler's *A Truer Liberty: Simone Weil and Marxism*, Ch. 5, 'Oppression', pp. 107–142.

4. See Martin Jay's discussion of Adorno in *The Dialectical Imagination*, Ch. 3 'The Integration of Psychoanalysis, pp. 80–112. See also Russell Jacoby's discussion in *Social Amnesia*, Ch. 4, 'Negative Psychoanalysis and Marxism', pp. 73–100.

5. It can be difficult to know how to read Simone Weil's *Spiritual Autobiography*, which was left with Father Perrin. It says most about the way that she was thinking while living in the South of France before leaving for America to join her parents. She had a tendency to interpret her past in the light of her present preoccupations. It is published in *Waiting On God*.

6. See the account of her experience of work and what led up to it in Simone Petremont's exhaustive biography *Simone Weil: A Life*, Ch. 8 'The Year of Factory Work (1934–1935)', pp. 214–147. See also *A Truer Liberty: Simone Weil and Marxism*, Ch. 8 'Work' pp. 143–93, which attempts to show how the experience of work helped form her later moral and political writings.

7. Simone Weil's letters from her period of factory work give crucial insights into the ways that it transformed her sense of herself as well as her personal and political relations with others. Her letters were collected by Richard Rees as *Seventy Letters*.

8. In the early sections of *The Need for Roots*, Weil tentatively explores those material and spiritual needs which we share as human beings. We gain intimations of a fuller moral psychology that recognises the moral pain and injuries caused to people that we often remain blinded to within our inherited utilitarianism.

9. Paolo Freire's *Pedagogy of the Oppressed* offers us a vital discussion of the different forms of social relations that go along with different conceptions of education. See also George Dennison's *The Lives of Children*.

10. Changes in the way that Simone Weil came to conceive the nature of power are discussed in Lawrence Blum and Victor Seidler's *A Truer Liberty: Simone Weil and Marxism*, Ch. 7 'Power', pp. 194–256.

11. *Gravity and Grace* collects remarks that were originally to be found in Simone Weil's notebooks. The introduction by Gustav Thibon gives a useful context to the writing. They were all written before May 1942 when Weil left Marseille for America.

12. Weil's experience in work made her aware of the shame that people often carry from their subordination at work. Often it is something that people want to leave behind them when they come home into the family. Often they do not take kindly to being reminded of it. It is a tension that many working class families learn to live with.

13. Weil was acutely aware of the failure of western culture to assign significant value to work. It was a weakness in Greek and Christian traditions that she otherwise praised. She failed to recognise it as a value in Hebrew culture because she was obsessed with identifying Hebrew and Roman cultures as organised around power. This blinded her to the Jewish resistance to Roman power.

14. The injustice involved in treating people equally who are in unequal situations is a theme in Victor Seidler's *Kant, Respect and Injustice: The Limits of Liberal Moral Theory*. See Ch. 4, 'Respect, Impartiality and the Moral Law', pp. 44–55. As the school children of Barbiana put it, 'Nothing is more unjust than to share equally among unequals' (*Letter to a Teacher*, p. 50).

7 Inequality and Justice

1. Simone Weil turned towards the *Iliad* to deepen her understanding of the workings of power and the ways that people can be reduced to matter. This was a text that she drew from in different ways as an inspiration at different points of her life. The Essay 'The *Iliad*, Poem of Might' (*L'Iliad ou le Poème de la Force*) was originally published as part of *La Source Grecque*, pp. 9–43. She insisted on making her own translations from

the Greek. It has been published as part of *Intimations of Christianity among the Ancient Greeks*, pp. 24–55. Changes in Weil's conception of power are discussed in Lawrence Blum and Victor Seidler's *A Truer Liberty: Simone Weil and Marxism*, Ch. 7, pp. 194–256.

2. Weil's vision of 'the supernatural virtue of justice' is developed in her essay 'Forms of the Implicit Love of God', probably written in the spring of 1942. It is reprinted in *Waiting On God*.

3. To understand the ways Weil comes to think of affliction, see her essay 'The Love of God and Affliction' in *Waiting on God*, pp. 16–94.

4. The intensity of Weil's insights into the ways that people can be reduced to 'not exist' through the workings of domination can be grasped through writings on slavery. See, for instance, Stanley Elkins' *Slavery*, Abram Kardiner and Daniel Ovesey, *The Mark of Oppression*, and Eugene Genovese *Roll, Jordan, Roll: The World the Slaves Made*. It can also be useful to set this against reflections on the conditions in the Nazi concentration camps so that some sense of the oppression suffered by blacks and Jews in the recent historical past is not marginalised within western culture. Both slavery and the Holocaust demonstrate a recurring challenge to modernity and the forms of philosophy and social theory that would render these experiences invisible. It is a strength of Simone Weil's work that she challenges the silences. See also Primo Levi's *If This is a Man* and *The Drowned and the Saved*, which carry a similar weight.

5. It can be useful to reflect on the essays gathered together in *Oppression and Liberty* for some of these were written right at the end of her life showing the different accent that she puts on things, as well as her continuing moral and political concerns. Some of these tensions are explored in *A Truer Liberty: Simone Weil and Marxism*, by Lawrence Blum and Victor Seidler.

6. The difficulties of assuming the autonomy and integrity of individuals as is usually done in theories of social contract, is an insight that Weil shares with Adorno and Benjamin, even if they approach it in quite different ways. The theme of 'individuality' and the silences of orthodox Marxist theory were what turned the Frankfurt School back to an interest in Kant, whatever the weaknesses of his formalist ethics. See, for instance, the illuminating discussion of the early development of Adorno and Benjamin in Susan Buck-Morss' *The Origin of Negative Dialectics*, Chs. 3 & 4.

7. It can seem as if justice negates the duty of charity. It can either seem within welfare capitalism that people do not have to give of themselves to others for this duty has been taken over by the state, or else within a state socialist society it can seem as if charity is insulting and in any case made redundant because the society is taken to be just with the abolition of private property and socialisation of the means of production. Michael Ignatieff explores some of the issues in *The Needs of Strangers*.

8. If charity is taken inevitably to fall short of justice it can be hard to acknowledge the need to give to others. Within a moral tradition that assumes it is 'natural' to be egoistic and that we require reasons to extend ourselves to others it can be difficult to give a different place to altruism

in our lives. Wittgenstein stands against such an Enlightenment tradition in his recognition of the 'naturalness' with which we can respond to the suffering of others. It is not behaviour that has to be mediated through a mental process of reasoning.

8 Respect, Rights and Injustice

1. Simone Weil makes us aware of the tensions that are carried within our moral and political traditions that can only be grasped through a sense of historical context. This is an insight she shares with Gramsci. This connection is explored in the concluding chapter to *A Truer Liberty: Simone Weil and Marxism*, entitled 'Morality, Truth and Politics'. This insight has the power to enrich an analytical philosophy tradition that has tended – at least in its early days – to analyse moral and political concepts as if they were bereft of a historical context and the workings of particular relationships of power and dominance.

2. The discussion of the tradition of positive rights has a place in *The Need for Roots* since Weil is convinced that the influence of this tradition over French moral and political culture has to be challenged if a different basis is to be discovered for the regeneration of France after World War 2.

3. Weil's conception of the person is challenging to a rationalist tradition that would define the individual as a rational self. There are wonderful insights, many of which remain unexplored, in her essay 'Human Personality', which she wrote in 1943. It appears in *Selected Essays 1934–43*, ed. Richard Rees, pp. 9–34.

4. The notion of rights has come to play a central role in expressing the nature of freedom and justice in recent moral and political philosophy, which has wanted to distance itself from a utilitarian inheritance. This tendency is discussed in an interesting way by H. L. A. Hart in 'Between Utility and Rights' in Alan Ryan (ed.) *The Idea of Freedom*, who would want to defend a modified utilitarianism. The primacy of rights is a central theme in the otherwise diverse traditions represented by John Rawls' *Theory of Justice*, Robert Nozick's *Anarchy, State and Utopia*, Charles Fried's *Right and Wrong* and Ronald Dworkin's *Taking Rights Seriously*. An attempt to explore a tradition that is not based either on utilitarianism or on rights theories is made in the concluding chapter to Victor Seidler's *Respect and Injustice: The Limits of Liberal Moral Theory* entitled 'Liberalism and the Autonomy of Morality'.

5. For a reading of Wittgenstein that appreciates this movement in his thought see the early parts of Stanley Cavell's *The Claims of Reason*. Some recognition of other resonances between the writings of Weil and Wittgenstein have been made by Peter Winch. See his introduction to *Lectures on Philosophy* and his study of Weil entitled *Just Balance: Reflections on the Philosophy of Simone Weil*.

6. A vision of justice that recognises the value of community and wants to

explore rights in the different contexts of community is provided by Michael Walzer, *Spheres of Justice*. It is also a theme in Michael Sandel's *Liberalism and the Limits of Justice*.

7. For some discussion of the sale of labour as a commodity within a Marxist tradition that attempts to consider the issue of rights, see Allen E. Buchanan, *Marx and Justice*. See also Richard W. Miller, *Analysing Marx: Morality, Power and History*. There is also a discussion of Marxism's relationship to rights in Steven Lukes' *Marxism and Morality* and his paper 'Can a Marxist believe in human rights?', *Praxis International*, vol. 1, no. 4, pp. 334–45.

8. The ways in which the powerless are dispossessed of their language is a theme explored in *A Truer Liberty: Simone Weil and Marxism*, Ch. 8, 'Power'. It is an insight that Bernard Williams expressed in an analytical tradition with the idea that the oppressed want to see themselves through the eyes of those who have power over them. See his paper 'The Idea of Equality' in *Problems of the Self*, pp. 230–49.

9. In her notebooks Weil says: 'We read, but also *we are read by*, others. Interferences in these readings. Forcing someone to read himself as we read him (slavery). Forcing others to read us as we read ourselves (conquest). A mechanical process. More often than not a dialogue between deaf people' ('Readings', *Gravity and Grace*, pp. 121–2).

10. To compare Weil's sense of the relationship of language to power with Gramsci, see the section of the *Prison Notebooks* entitled 'The Study of Philosophy', pp. 322–77. Together they provide a challenge to a post-structuralist tradition, partly represented by Foucault, that fails to illuminate the contradictions in lived experience since it takes experience itself to be an effect of discourse.

11. The contrast between the 'personal' and the 'impersonal' becomes important in her later writings, especially as she is clarifying her objections to the personalism of Mournier. This is explored in her essay 'Human Personality'. It helps illuminate the ways she questions psychologistic accounts, since she does not want to separate them from their moral and spiritual contexts.

12. For a historical account of the development of 'personalism' in France, see John Hellman, *Emmanuel Mournier and the New Catholic Left, 1930–1950*.

13. Marx talks about the relationship of commodity exchange to a language of rights in the early sections of his 'The Chapter on Capital', pp. 239–75, in *The Grundrisse: Foundations to the Critique of Political Economy*.

14. See the discussion in Bernard Williams' 'Persons, Character and Morality' in *Moral Luck*, pp. 1–19. This paper originally appeared in *Identities of Persons*, ed. A. O. Rorty.

15. For an introductory discussion of Freud, see Sigmund Freud's *Introductory Lectures in Psychoanalysis*. See also Richard Wollheim, *Freud*, O. Mannoni, *Freud*, and the taped conversations with Wilhelm Reich published in *Reich Speaks of Freud*.

16. A need to come to terms with the failures of traditional political theory
to illuminate the moral realities of assembly-line production was also felt
by Gramsci. See his 'Americanism and Fordism' in *The Prison Papers*
p. 277–318.

9 Morality, Subordination and Oppression

1. Alexis de Tocqueville realised in *Democracy in America* that 'small
aristocratic societies that are formed by some manufacturers in the midst of
the immense democracy of our age' would mean that 'if ever a permanent
inequality of conditions and aristocracy again penetrates into the world, it
may be predicted that this is the gate by which they will enter' (vol. 2,
p. 170–71).
2. How relationships of power and subordination bring into question an
autonomy of morality that is otherwise assumed within liberal moral
theory is a central theme in Victor Seidler's *Kant, Respect and Injustice;
The Limits of Liberal Moral Theory*.
3. The ways in which people can be reduced and undermined through the
workings of relations of power and subordination cannot be illuminated
within a post-structuralist tradition that treats individuality as an effect of
relations of power. It loses the crucial connections between trusting our
experience and defining our identities. It tends to be dismissive of any
language of experience, held as it often is, within structuralist assumptions
that can only discern a threat of essentialism. It has been a strength of
feminist work, when it has resisted a structuralist reading, to insist on
a connection between experience, power and identity. These issues are
discussed further in Victor Seidler's *Rediscovering Masculinity; Reason,
Language and Sexuality*.
4. See, for instance, Sheila Rowbotham's *Hidden from History* and Barbara
Taylor's *Eve and the New Jerusalem*.
5. James Connolly's essay on women reprinted from the *Reconquest of
Ireland* (Dublin 1916) in *James Connolly: Selected Writings*, edited
by P. Berresford Ellis. I thank Sheila Rowbotham for pointing out the
significance of this issue to me.
6. See the interesting discussion about a woman's right to choose provided
by Eileen Fairweather's article, 'Abortion – the Feelings behind the
Slogans', *Spare Rib* Issue 87, October 1979, and by *Spare Rib* Issue 90,
January 1980.
7. For insights into the development of gender identity see Nancy Chodorow,
*The Reproduction of Mothering: Psychoanalysis and the Sociology of
Gender*, and Joyce Treblicot, *Mothering: Essays in Feminist Theory*.
See also Victor Seidler *Rediscovering Masculinity: Reason, Language
and Sexuality*, Ch. 6, 'Identity'.
8. Weil tries to develop a sense of the different levels at which individuals
can be injured so suffering different forms of injustice. This opens a space

for connecting our moral and political theory with insights drawn from therapeutic theory and practice, in a way barely possible within a utilitarian tradition.

9. We are so used to identifying justice with distributive justice that it can be difficult to recognise that there might be other traditions that give priority to the injuries that people can do to each other. Weil recognised sources in the Greek conception of justice, particularly in Sophocles. It might be that such a tradition has to be reawakened if we are to appreciate the harm that we do to the natural world in terms of justice.

10. For a sense of Weil's detailed investigations of factory production, see 'A Factory Journal' – *'Journal d'Usine'*, translated and edited by Dorothy Tuck McFarland and Wilhelmina Van Ness in *Simon Weil: Formative Writings, 1924–1941*.

11. For a discussion of Weil's changing vision of freedom, see Lawrence Blum and Victor Seidler, *A Truer Liberty: Simone Weil and Marxism*, Ch. 4, 'Liberty', pp. 80–106.

12. See Harry Braverman, *Labor and Monopoly Capital*, and the collection of articles published by the Conference of Socialist Economists as *The Labour Process and Class Struggle*. For a fuller picture of work in a car assembly plant in the 1970s, see Huw Benyon's *Working for Ford*.

13. For a fuller discussion of Simone Weil's experience of work and the ways that it shaped her moral and political thought, see *A Truer Liberty: Simone Weil and Marxism*, Ch. 6 'Work', p. 143–93.

14. See Karl Marx's discussion of 'estranged labour', pp. 64–78, as well as the earlier discussion on 'wages and labour', pp. 23–36 in *Economic and Philosophical Manuscripts of 1844*.

15. Some of Weil's insights into the relationship of language and power have been explored within recent feminist discussions of language. See, for instance, some of the discussion provoked by Dale Spender's *Man-Made Language* and Deborah Cameron's *Feminism and Linguistic Theory*. The relation of masculinity to language is tentatively explored in Victor Seidler's *Rediscovering Masculinity: Reason, Language and Sexuality*, Ch. 8, 'Language', pp. 123–42.

16. It is partly as a response to working-class opposition that the 1980s have seen the development of 'post-Fordism' which has involved the break-up of large units of factory production and the increasing importance of part-time work. For a critical discussion of literature on post-Fordism, see Michael Rustin 'The Politics of Post-Fordism: or, the trouble with the "New Times"', *New Left Review* 175, May/June 1984, pp. 54–78.

17. Simone Weil's reflections on the meaninglessness of work could prove crucial in the remaking of socialist politics in both western and eastern Europe, where talk of the dignity of work has so often been for different reasons empty and rhetorical and where it seems that capitalist production has at least been able to provide full shops and consumer goods. Questions of freedom, incentive and responsibility have become central to the renewal of socialism.

18. See the discussion in Victor Seidler, 'Kant: Respect, Individuality and Dependence' in *Kant's Practical Philosophy Reconsidered*, ed. Y. Yovel, pp. 235–54.

10 Love, Dignity and Oppression

1. The inadequacy of the prevailing political distinctions of 'left' and 'right' to illuminate the moral and political realities that we face is a theme in the conclusion, 'Morality, Truth and Politics' to *A Truer Liberty: Simone Weil and Marxism*, by Lawrence Blum and Victor Seidler.
2. The relationship of the Enlightenment to a liberal sense of modernity has become a central theme in the discussions around the ambiguous idea of 'post-modernity'. See, for instance, Michel Foucault's 'What is Enlightenment?' in Paul Rabinow (ed.) *The Foucault Reader* and Jurgen Habermas' 'Taking Aim at the Heart of the Present' in David Couzens Hoy (ed.) *Foucault: A Critical Reader* pp .103–8. See also Martin Jay, 'Habermas and Modernism', in Richard Bernstein (ed.) *Habermas and Modernity*, pp. 123–39.
3. A sense of the growth and development of modern feminism can be gleaned from Sheila Rowbotham's *Dreams and Dilemmas* and Lynne Segal's *Is the Future Female?*. For a sense of the different strains of feminist theory see Alison Jaggar, *Feminist Politics and Human Nature*.
4. An interesting discussion of the relationship of feminism to our inherited sense of politics and the public sphere is provided by *Feminism as Critique*, ed. Seyla Benhabib and Drucilla Cornell. see also *Women in Western Political Philosophy*, ed. E. Kennedy and S. Mendus.
5. It becomes crucial to investigate the nature of the challenges that different forms of feminism make to our inherited sense of modernity. We fail to get this challenge in true perspective if we regard feminism as part of a modernity that has to be broken with. This becomes the rationale for empty talk of a 'post-feminism'. In large part the issues of experience, power and identity that have been raised by feminism have been marginalised within a rationalistic philosophical culture.
6. A useful introduction to the Frankfurt School within the tradition of a history of ideas is provided by Martin Jay's *The Dialectical Imagination: A History of the Frankfurt School and the Institute of Social Research 1923–50*. It is significant that the discussion around post-modernity has largely been reached through a movement within French social thought and its break with a structuralist tradition. This has largely shaped the framework within which the discussion has taken place. More recently resonances with Adorno and Benjamin have been appreciated. See, for instance, Peter Dews' *Autonomy and Solidarity: Interviews with Jurgen Habermas*.
7. Spinoza allows for developing a more substantial conception of the person for he acknowledges emotional life and the miseries it can create. He

remains in tension with Descartes and with various ways that a rationalist tradition of philosophy has been conceived. The significance of Spinoza as representing a challenge to various aspects of the Enlightenment tradition in essentially a secularised form of Christianity is still to be explored. It is interesting to note the resonance that Freud also felt with Spinoza. This has been noted by Siegfried Hessing, 'Freud's Relation to Spinoza', in *Speculum Spinozanum 1677–1977*, ed. Siegfried Hessing, pp. 224–39.

8. The relationship between masculinity, language and power could suggest that men can experience difficulties in communicating at an emotional level. Frustration can lead men to use their power to act out violently. If problems of abuse are often understood as relating to communication blocks within the family, they are rarely connected directly to issues of masculinity. Some background ideas that would help explore an education into masculinity are set out in Victor Seidler's *Rediscovering Masculinity: Reason, Language and Sexuality*.

9. The failure to take seriously a connection between dominant forms of masculinity and particular forms of reason has made the discussion around masculinity less fruitful. It has also meant that the insights and challenges of feminism remain marginalised. See, for instance, the connections made by Susan Griffin in *Pornography and Silence*.

10. Simone Weil recognises how the distinction between the sciences and the humanities has crucially organised the terms of modernity. It is a significant theme in *The Need for Roots*.

11. Since the Enlightenment was supposed to render Jews, blacks and women as equal citizens it was supposedly a development that should be welcomed. It has been much harder to discern the anti-Semitic and racist assumptions that underpinned the 'Age of Reason'. In this sense modernity has to be investigated before it can be transcended. It is only through grasping the realities of slavery as part of the lived history of black people, and the Holocaust for Jews, that we can begin an exploration of modernity and its discontents. It is a strength of Franklin Littell that he raises some of these uncomfortable issues, at least as far as the Jewish people in their relationship to Christianity, are concerned. See *The Crucifixion of the Jews*. See also *Faith and Freedom; A Tribute to Franklin H. Littell*, ed. Richard Libowitz.

12. See the essays by Isaiah Berlin, 'Benjamin Disraeli, Karl Marx and the Search for Identity' and 'The Life and Opinions of Moses Hess', in *Against the Current; Essays in the History of Ideas*, pp. 252–87 and 213–51.

13. In contrast to the impact of World War I on the culture of the 1920s, this silence in recent philosophical and intellectual culture about the Holocaust was raised by Saul Friedlander's address to the Oxford Conference, Remembering for the Future, Oxford, 10–13 July 1988.

14. 'Encounter with the Old Testament', 62, *The Chicago Theological Seminary Register* (1972) 2:1.

15. See John Stuart Mill, *On Liberty*, Ch. III, and the discussion in Alan Ryan

J. S. Mill and Isaiah Berlin, 'John Stuart Mill and the Ends of Life' in *Four Essays on Liberty*, pp. 173–206.

16. To think about the place of love and friendship in contrast to the recognition it has been given in previous times, see Iris Murdoch, *Sovereignty of Good*, Lawrence Blum, *Friendship, Altruism and Morality*, Martha Nussbaum, *The Fragility of Goodness*, and Barrington Moore, *Privacy*.

17. For an introduction to some Chasidic ideas, see Martin Buber's *Tales of the Hasidism*. For a contrasting view see Gershom Scholem, 'Martin Buber's Interpretation of Hasidism', in *The Messaianic Idea in Judaism*, pp. 228–50.

18. Jan Blonski's article paraphrases the title of Milosz's poem 'A Poor Gentile looks at the Ghetto'. The discussion in Tygodnik Powczechny raised issues about the millenial relationship between Poles and Jews that had been silenced since the war. Since Polish identity was so closely tied up with the history of the Catholic church, it was always difficult for Jews to be recognised as Poles, despite the influence of the Enlightenment. For some understanding of this difficult relationship, see Rafael Scharf, 'In Anger and in Sorrow', *Polin: A Journal of Polish-Jewish studies*. See also Nechama Tec, *Dry Tears*, for a personal account of a wartime childhood.

19. The relationship of identity to history can be difficult to grasp within a structuralist tradition. It fails to recognise that we often have to *work* through a history that we have not chosen for ourselves. Slavery is an inescapable experience for blacks as the Holocaust is for Jews. If we are not to be crushed by these histories we need to find ways of working with them. This rejects the notion that we can simply turn our backs on history we would prefer to forget. If Hegel helps us appreciate that it is not an either/or situation, he traps us in his identification of history, freedom and progress.

20. For reflections on black identity see, for instance, C. L. R. James, *The Future in the Present*, The Autobiography of Malcolm X, Franz Fanon, *Black Skin, White Masks*, and Paul Gilroy, *The Empire Strikes Back*.

21. For some exploration of the relationship of power, marginality and knowledge, see J. Baker Miller, *Towards a New Psychology of Women*, Susan Griffin, *Pornography and Silence*, and Jean Baudrillard, *The Mirror of Production*.

22. For a discussion of some of the implications of Kant's theory of education see Victor Seidler's 'Fathering, Authority and Masculinity' in *Male Order*, ed. R. Chapman and J. Rutherford, pp. 292–302, which is part of a larger study of the relationship of masculinity to authority.

23. Simone Weil was influenced by her relationship with Paul Nizan, who, as a student, became involved with struggles against colonialism. See Paul Nizan, *Aden Arabie*, and the essay by Jean Paul Sartre on 'Paul Nizan', *Situations*, pp. 115–73.

24. For some discussion of Wittgenstein on issues of criteria see: Rogers Allbritton, 'On Wittgenstein's Use of the Term "Criterion"'; Stanley Cavell, 'The Availability of Wittgenstein's Philosophy'; and Barry Stroud,

'Wittgenstein and Logical Necessity'; all reprinted in *Wittgenstein: A Collection of Critical Essays*, ed. George Pitcher.

25. Whether there is a particular relationship of masculinity to a Kantian moral framework is discussed in Victor Seidler's *Rediscovering Masculinity: Reason, Language and Sexuality*, and in Carol Gilligan's *In a Different Voice*.

26. Whether issues of care and concern can be positioned within a rationalistic moral framework or whether it brings such a framework into question is an issue that affects the evaluations of schemes of moral development, such as those developed by Lawrence Kohlberg. See, for instance, Lawrence Kohlberg's *The Philosophy of Moral Development* and *Psychology of Moral Development*. In the area of moral development the boundaries between moral psychology and moral philosophy are quickly dissolving.

27. For an exploration of the relationship of Kierkegaard to Hegel see Niels Thulstrup, *Kierkegaard's Relation to Hegel*. See also Mark C. Taylor, *Journeys to Selfhood: Hegel and Kierkegaard*.

28. See Walter Benjamin, 'Theses on the Philosophy of History' in *Illuminations*, pp. 255–66.

29. These issues of translation in Kant scholarship were raised for me by Hans Fink. See his brief discussion in *Social Philosophy*. See also the discussions of Kant in Genevieve Lloyd, *The Man of Reason: 'Male' and 'Female' in Western Philosophy*, and Susan Mendus' 'Kant; An Honest but Narrow-Minded Bourgeois?' in Ellen Kennedy and Susan Mendus, *Women in Western Political Philosophy*.

30. The place of women in the story of creation and the ways that Eve is blamed for bringing evil into the world and for the exclusion of humanity from the Garden of Eden remains a crucial issue for feminist explorations in theology. See, for instance, the important work by Elaine Pagels, *Gnostic Gospels*, and *Feminist Interpretation of the Bible*, ed. Letty M. Russell. This remains a crucial issue for our understanding of the relationship of modernity to gender.

31. Some of the vital discussions in Judaism deserve to be better known for they have a crucial bearing upon the whole relationship of modernity to Christianity. To what extent has the philosophical tradition that has deemed itself as 'modern' and claimed itself to be 'universal' because it is rational legitimated a secular form of Christianity? To what extent has it made it difficult to recognise the integrity of different traditions that have unwittingly been marginalised within an Enlightenment tradition? The plurality of an earlier period that more easily recognised the claims of Jewish, Islamic and Christian thought was lost in the centralising and universalistic tradition of the Enlightenment. These tensions have been inherited within Jewish thought. Where we can recognise both the heartfelt rationalism of David Hartman, *The Living Covenant*, as well as the mystical insights in Adin Steinsaltz's *The Thirteen Petalled Rose*.

32. Some interesting connections between Plato and Kant are drawn by Richard Rorty in *The Consequences of Pragmatism*.

33. For some interesting discussions on Max Weber's *The Protestant Ethic and the Spirit of Capitalism*, see Donald MacRae, *Weber*, and Frank Parkin, *Max Weber*.

34. For some sense of the feminist critique of Lawrence, see Kate Millet, *Sexual Politics*, Ch. 5, 'D. H. Lawrence', pp. 237–93. See also P. A. Lea, *in the Wilderness*, Ch. 4, 'David Herbert Lawrence 1885–1930', pp. 120–66.

35. The ways that Simone Weil's thinking was changed by her experience of the Spanish Civil War is discussed in *A Truer Liberty: Simone Weil and Marxism*, Ch. 7, 'Power', pp. 194–256.

36. The recognition of the body in more recent social theory, partly under the influence of Foucault's sense of the ways that regulation of the body is integral to social control, has yet to appreciate some of the crucial insights made by Reich. See Myron Sharaf, *Fury on Earth: A Biography of Wilhelm Reich*, David Boadella, *Wilhelm Reich: The Evolution of his Work*, and Stanley Kellerman, *Somatic Reality*.

37. printed in the *Catholic Worker*, Dec. 1988, p.8, vol. LV, no. 8).

38. 'Interwar Poland: Good or Bad for the Jews?' in *The Jews In Poland* cited by Abramsky, Jachimczyk and Polonsky (Blackwell, Oxford 1986).

39. reprinted in 'Waking from a dream – Thomas Merton and the Catholic Worker', by Jim Forest, Dec. 1988, vol. LV, no. 8)

40. A language of the soul has remained as part of a black experience of resistance as well as part of black scholarship. See, for instance, W. E. B. DuBois, *The Souls of Black Folk* and *Black Reconstruction*. This point was made by Paul Gilroy in a talk at Goldsmiths' College, University of London on 'Identity, Politics, Culture', March 1989. See also James Baldwin, *Price of the Ticket*, Michael Joseph, 1985.

41. Issues of responsibility, blame, power and oppression have been raised by feminist theory and practice in a way that is bringing into question central themes in our moral and political tradition. See, for instance, Susan Moller Okin, *Women in Western Political Thought*, and Alison Jaggar, *Feminist Politics and Human Nature*.

Bibliography

ARIES, Philip, *Centuries of Childhood* (Harmondsworth: Penguin Books, 1975).

BAECK, Leo, *Judaism and Christianity* trans. Walter Kaufman (New York: Atheneum, 1981).

BALDWIN, James, *The Price of the Ticket* (London: Michael Joseph, 1985).

BAUDRILLARD, Jean, *The Mirror of Production* (New York: Telos Press).

BENDIX, R. and LIPSET, M., *Class, Status and Power* (New York: The Free Press, 1966).

BENHABIB, S. and CORNELL, D., *Feminism as Critique* (Oxford: Polity Press, 1987).

BENJAMIN, Walter, *Illuminations*, trans. Harry Bohn (London: Collins/Fontana Books, 1973).

BENJAMIN, Walter, *One-Way Street* (London: New Left Books, 1979).

BENYON, Huw, *Working for Ford* (Harmondsworth: Penguin Books, 1973).

BERLIN, Isaiah, *Against the Current* (Oxford: Oxford University Press, 1981).

BERLIN, Isaiah, *Four Essays on Liberty* (Oxford: Oxford University Press, 1969).

BERLIN, Isaiah, *Vico and Herder: Two Studies in the History of Ideas* (New York: Random House, 1976).

BERNSTEIN, Richard, *Habermas and Modernity* (Oxford: Polity Press, 1985).

BLUM, Lawrence, *Friendship, Altruism and Morality* (London: Routledge, 1980).

BLUM, Lawrence and SEIDLER, Victor J., *A Truer Liberty: Simone Weil and Marxism* (New York: Routledge, 1989).

BOADELLA, David, *Wilhelm Reich: The Evolution of his Work* (London: Vision, 1985).

BRAVERMAN, Harry, *Labor and Monopoly Capital* (New York and London: Monthly Review Press, 1974).

BUBER, Martin, *Tales of the Hasidim* (New York: Schocken Books, 1948).

BUCHANAN, A. E., *Marx and Justice: The Radical Critique of Liberalism* (London: Methuen, 1977).

BUCHANAN, Allen E., *Marx and Justice: The Radical Critique of Liberalism* (Totowa, New Jersey: Rowan and Allanfield, 1982).

BUCK-MORSS, Susan, *The Origin of Negative Dialectics* (Brighton: The Harvester Press, 1977).

CAPLAN, Pat (ed.) *The Cultural Construction of Sexuality* (London: Tavistock, 1987).

CARTLEDGE, S. and RYAN, J., *Sex and Love* (London: The Women's Press, 1983.

CAVELL, Stanley, *The Claims of Reason* (Oxford: Oxford University Press, 1980).

CAVELL, Stanley, *Must We Mean What We Say?* (New York: Scribners, 1969).

CHAPMAN, R. and RUTHERFORD, J., *Male Order: Unmasking Masculinity* (London: Lawrence and Wishart, 1988).

CLARKE, S., LOVELL, T., ROBINS, K., and SEIDLER, V. J., *One-Dimensional Marxism* (London: Allison and Busby, 1980).

COHEN, G., *Karl Marx's Theory of History: A Defence* (Oxford: Oxford University Press, 1978).

COLES, Robert, *Simone Weil: A Modern Pilgrimage* (Reading, Massachusetts: Addison-Wesley, 1987).

CONNOLLY, James, *Selected Writings* P. Beresford Ellis (ed.) (Harmondsworth: Penguin Books, 1973).

C.S.E., *The Labour Process and Class Struggle* (London: Stage, 1987).

DAHRENDORF, Ralf, *Class and Class Conflict in Industrial Society* (Stanford: Stanford University Press, 1959).

DAVIDSON, Alastair, *Antonio Gramsci: Towards an Intellectual Biography* (London: The Merlin Press, 1977).

DENNISON, George, *The Lives of Children* (Harmondsworth: Penguin Books, 1974).

DEWS, Peter (ed.), *Habermas, Autonomy and Solidarity* (London, New Left Books, 1986)

DRURY, M. O'C., *The Danger of Words* (London: Routledge and Kegan Paul, 1983).

DU BOIS, W. E. B., *The Souls of Black Folk* (Chicago: McClure, 1903).

DU BOIS, W. E. B., *Black Reconstruction in America* (New York, 1934)

DUNAYEVSKAYA, Raya, *Marxism and Freedom* (London: Pluto Press, 1971).

DWORKIN, R., *Taking Rights Seriously* (London: Duckworths, 1977).

DWORKIN, R., *The Philosophy of Law* (Oxfrod: Oxford University Press, 1977).

ELKINS, Stanley M., *Slavery* (Chicago: University of Chicago Press, 1959).

ELSHTAIN Jean Bethke, *Public Man, Private Woman* (Princeton University Press, 1986).

FABRICIUS, Cajus, *Positive Christianity in the Third Reich* (Dresden: Puschel, 1937).

FANON, Franz, *Black Skins, White Masks* (London: Paladin Books, 1972).

FEINBERG, Joel, *Moral Concepts* (Oxford: Oxford University Press, 1969).

FINK, Hans, *Social Philosophy* (London: Methuen, 1981).

FOOT, Philippa, *Virtues and Vices* (Oxford: Blackwell, 1978).

FREIRE, Paolo, *Pedagogy of the Oppressed* (Harmondsworth: Penguin Books, 1974).

FREUD, Sigmund, *Introductory Lectures on Psychoanalysis* (London: Allen and Unwin, 1922).

FRIED, Charles, *Right and Wrong* (Harvard University Press, 1978).

FRISBY, D., *The Positivist Dispute in German Sociology* (London: Heinemann, 1976).

FROMM, Erich, *Fear of Freedom* (London: Routledge and Kegan Paul, 1942.

GENOVESE, Eugene, *Roll, Jordan, Roll – The World the Slaves Made* (New York: Random House, 1974).

GERAS, Norman, *Human Nature in Marx* (Loondon: New Left Books, 1984)

GERTH, Holms and MILLS, C. S., *From Max Weber: Essays in Sociology* (London: Routledge, 1958).

GIDDENS, Anthony (ed.), *Positivism and Sociology* (London: Heinemann Educational Books, 1974).

GILLIGAN, Carol, *In a Different Voice* (Harvard University Press, 1982).

GILROY, Paul, *The Empire Strikes Back* (London: Hutchinson, 1988)

GRAMSCI, A., *Selections from the Prison Notebooks* (ed. and trans. Q. Hoare and G. Nowell-Smith; London: Lawrence and Wishart, 1971).

GRIFFIN, Susan, *Made From This Earth* (London: The Women's Press, 1982).

GRIFFIN, Susan, *Pornography and Silence* (London: The Women's Press, 1980).

HARTMAN, David, *A Living Covenant* (New York: The Free Press, 1985).

HELLMAN, John, *Emmanuel Mournier and the New Catholic Left 1930–1950* (Toronto University Press, 1981).

HELLER, Agnes, *The Theory of Need in Marx* (London: Allison and Busby, 1974).

HESSING, Siegfried, *Specumulum Spinozanum. 1677–1977* (London: Routledge and Kegan Paul, 1977).

HEYD, David, *Supererogation* (Cambridge: Cambridge Studies in Philosophy, 1982).

HONDERICH, Ted, *Morality and Objectivity* (London: Routledge and Kegan Paul, 1985).

HOY, David Couzens, *Foucault: A Critical Reader* (Oxford: Blackwell, 1986).

IGNATIEFF, M., *The Needs of Strangers* (London: Chatto and Windus, 1984).

JACOBY, Russell, *Social Amnesia* (Boston: Beacon Press, 1975).

JAGGAR, Alison, *Feminist Politics and Human Nature* (Sussex: The Harvester Press, 1983).

JAMES, C. L. R., *The Future in the Present* (London: Allison and Busby, 1977).

JAY, Martin, *The Dialectical Imagination* (London: Heinemann Educational Books, 1973).

JOSEPH, Keith, and SUMPTON, Jonathan, *Equality*.

KANT, Immanuel, *Foundations of the Metaphysic of Morals*, trans. Lewis White Beck (Indianopolis and New York: Bobbs-Merril, 1959).

KANT, Immanuel, *Critique of Practical Reason*, trans. Lewis White Beck (Indianapolis and New York: Bobbs-Merril, 1956).

KANT, Immanuel, *Religion Within The Limits Of Reason Alone* trans. Greene and Hudson (New York: Harper and Row, 1960).

KANT, Immanuel, *The Doctrine of Virtue* trans. Mary J. Gregor (New York: Harper and Row, 1964).

KARDINER, A., and OVESEY, D., *The Mark of Oppression* (New York: Meridan Books, 1962).

KELLERMAN, Stanley, *Somatic Reality* (Berkeley, California: Center Press, 1979).

KENNEDY, E., and MENDUS, S., *Women in Western Political Philosophy* (Sussex: Wheatsheaf Books, 1987).

KIERKEGAARD, Soren, *Philosophical Fragments* (Princetown: University Press, 1967).

KIERKEGAARD, Soren, *The Concept of Dread* (Princeton: University Press, 1955).

KIERKEGAARD, Soren, *World of Love* trans. Howard and Edna Home (New York: Harper and Row, 1962).

KIERKEGAARD, Soren, *The Present Age* (London: Fontana, 1962).

KIERKEGAARD, Soren, *Purity of Heart*, trans. Douglas Steere (London: Fontana, 1961).

LAKE, Frank, *Clinical Theology* (London: Dartman, Longman and Todd, 1966).

LEA, P. A., *Voices in the Wilderness* (London: Brentham Press, 1975).

LEWIS, C. S., *The Screwtape Letters* (Fontana: London, 1953).

LIBOWITZ, Richard (ed.), *Faith and Freedom: A Tribute to Franklin H. Littell* (Oxford: Pergamon Press, 1987).

LITTELL, Franklin H., *The Crucifixion of the Jews* (New York: Harper and Row, 1975).

LLOYD, Genevieve, *The Man of Reason: 'Male' and 'Female' in Western Philosophy* (London: Methuen, 1984).

LOVEJOY, A. O., *The Great Chain of Being* (New York: Harper and Row, 1936 [1960])

LUKES, Steven, *Marxism and Morality* (Oxford: University Press, 1985).

LUKES, Steven, 'Can a Marxist Believe in Human Rights?', *Praxis International* vol. 1, no. 4, Jan. 1982, pp. 334–45.

MACPHERSON, C. B., *The Political Theory of Possessive Individualism* (Oxford: University Press, 1962).

MACINTYRE, Alasdair, *After Virtue* (London: Duckworths, 1983)

MACRAE, Donald, *Weber* (London: Fontana, 1974).

MALCOLM, Norman, *Nothing is Hidden* (Oxford: Blackwell, 1986).

MALCOLM, X, *The Autobiography of Malcolm X* (Harmondsworth: Penguin Books, 1968).

MANNONI, O., *Freud* (New York: Random House, 1974).

MARCUSE, Herbert, *Reason and Revolution* (Routledge and Kegan Paul: London, 1967).

MARX, Karl, *Capital*, vol. 1 (Harmondsworth: Penguin Books, 1976).

MARX, Karl, *Economic and Philosophical Manuscripts of 1844* (London: Lawrence and Wishart, 1954).

MARX, Karl, *The Grundrisse: Foundations to the Critique of Political.* (Harmondsworth: Penguin Books/New Left Books, 1973).

MIDGLEY, M., and HUGHES, J., *Women's Choices* (London: Weidenfeld and Nicolson, 1983).

MILLER, Jean Baker, *Towards a New Psychology of Women* (Harmondsworth: Penguin Books, 1982).

MILLER, Richard W., *Analyzing Marx: Morality, Power and History* (Princeton: University Press, 1984).

MILLET, Kate, *Sexual Politics* (London: Virago, 1977).

MOMMSEN, Wolfgang J., *The Age Of Bureaucracy* (Oxford: Basil Blackwell, 1974).

MURDOCH, Iris, *The Sovereignty of Good* (London: Routledge and Kegan Paul, 1970).

NIZAN, Paul, *Aden Arabie* (Paris: Editions Maspero, 1960).

NOZICK, Robert, *Anarchy, State and Utopia* (New York: Basic Books, 1974).

NUSSBAUM, Martha C., *The Fragility of Goodness* (Cambridge: University Press, 1986).

OKIN, Susan Moller, *Women in Western Political Thought* (London: Virago, 1980).

O'NEIL, John, *Sociology as a Skin Trade* (London: Heinemann Educational Books, 1972).

PAGELS, Elaine, *The Gnostic Gospels* (Harmondsworth: Penguin Books, 1982).

PARKIN, Frank, *Max Weber* (London: Tavistock, 1982).

PASHUKANIS, Eugene, *Law and Marxism: A General Theory* (London: Ink Links, 1978).

PETREMENT, Simone, *Simone Weil: A Life* (New York: Pantheon, 1976).

PITCHER, George, *Wittgenstein: A Collection of Critical Essays* (London: Macmillan, 1968).

PIVEN, Frances Fox, and CLOWARD, R., *Regulating the Poor* (New York: Vintage, 1971).

PIVEN, Frances Fox, and CLOWARD, R., *Poor People's Movements*, (New York: Pantheon, 1977).

RABINOW, Paul (ed.), *The Foucault Reader* (New York: Pantheon, 1984).

REICH, Wilhelm, *Reich Speaks of Freud* (London: Souvenir Press, 1972).

RHEES, Rush, *Ludwig Wittgenstein: Personal Recollections* (Oxford: Blackwell, 1981).

RORTY, Amelie O., *The Identities of Persons* (Berkeley: University of California Press, 1976).

RORTY, Amelie O., *Explaining Emotions* (Berkeley: University of California

Press, 1980).
RORTY, Richard, *The Consequences of Pragmatism* (Sussex: Harvester Press, 1982).
ROWBOTHAM, Sheila, *Dreams and Dilemmas* (London: Virago, 1983).
ROWBOTHAM, Sheila, *Woman's Consciousness, Man's World* (Harmondsworth: Penguin Books, 1973).
ROWBOTHAM, Sheila, *Hidden from History* (London: Pluto Books, 1973).
RUBIN, Lillian Breslow, *Worlds of Pain* (New York: Basic Books, 1976).
RUITENBECK, Henrik M. (ed.), *Psychoanalysis and Existential Philosophy*, (New York: E. P. Dutton, 1962).
RUSSELL, Letty M., *Feminist Interpretations of the Bible* (Oxford: Blackwell, 1983).
RYAN, Alan, *J. S. Mill* (London: Routledge and Kegan Paul, 1984).
RYAN, Alan (ed.), *The Idea of Freedom* (Oxford: University Press, 1979).
RYAN, William, *Blaming the Victim* (New York: Random House, 1971).
SARTRE, Jean-Paul, *Anti-Semite and Jew* (New York: Schocken Books, 1960).
SARTRE, Jean-Paul, *Situations* (London: Hamish Hamilton, 1965).
SCHELER, Max, *Formalism in Ethics and Non-Formal Ethics of Values* (Chicago: Northeastern Press, 1973).
SCHELER, Max, *Resentiment*, trans. William W. Holdheim (New York: Schocken Books, 1972).
SCHELER, Max, *Man's Place in Nature*, trans. Hans Meyerhote (New York: Noonday Press, 1965).
SCHOLEM, Gershom, *The Messianic Idea in Judaism* (New York: Schocken Books, 1971).
SEGAL, Lynne, *Is the Future Female?* (London: Virago, 1987).
SEIDLER, Victor J., *Kant, Respect and Injustice: The Limits of Liberal Moral Theory* (Routledge: London, 1986).
SEIDLER, V. J., *Recreating Sexual Politics: Men, Feminism and Politics* (Routledge: London, 1991)
SEIDLER, V. J., *Rediscovering Masculinity: Reason, Language and Sexuality* (Routledge: London, 1989).
SENNETT, Richard, and COBB, Jonathan, *The Hidden Injuries of Class* (Cambridge: University Press, 1973).
SHARAF, Myron, *Fury on Earth: A Biography of Wilhelm Reich* (New York: St. Martin's Press, 1983).
STAUDE, John R., *Max Scheler 1874-1928* (New York: The Free Press, 1967).
STEINSALTZ, Adin, *The Thirteen Petalled Rose* (New York: Basic Books, 1980).
TAYLOR, Barbara, *Eve and the New Jerusalem* (London: Virago Press, 1983).
TAYLOR, Charles, *Hegel and Modern Society* (Cambridge: Cambridge University Press, 1979).
TAYLOR, Charles, *Philosophy and the Human Sciences, Philosophical*

Papers 2 (Cambridge: Cambridge University Press, 1985).

TAYLOR, Mark C., *Journeys to Selfhood: Hegel and Kierkegaard* (California: University Press, 1980).

TEC, Nechama, *Dry Tears* (Oxford: University Press, 1984).

THOMAS, Keith, *Religion and the Decline of Magic* (Lonodon: Allen Lane, 1971).

THOMSON, J. J., and DWORKIN, G., *Ethics* (Harper and Row: New York, 1968).

THOMPSON, Edward, *The Poverty of Theory* (London: Merlin Press, 1979; Cambridge University Press, 1985).

THULSTRUP, Riels, *Kierkegaard's Relation to Hegel* trans. George Stengren (Princeton: University Press, 1980).

TOCQUEVILLE, Alexis de, *Democracy in America* (New York: Vintage, 1952).

TREBLICOT, Joyce, *Mothering: Essays in Feminist Theory* (Totowa, New Jersey: Rowan and Allanheld, 1984).

URMSON, J. O., 'Saints and Heroes' in *Essays in Moral Philosophy* ed. A. H. Malden (Seattle: University of Washington Press, 1958).

WALZER, Michael, *Spheres of Justice* (New York: Basic Books, 1983).

WEBER, Max, *The Protestant Ethic and the Spirit of Capitalism* (London, 1930).

WEIL, Simone, *Gravity and Grace* (London: Routledge and Kegan Paul, 1952).

WEIL, Simone, *Lectures on Philosophy* trans. Hugh Price (Cambridge: Cambridge University Press, 1970)

WEIL, Simone, *Oppression and Liberty* (London: Routledge and Kegan Paul, 1958).

WEIL, Simone, *Waiting on God* (London: Fontana Books, 1959).

WEIL, Simone, *Selected Essays 1934–43* ed. Richard Rees (Oxford: University Press, 1962).

WEIL, Simone, *Seventy Letters* (Oxford: University Press, 1965).

WEIL, Simone, *The Need for Roots* (London: Routledge and Kegan Paul, 1972).

WIESEL, Elie, *Souls on Fire* (Harmondsworth: Penguin Books, 1984).

WILLIAMS, Bernard, *Problems of the Self* (Cambridge: University Books, 1973).

WILLIAMS, Bernard, *Morality* (Cambridge: University Press, 1972).

WILLIAMS, Bernard, *Ethics and the Limits of Philosophy* (London: Fontana, 1985).

WILLIAMS, Bernard, *Moral Luck* (Cambridge: University Press, 1981).

WINCH, Peter, *Just Balance: Reflection on the Philosophy of Simone Weil* (Cambridge: University Press, 1989).

WITTGENSTEIN, Ludwig, *Philosophical Investigations* trans. G. E. M. Anscombe (Oxford: Blackwell, 1958).

WOLLHEIM, R., *The Thread of Life* (Cambridge, Massachusetts: Harvard University Press, 1984).

WOLLHEIM, R., *Freud* (London: Fontana, 1971).
YOVEL, Y., *Kant's Practical Philosophy Reconsidered* (The Hague: Kluwer Academic Publishers, 1989).

Index

abilities 10, 88
  abstract 182
  confidence/trust in 21, 120, 145, 147
  differences of 60, 68
  individual 56, 99, 161–2, 168
  of others 31
abstraction(s)/abstracting 4, 10, 92, 164, 175, 178, 185, 197, 201–2, 213 n.8
  from differences/distinctions/ personal qualities 18, 54, 113, 174
  from earthly/everyday life/ empirical world/social life 32, 44, 56, 67, 76, 86, 92, 96–7, 106, 109, 194
  from history/culture 91, 174–5
  from power/social/unequal relations/of domination/subordination/dependency (xii), 5, 8, 12, 17, 20, 22, 46, 74–7, 81, 92, 99, 144, 165, 167, 179, 191, 211 n.9, 11
  of the sacred 10
  of the society 24
  abstract abilities, 182
    acknowledgement of others 9
    bearers of rights 9, 174
  choices 153
    from feelings 41
    equality 70, 92–3
    love 196
    principles 93
    quality of respect 9
    subject 10
    universality of spirituality 177
achievements
  individual 67, 87, 104
  identified with success (xiii), 24, 431
  of others 31
Adam 195

Adorno, T. W. 100, 213 n.4, 215 n.6
advantage(s) 66, 78–9, 93–5
affliction 20, 90, 96, 101–2, 117, 119–22, 150–1, 182, 215 n.3
  the afflicted 163, 178
Africa 181
almsgiving 118
altruism 17, 197, 209 n.5
  altruistic emotions 208 n.11, 209 n.7, 215 n.8
Amazon forest 187
anger 90, 179, 183, 198, 201
  of the poor 96
animals 187
  animal natures 28, 30, 33, 40, 62, 179
  animal wants/needs 43
anti-Semitism 175–7
Aristotle 17
  Aristotelian ethics 17
Asians 173
assembly line 66, 109, 139, 156, 162, 164, 218 n.16
assimilation 175, 181
attention 77, 117, 120, 139–40, 150, 181, 195
attitude 147
  we take up to others/in relations 8, 11–12, 18–9, 21, 30–2, 47–9, 98, 103, 106, 113–4, 122, 152, 166, 170, 179, 182, 208 n.13
  to ourselves (xi), 14
  of others 201
Auschwitz (ix), 173
Austin, J. 91, 212 n.6
authoritarian regimes 147
authority/authorities 4, 57, 67, 77, 87, 110, 178, 193
  of reason (x)
  of the state 4
autonomy 20, 170, 178, 182, 186, 193
  of civil society (xi)
  of individual(s) 4, 12, 99, 179,

95, 116, 123
to self/ourselves 16–7, 48–9, 86,
    149, 202
of soul and society 3
to time 111
of/at work 109, 111–2, 151
relativism (x), 125, 187
religion/religiosity (xii), 3, 5, 102,
    172–3, 175, 177, 185
renunciation 117
respect (ix), 1, 8–9, 11–2, 16, 18–9,
    22–3, 25–7, 31–5, 45–6, 56,
    77, 79, 87, 97–8, 100–1, 103–4,
    107–8, 112, 124, 127, 129, 133,
    139, 146, 149, 156–7, 165–7,
    169–70, 174, 181–3, 204 n.1,
    211 n.9
for affliction 122
as distance/non-interference 5, 7,
    9, 11, 21, 23, 27, 33–4, 37, 44,
    78–9, 98–9, 123, 127, 136, 143
hierarchical sense of 9, 26, 34
for the moral law 9
as negative duty 25
for/owed to others/human
    beings 8–10, 12, 16, 18, 21–2,
    25–8, 30–1, 33–4, 37, 48–9,
    56, 62, 75, 82, 98–9, 103, 106,
    108, 110–1, 113–5, 120, 124,
    127–9, 143–4, 152, 159, 162,
    166–7, 174, 213 n.2
for ourselves (xiii) *see also* self-
    respect
for rights 127, 129, 130, 139
of selves by women 147
at work 111–2, 154–5, 165
responsibility 22, 44, 112, 129–30,
    146, 169, 187, 190–4, 203,
    224 n.41
of capitalists 112, 160
to defend 102, 158
in relationships 53–4, 186
revolutions in Eastern Europe 147,
    163
rich 108–9
rich and poor 5, 7, 20, 34, 45,
    55–6, 72–3, 79, 87, 95, 99, 109,
    116, 121, 123
right(s) 25, 84, 100, 102, 123–37,
    139, 143–8, 152, 158, 163, 169,
    174, 213 n.1, 216 n.4, 217 n.7
abstract 9–10
to emotions/feelings 183
equal 145, 150
individual/personal 21, 100, 137,
    140, 161, 163
individuals/people/women existing
    in their own 29, 145–6, 169,
    182
infringed/infringement of 19, 126,
    129–31, 134, 136–9, 157, 170
language of 19–21, 125–6, 128–32,
    134–40, 143–5, 147, 157, 168,
    217 n.13
legal and political 109, 111, 128,
    145, 150, 152, 160, 168, 174,
    197
of man 10
positive 124–5, 130–1, 142,
    216 n.2
to strike 156
of workers/capitalists 141
role theory 81, 212 n.1
    roles 82–3, 87, 89, 91
romantic tradition 15
Romans/Roman law 102, 131,
    214 n.13
Rousseau, J.J 4
Ruddick, Sarah 203
sacred/the sacred 10, 18, 20, 127,
    133–4, 148, 178
Sartre, J.-P. 174–5
schools/schooling/schoolteachers 107,
    148, 154, 182
salvation 3, 5, 28–9, 62, 64–5, 67, 74,
    91, 165, 194, 200
Scheler, M 16, 35–6, 206 n.17,
    208 n.19
science 15, 139, 173, 183, 187
human 187
moral 33, 221 n.10
scientific, discourse 88
management 164
Marxism 24
Second World War (ix)
secularism/secularised culture /
    forms (ix), (xii), 2–5, 12–3,
    29, 172–3, 175, 186, 190, 197

of women 145–6, 181
see also relations of dependency/
subordination
suffering/ways people suffer (ix),
(xiii), 1, 22–3, 60, 64, 74, 76,
87, 89, 101–2, 114, 117–8, 121,
130–1, 133–4, 136–7, 154,
156–7, 159, 162–3, 166, 182,
185, 203, 216 n.8
of women 169, 171
supernatural, compassion 119
gratitude 119
love of neighbour 117
strength 113
virtue of justice 113, 115–6
surplus value 141, 157
sympathy 35, 38–9, 41
of the weak for the strong 119

Taylor, Charles 11
technology 155
technical progress 18
Thévenon, Albertine 101
de Tocqueville, A. 2, 143
Treaty of Versailles
Trotsky, L. 153
truth(s) (x), (xiii)/(xiv), 23, 50, 65,
68, 76, 83, 132–3, 139, 160,
163, 176, 189, 201

universalism/universality 10–2,
25, 39, 162, 173, 175–7, 185,
187–8
in Marxism 21
of reason (x), (xii), 5
universal, claims of Christendom
(xiii)
ethical theory (ix), 4, 12
language 14–5, 148, 158
law 11, 41
love 38, 177–8
rights 174
principles 49
spirituality 177
victimisation 203
utilitarianism/utilitarian theory /
tradition (ix), 11, 106, 136, 138,
168, 190, 197, 214 n.8, 216 n.4,
219 n.8

utilitarian,conception of the
person 139
conception of social life 85
language 19, 84
moral psychology 148–9

value(s) 13–15, 17, 22, 35–6, 41,
99–100, 181, 184–5
of experience 66
of human relations (xiii)
of life 185
of love 35
of the market 19
of our natures 188
of women (ix), (xii), 172
violation 20, 135, 138–40, 151, 157,
160, 162, 168, 170–1, 182
Voltaire 175

Walewska, J. 180
wants (xii), 6, 9, 11, 22, 24, 28–30,
39, 43–4, 49, 59, 62, 68, 76,
104, 147–9, 168, 190
wealth 5, 7, 18, 56–7, 60, 63, 68–70,
72–7, 91, 93, 99, 122, 131, 134,
161, 168, 174
Weber, M. (xiii), 14, 31–2, 194,
215 n.13, 206 n.18, 224 n.33
Weberian tradition 17
Weil, Simone (xi)/(xiii), 1–3, 8–10,
14, 17–23, 56–7, 63, 69, 72,
84, 96–146, 148–71, 173,
178, 182–5, 192, 195, 197,
201–3, 206 n.20, 213 n.10,
1, 3, 5–6, 214 n.7, 8, 10–13,
1, 215 n.2–6, 216 n.1–3,
217 n.8–9, 11, 218 n.8,
219 n.9–11, 13, 15, 17,
221 n.10, 222 n.23, 224 n.35
Wiesel, E. 179
will/willing 11–2, 14, 16, 35, 47, 49,
73, 88, 94, 118, 141, 173, 188,
191, 200, 202
of God 20, 121, 211 n.7
of the strong 114
Williams, B. (x)/(xi), 75
Wittgenstein, L. (x), (xiv), 14, 46,
86, 91, 129, 136, 183, 198,
205 n.15, 209 n.1–2, 212 n.3,